Criticism in the Borderlands

Post-Contemporary Interventions
A series edited by Stanley Fish
and Fredric Jameson

Criticism in the Borderlands

Studies in Chicano Literature, Culture, and Ideology

Edited by Héctor Calderón and José David Saldívar

with a Foreword by Rolando Hinojosa ✿ Selected and

Annotated Critical Bibliography of Contemporary

Chicano Literary Criticism Compiled by Roberto Trujillo,

José David Saldívar, and Héctor Calderón

Duke University Press ✿ Durham and London 1991

Third printing, 1998
© 1991 Duke University Press
All rights reserved
Printed in the United States of America
on acid-free paper ∞
Typeset in Trump Mediaeval
Library of Congress Cataloging-in-Publication Data
appear on the last printed page of this book.

For all who came before us

Contents

Acknowledgments

Many Stanford friends and colleagues had a hand in the realization of this volume during the academic year 1986–87 while Calderón was a Ford Fellow at the Stanford Humanities Center and Saldívar was a National Research Council Fellow at the Stanford Center for Chicano Research. We would like to take this opportunity to express our appreciation to Bliss Carnochan and Mort Sosna, director and associate director of the Humanities Center, and Renato Rosaldo and Armando Valdez, director and associate director of the Center for Chicano Research, for their cooperation in sponsoring "Chicano Literary Criticism in a Social Context," the May 1987 conference which brought together many of the contributors to this volume. We also want to acknowledge the enthusiastic support and generous funding received from Fernando de Necochea, assistant provost, the entire Chicano student and scholarly community, and the departments of English, history, Spanish and Portuguese, comparative literature, modern thought and literature, American studies, feminist studies, and Latin American studies. A special debt of gratitude is owed to Dee Márquez, of the Stanford Humanities Center, and José Antonio Burciaga, resident fellow of Casa Zapata, and Victoria Calderón for their assistance in making the conference a success.

Roberto Trujillo, Curator of Mexican-American Collections for Stanford University Libraries, was kind enough to lend his expertise and assistance in preparing the selected and annotated bibliography of Chicano literary criticism. His fine staff made our tasks of editing and revising our selections much easier: in 1988 Gary Cordova wrote the original annotations; Janet Goitia prepared the manuscript version of the bibliography and also assisted in editing the annotations.

We would also like to acknowledge the encouragement and support received from Gloria Anzaldúa, Houston A. Baker, Jr., Paul Lauter, Werner Sollors, and William Mills Todd III. Reynolds Smith, our editor at Duke, and Fredric Jameson helped improve the book in many ways. Just in time, Robert Mirandon wrote a wonderful index for the book. And, finally, we would like to thank the authors of the essays for making this anthology possible.

In 1988 the original preparation of the manuscript was made possible by a grant from the A. Whitney Griswold Faculty Research Fund of the Whitney Humanities Center, Yale University.

Portions of the following essays have appeared in the following publications: Angie Chabram's "Conceptualizing Chicano Critical Discourse" in "Chicano Critical Discourse: An Emerging Cultural Practice," *Aztlán* 18, no. 2 (1987):45–90. Renato Rosaldo's "Fables of the Fallen Guy" in his *Culture and Truth: The Remaking of Social Analysis*, Boston: Beacon Press, 1989. Ramón Saldívar's "Narrative, Ideology, and the Reconstruction of American Literary History" in his *Chicano Narrative: The Dialectics of Difference*, Madison: University of Wisconsin Press, 1990. Héctor Calderón's "Criticism in the Borderlands" in "At the Crossroads of History, on the Borders of Change: Chicano Literary Studies Past, Present, and Future," *Left Politics and the Literary Profession*, ed. Leonard J. Davis and M. Bella Mirabella, New York: Columbia University Press, 1990, and "Reinventing the Border," *American Mosaic: Multicultural Readings in Context*, ed. Barbara Rico and Sandra Mano, Boston: Houghton Mifflin.

An earlier version of Norma Alarcón's "The Theoretical Subject(s) of *This Bridge Called My Back* and Anglo-American Feminism" appeared in *Making Face, Making Soul/Haciendo Caras: Creative and Critical Perspectives By Women of Color*, ed. Gloria Anzaldúa. © 1990. Reprinted by permission of Aunt Lute Books ([415] 558–8116).

Foreword
Redefining American Literature

In the fall of 1896, William Lyon Phelps was an assistant professor at Harvard, and he introduced the concept of an American literature in the United States for the very first time. He chose Poe and Hawthorne, Melville, Whitman, and Dickinson. In the ensuing semester he was told to stop teaching, and I'm quoting, that "so-called American literature." He was threatened with dismissal. Phelps went on, of course, as we already know, to agitate for the inclusion of American literature in American colleges and universities. That "so-called literature" phrase may sound familiar when one thinks of Américo Paredes, for one, who established the Center for Mexican-American Studies at the University of Texas, Austin, and of the men and women at other institutions who established Chicano Studies programs in the late sixties.

Now, as for Phelps, I doubt very much if it entered his head to include, say, African-American literature or to wonder if there were any other American literatures except his New England variety. However, his stance is understandable. American literature, though, even the New England variety, was by no means widely accepted in the United States, or rather in university curricula, despite the later presence of Crane, Twain, Dean Howells, Dreiser, and so on. I should like to add two additional facts. The first is that the first Ph.D. in American literature is a twentieth-century phenomenon. The second is that it wasn't until after World War II that a degree in that literature was added to the curriculum in America's heartland, Kansas and Missouri.

American literature professors of the time faced the same problems, headaches, and opposition to its offerings as did the professors of Hispanic-American literature in the Romance language departments in this country for the first fifty years of this century. It wasn't until after 1957 that

Hispanic-Americanists began to carve out their own territory in Romance language departments. The National Defense Education Act was largely responsible for the widening of Hispanic-American literature. The newness of Hispanic-American literature offerings in departments of Spanish and Portuguese may be appreciated when one learns that Luis Leal, one of the contributors to this volume, produced over fifty Ph.D. theses while at the University of Illinois (he's still very much alive and kicking at the University of California, Santa Barbara) and that the first thesis on Carlos Fuentes was not published until the sixties under his guidance.

The offerings in the Hispanic-American literature were augmented by waves of Central and South American literary scholars who migrated to the United States and taught in U.S. universities. The opposition by Peninsularists is a well-known recorded and unalterable fact. Their opposition does not differ much from that of the British literature specialists vis-à-vis Americanists. I don't pretend to know the entire history in this regard, but in the mid-fifties, when I was an undergraduate student at the University of Texas, the Romance language department offered two survey courses: a third-year junior course and a fourth-year senior and graduate course, both in Peninsular literature. The Hispanic-American literature courses were the following: the novel, including *Los de abajo (The Underdogs)*, *La vorágine (The Vortex)*, *Don Segundo Sombra*, and *Doña Bárbara*; two courses in the short story, both taught by Ms. Nina Weisinger, an adjunct professor who'd been an adjunct for forty years; and a senior graduate course, Mexican Literature, taught by Dorothy Schons. I also took *El Periquillo Sarniento (The Itching Parrot)* as a seminar, but that was the extent of the offerings of Hispanic-American literature in that Romance language department of so many years ago.

I'm offering this bit of archaeology to remind us that entering into the curriculum has never been easy for anyone. With the admission of a few courses in American literature at a few United States universities, one may be quite right in inferring that African-American literature was not offered at the time. Personally, I also doubt if anyone thought of it as an offering. I've not studied some of the offerings at Howard or Bishop College or at some of the other black institutions, but I think it would be instructive for all of us to do so—to see what it was that they were offering at the time.

Certain historical processes were going on in this country in the decade of the sixties. While the processes addressed the increase of enrollment of Americans of Mexican descent in U.S. colleges and universities, an adjunct to this was a demand for the hiring of Chicano professors and the teaching of college courses with reference and with relevance to our historical presence in our native land, the United States. The opposition to these demands was not long in coming; for a decade or so, well into the seventies, the demands were met at times, forgotten and fought, resisted, addressed repeatedly, admitted, rejected, and so on. None of this is over, yet. But the modest increase of students was, and is, a visible piece of evidence. Not so is the increase of professors, but time may take care of this.

As for the course offerings, these are placed mostly in the college of liberal arts and within the colleges in departments, in centers, and in programs. The opposition to the inclusion of Mexican American literature was understandable, if one accepts the opposition on academic grounds. That is, is there such an American literature? Who are its contributors? Is there a body of criticism? And so on. The answer to the last question was "no"—there was no body of criticism. But the answer was "yes" to the first two questions—the literature existed and exists, and people were contributing and had contributed to it. The next question: "Is it any good?" was also brought up. Well, none of us knew the answer to that, nor did William Lyon Phelps back in 1896. He had, of course, touched on William Bradford and Edward Taylor and Jonathan Edwards, William Cullen Bryant, and James Fenimore Cooper. But he had focused on Poe, Hawthorne, Melville, Whitman, and Dickinson.

Now, as to its worth and the widening of this American literature, this lies with time, and that's the only answer that anyone can actually say and admit because time is the great leveler, and it usually decides what will live and what will not. It so happens, however, that universities are repositories of learning and that our time in the academy is different from the time of those outside the university. It takes us a longer time to admit or to reject ideas or theories. We're not a shopping mall with bright lights and colors and soft music to persuade us toward one item or another. We're deliberate, and we debate, and we study, we argue, and we assess. Time is on our side, and long after the popular mind has dismissed or has forgotten that which is transitory, the academy investigates and meets, and it tables or acts upon it. We're often accused of talking something to death, and we may be found guilty of that, too. But we also have higher responsibilities, we are a university. We're not a supermarket where the customer is always right. The inclusion of any course or program brings curiosity and questions. It may also bring blind opposition. But then our universities are populated by all manner of colleagues who also possess all manner of ideas and opinions. Some, of course, are also paranoic, but we live with them, too.

The proposal to adopt African-American literature and literature of the Native American and the Asian-American and so on came in the sixties. The opposition on academic grounds was wanting, but the opposition on the basis of racism was something else. There was some of both; there was also some paranoia on both sides. But worse than paranoia, there was arrant racial prejudice and, as always in life, there was irony. Opposition came also from some Americanists who were teaching American literature—American literature in its narrowest sense, of course. For if one thinks that New England literature looked kindly upon Southern White literature, one would be mistaken, and let me remind us that it is not until the fifties that systematic studies in American literature began to appear in public institutions. Regarding Southern literature, at the time of Faulkner's winning of the Nobel Prize almost all of his books were out of print. The year was 1949, and American literature became a growing concern in the fifties.

The greater demand for American literature, the New England and the Southern variety, coincided with the increased enrollment in U.S. institutions after 1957. The enrollment, too, was selective, but I'm going to let that pass for a more important consideration: academic amnesia. Those who inherited ready-made degree programs in American literature opposed the widening of American literature. Since this is a young field, we have every right to suspect that many of these colleagues had not yet won their own spurs and here they were unwilling to read, let alone teach, Richard Wright, Langston Hughes, the younger Ralph Ellison, James Baldwin, Tomás Rivera, Lucy Topahanso, Denise Chávez, Jenny Chin, Wendy Rose, and so on. One of the chief reasons was that American literature was still insecure as to its own place and standing in the curriculum, and because of this, it covered its own flanks and retrenched. While William Lyon Phelps had ample reason for his ignorance and for his narrow selection, our contemporary colleagues did not. They chose instead to retrench, to reject out of hand, and mistakenly, they went on to the other side of our other colleagues in British literature.

But let us see what happened. In 1968 the Modern Language Association was headed by Henry Nash Smith; that's a brief twenty-three years ago. In the late seventies Smith, along with Bill Schaefer, began to widen MLA representation and representative curriculum. Many of us know that Henry Nash Smith died not too long ago and those of us who knew him mourn his passing. Because it was he who, as a very strong force in the MLA, oversaw the changes in this country's curriculum in higher education. It would be an exaggeration to claim that Smith caused the changes, and he would not have made the claim, anyway; but as a leader, he recognized that the changes had to be made, and he facilitated those changes which paved the way for wider participation by women in the profession and the likewise important participation by other members of the MLA, who heretofore had not been included in any participatory capacity. Those other members of MLA included us—the Mexicans, that is Americans of Mexican descent—as well as native African-Americans, Native Americans, Asian-Americans, all members of the MLA.

Along with this decision came the inclusion of other American literatures which had been ignored and fought and derided and insulted. But time brought changes. Because in time younger and not so young Americanists widened American literature. I've heard it said, quite mistakenly, that it was the swing of the pendulum. I have to say that there's no such thing. I don't believe in cosmic changes. It isn't, and it wasn't, a pendulum. It was an effective breach which was widened to include the whole of the United States literature, irrespective of language.

Nevertheless, changes are constant, and it is the widening of the curriculum that has produced a vibrancy, once again, to American literature. The vibrancy has produced a breach in some of the old ideologies and in some of the old intramuralism and has served to introduce other voices.

I've no idea where it will end, but the ideas of 1967 regarding American literature are not those of 1991. This is the way it should be, since literature is meant to reflect values held and decisions taken by men and women and not by caricatures of them.

Rolando Hinojosa
Austin, Texas

Criticism in the Borderlands

Editors' Introduction
Criticism in the Borderlands

We have witnessed in recent years the need for a new history of American literature, one that would include the contributions of women and cultural groups ignored by the academy. Much work still lies ahead, however, especially in the field of Chicano literature; although many men and women have entered the academy, our literature and scholarship have yet to receive full institutional support or national attention. No doubt, other fields have benefited from the widening of the literary canon, most notably women's studies and African-American studies. That these area studies of research have received the most attention from the academy and its allied publishing sector can be verified by strolling through the book exhibits at the annual Modern Language Association national convention or by noting the names of women and African-American scholars present on the editorial boards of legitimating literary journals. We encourage and support this interest in African-American and feminist scholarship, for it arises out of concrete social conditions and will eventually influence classroom teaching and the emergence of an alternative canon. However, we lament the fact that such recognition has not been achieved by Chicano, as well as by Asian-American, Native American, and Puerto Rican men and women.

As this exclusion from the national critical scene continues, Chicano culture is increasingly drawing the attention of foreign scholars as witnessed by the biennial conferences in Germersheim (1984, 1990), Paris (1986), Barcelona (1988), and Madrid (1992) on U.S. Hispanic cultures; the annual *encuentros* between Mexican and Chicano scholars in Mexico City and in cities along the U.S.-Mexican border; and the participation of Chicano scholars, writers, artists, actors, and film makers in conferences and festivals throughout Latin America. Indeed, the idea for *Criticism in the Borderlands* first surfaced in 1985 as a response to the growing international interest in Chicano literature.

I

Chicano culture, as viewed by Chicana and Chicano critics as well as by European and Latin American scholars, is an expression of a social group that has given *the* distinctive cultural feature to the American West and Southwest. If we limit Chicano or Mexican-American artistic forms to political boundaries, they have existed in oral and written form since the Texas-Mexican War (1836) with greater awareness of cultural differences from Mexico after the U.S.-Mexican War (1846–48). Although colonial Novohispano and Mexican cultures in this region date back to the mid-sixteenth century and beyond, taking into account Native American *mestizo* roots, the literature produced by these groups should be ideologically and institutionally situated within the national literatures of Spain and Mexico. A Spanish chronicler of the area which was later to form the northern regions of the viceroyalty of New Spain, like Cabeza de Vaca or Coronado writing in the sixteenth century, regardless of whatever sympathy he may have had for Native Americans, is not a Chicano but a Spaniard. A similar situation holds true for Mexican writers. While Mexican literature flourished in the northern Mexican borderlands prior to and after 1848, until recently Mexican writers and scholars, expatriates and travelers in the United States have taken an unsympathetic view of their northern brethren judging them as Anglicized, inauthentic Mexicans.

Although the "unsettled" Southwest may have been discovered and, indeed, invented for an Anglo-American popular readership at the end of the nineteenth century by easterner Charles F. Lummis in books like *A New Mexico David* (1891), *The Land of Poco Tiempo* (1893a), and *The Spanish Pioneers* (1893b), greater scholarly knowledge of Hispanic culture in the Southwest accumulated rapidly early in this century through Aurelio M. Espinosa's "Romancero nuevomejicano" (1915–17) and Arthur L. Campa's "The Spanish Folksong in the Southwest" (1933). And J. Frank Dobie, instrumental in the development of Western folklore societies, was the first to teach a course on the Southwest, "Life and Literature of the Southwest," at the University of Texas, Austin, a course now taught by Chicano writer Rolando Hinojosa. However, all these early efforts stressed a virtually uninhabited landscape and an unreflected, storied Spanish or Mexican past at the expense of African-Americans, Asian-Americans, Native Americans, and Chicanos, many of whose ancestors had worked the Western soil for generations.

Contemporaries Lummis and Espinosa merit further examination for they greatly influenced the development of institutional studies on the borderlands in the twentieth century. In 1925, three years prior to his death,

Lummis boasted in *Mesa, Cañon and Pueblo* that he had been the first to apply the generic name "Southwest," or more specifically, "Spanish Southwest," to the million square miles that include New Mexico, Arizona, southern California, and parts of Colorado, Utah, and Texas. In a span of nine years, from 1891 to 1900, Lummis published eleven books, changing what was a physical and cultural desert into a land internationally known for its seductive natural and cultural attractions. Though an amateur inclined toward self-promotion and hyperbolic writing, Lummis became the founder of the "Southwest genre," recognized by both professionals and the popular media as the undisputed authority on the history, anthropology, and folklore of the Southwest.

In 1884 upon his arrival in Santa Fe, Territory of New Mexico, Lummis discovered for his readers a culture much like the fictional characters and settings of romantic literature. Unlike his native Massachusetts, the West had an authentic folk culture of simple and picturesque souls still existing undisturbed by the modern world. So taken was Lummis by the alien culture he encountered that he adopted it as his own, learned Spanish and took the name of Don Carlos. He founded the Southwest Museum in Los Angeles, promoted "Spanish" architecture, and established the Landmarks Club to revive the California missions. However, like other foreigners who make native culture their own, Lummis had a conservative and patronizing side, intent on writing about the most folkloric and romantic elements of Native American and *mestizo* culture. Through his first books Lummis reveals his attractions for courtly dons, beautiful señoritas, innocent Indian children, kind Mexican peons, witches, and penitents. So taken was Lummis by his "child-hearted" Spanish that he became an apologist for the Spanish conquest of the Americas. His *Spanish Pioneers* (1893b) is a vindication of the heroic padres and gallant Spaniards who brought God and civilization to the Americas.

Aurelio M. Espinosa, from Colorado, who once chaired the Department of Spanish and Portuguese at Stanford University is also particularly significant, for he rose to prominence as an internationally recognized scholar at the inception of Romance language studies on the West Coast. His goal in scholarship was to demonstrate that the folklore of the Spanish-speaking people of the Southwest was principally and fundamentally of Peninsular origin. Using positivistic methods, he quantified parallel motifs of New Mexican songs and tales with those from different regions of Spain. We cannot deny that much Mexican-*mestizo* folklore is Peninsular in origin, but can one ignore altogether the different historical and social contexts that made the materials collected by Espinosa as much Mexican as Spanish. What changes had occurred in Novohispano society that affected the transmission of oral tradition in the intervening years between the conquest of Mexico in 1521 and the establishment of Santa Fe in 1610 or what changes had occurred by the time of collection in the twentieth century? Of these issues virtually nothing was written until the Chicano period.

The political consequences of emphasizing the Spanish past were quite damaging. The historical fact that the Southwest was conquered Mexican territory was completely ignored. It was as if Spain had become the United States without centuries of racial and cultural mixture. Yet this interpretation of the conquest and colonization of Arizona, California, New Mexico, and Texas is still accepted by many Anglo-American critics as the golden age of Hispanic culture in the Southwest and continues to flourish in the present in the popular imagination in literature, mass media images, Hollywood films, and in the celebration of Spanish fiesta days throughout the Southwest.

The same romantic, even quaint, view of Spanish-Mexican experience on both sides of the international border was held by many Mexican-American writers, both men and women, during the first fifty years of this century. Writers of English expression like Nina Otero de Warren (*Old Spain in Our Southwest*, 1936), Cleofas M. Jaramillo (*Shadows of the Past/Sombras del Pasado*, 1941), Josephina Niggli (*Mexican Village*, 1945), and Fabiola Cabeza de Baca (*We Fed Them Cactus*, 1954) held conventional Anglo-American views of their culture. This is a literary period that awaits further scholarly studies, and Genaro Padilla's essay in this volume is an indication that a reassessment is clearly under way.

Although we are not dismissing the various ideological discourses on the borderlands prior to mid-twentieth century, we are arguing in this volume for a Mexican-American or Chicano intellectual perspective as found in the Arizona writer Mario Suárez who wrote short stories and sketches about his Tucson barrio for the *Arizona Quarterly* (1947, 1948, 1950). From our vantage point in the twentieth century, we can posit that such a perspective must have emerged in the borderlands in mid-nineteenth century when Mexican-Americans, Chicanos, or *mestizos* began to project for themselves a positive, yet also critical, rendering of their bilingual and bicultural experience as a resistive measure against Anglo-American economic domination and ideological hegemony.

For many compelling historical and sociological reasons, including overt racism, economic exploitation, and the lack of educational opportunities, it is not surprising that Mexican-American experience, thought, and writing did not receive their proper share of attention from universities prior to the Chicano movement of the sixties. We must, however, pay tribute to some outstanding scholars who through their individual efforts laid the groundwork for later research and writing. Jovita González's early study of Texas-Mexican society (1930) and collections of Texas-Mexican tales (1954), George I. Sánchez's dissertation on bilingual education (1934) and his *Forgotten People: A Study of New Mexicans* (1940), Luisa Espinel's collection of traditional folksongs from southern Arizona, *Canciones de Mi Padre* (1946), Américo Paredes's classic work on Texas border balladry, *"With His Pistol in His Hand": A Border Ballad and Its Hero* (1958), and Ernesto Galarza's political and scholarly activism on behalf of California farm workers (1964) all speak well for individual scholarly research combined with the interests of a bicultural, working-class community, a combination that helped mold Chicano studies in the seventies. The presence of Paredes is especially evident throughout our volume, for his book, *"With His Pistol in His Hand,"* was a highly conscious, imaginative act of resistance that redefined the border, which is to say, not the "Old Spain in Our Southwest" invented by Anglo-Americans, but a historically determined geopolitical zone of military, linguistic, and cultural conflict.

The tradition of Chicano literary studies that both of us inherited when we began our teaching and research careers in the early eighties was a product of the Chicano movement of the sixties, taking shape from a cultural and an institutional politics that called for the affirmation of a working-class, Mexican-*mestizo* heritage as well as for the establishment of centers of research and curricular programs in the universities and colleges of the United States. Chicano literature survived its early years of the late sixties with a canon to be discussed, debated, and questioned. And Chicano literary criticism which thrived early in ephemeral and sporadically published ethnic journals now constitutes a body of work with a variety of theoretical tendencies. As Rolando Hinojosa argues in the Foreword to this volume, this institutional success is owed not so much to the academy, but to the persistence of committed women and men who in addition to their "normal" professional duties and interests established curricular programs in Chicano literary studies.

II

Criticism of Chicano and Chicana writing over the last ten years reflects important shifts in argument and commitment. This book was conceived as a complement to Joseph Sommers's and Tomás Ybarra-Frausto's ground-breaking *Modern Chicano Writers* (1979) and Vernon E. Lattin's *Contemporary Chicano Fiction* (1986). With Sommers, Ybarra-Frausto, and Lattin we share an interest in addressing the status of Chicano criticism, but each anthology reveals a different ideological project, corresponding to a cultural conversation that has evolved since the late seventies over the nature of literary and paraliterary approaches to Chicano texts and culture. Sommers and Ybarra-Frausto's book was the first to postulate the existence of a distinct folk and communal tradition in Chicano literature. Américo Paredes's now classic essay, "The Folk Base of Chicano Literature," from their collection, demonstrates how folklore is of importance to minority discourse and groups because their basic sense of self is expressed in a language with an "unofficial" status. Like Paredes's article, the essays in *Modern Chicano Writers* survey the terrain of that unofficial and undocumented literary continent, but with the exceptions of Paredes's intervention and Sommers's dialectical essay on Tomás Rivera, they do so without providing the metacommentary that would prepare for a theory of Chicano literature. Lattin's *Contemporary Chicano Fiction*, as the title suggests, investigates, some seven years later, the growth of Chicano narrative in a pluralistic and somewhat theoretical manner. However, issues of race, class, and gender are only sporadically addressed, and the more complex predicament of theories and theorists in terms of location and self-positioning are absent.

Dialogic in intention, our book gathers a range of varying ideological, feminist, and cultural studies perspectives. That is, we present Chicano/a theory and theorists in our global borderlands: from ethnographic to postmodernist, from Marxist to feminist, from cultural materialist to New Historicist critical perspectives. In addition, our book strives to construct and elicit allegiances outside the immediate sphere of Chicano studies; we do so, let us add, because ideology itself involves networks of meaning and borders through which society is knitted together. By recovering neglected authors and texts, by challenging conservative habits of mind, by opening new perspectives on American literary history, ethnicity, gender, culture, and literary process itself, our book contributes in many ways to the new, albeit incomplete, American literary histories currently under reconstruction.

Moreover, we view our book paired with the recent books by Moraga and Anzaldúa (1983) and Herrera-Sobek and Viramontes (1988) in Latina feminist studies, Arnold Krupat (1989) and Gerald Vizenor (1988) in Native American studies, Houston A. Baker, Jr. (1987) and Hazel V. Carby (1987) in African-American studies, and Fernández-Retamar (1989) and Pérez-Firmat (1990) in the new comparative American studies as a form of what Elizabeth Fox-Genovese calls a "collective autobiography" (1986, 133). We concur with her that "The canon, or the power to speak in the name of the collectivity, results from social and gender relations and struggles, not from nature" (1986, 141). The first section of our volume, "Institutional Studies

and the Literary Canon," addresses the problem of the American canon
from perspectives as varied as narrative theory and ideology (R. Saldívar),
ethnicity and multiculturalism (Leal), and women-of-color feminisms and
subjectivities (Alarcón). "Representations of the Chicana/o Subject," addresses Fabiola Cabeza de Baca's and Cleofas Jaramillo's colonial discourse
in New Mexico (Padilla), Alma Villanueva's revisions of the physical power
of women (Ordóñez), Chicana *mestizaje* and the construction of identity
(Quintana), and the politics of culture in the recent short story cycles by
Sandra Cisneros, Denise Chávez, and Alberto Ríos (Rosaldo). "Genre, Ideology, and History" relates particular products of Chicano literature—narrative and literary criticism especially—to the variety of cultural (Calderón),
social and gendered (Sánchez), institutional and disciplinary (Chabram),
collective local and global (Harlow) borders that these products traverse.
The last section, "Aesthetics of the Border," reaches for new critical configurations in literary criticism and cultural studies: the Chicano border narratives by Américo Paredes, Tomás Rivera, and Rolando Hinojosa as national allegories and cultural critique (J. D. Saldívar), social dramas in
various *corridos* or ballads of border conflict (McKenna), the interesting
border disputes among women of color and white feminists (Saldívar-Hull),
and the ethnographic political unconscious in Mexican-American south
Texas (Limón). The volume as a whole thus aims at generating new ways of
understanding what counts as culture and "theory" and who counts as
(cultural) theorists.

Criticism in the Borderlands is an invitation, we hope, for readers—
(Pan-)Americanists, cultural studies critics, feminists, historians, and anti-
racists—to remap the borderlands of theory and theorists. Our work in the
eighties and nineties, along with that of other postcolonial intellectuals
moves, travels as they say, between first and third worlds, between cores
and peripheries, centers and margins. The theorists in this book see their
text always "written for" in our local and global borderlands.

This collection, therefore, should offer an important cultural perspective absent to an international scholarly community. We view this volume
as a Chicana and Chicano contribution to a new awareness of the historical
and cultural interdependence of both northern and southern American
hemispheres. We feel that at the present moment, any glossy version of a
postmodern, postindustrial "America" must be reinterpreted against the
influx of Third World immigrants and the rapid re-Hispanicization of important regional sectors of our Mexican America and the wider United
States. It should also be clear from this collection that future models of
"American" culture and reconstructions of "American" literary history that
fail to take into account the four hundred years of a Mexican-*mestizo*
presence in our borderlands will of necessity be incomplete.

Part I

Institutional Studies

and the

Literary Canon

Ramón Saldívar

Narrative, Ideology, and the Reconstruction of American Literary History

Before I present a more detailed analysis of narrative forms, ideology, and American literary history, I should say something about the coordinates of this essay. I think that we have reached a point in literary studies where it is no longer fruitful, nor even accurate, for us to assume that we can go directly to a text without first considering the critical presuppositions that we bring to our reading of a text. This is as true for noncanonic texts as for those of the established canon.

It is especially true, I believe, in the case of Chicano literature and its literary criticism as it produces texts that have been systematically excluded from the traditional framework of American literature. Works by Mexican-American authors are absent from the American literary histories, the anthologies of American literature, and from the syllabi of courses on American literature. Spanish departments in American universities have also participated in this strategy of exclusion. This exclusion is by no means innocent. Its effect has been very similar to that of the exclusion from the American canon of African-American art, where as Henry Louis Gates, Jr., describes it "logocentrism and ethnocentrism marched together in an attempt to deprive the black human being of even the potential to create art, to imagine a world and to figure it" (1984, 7).

I wish to suggest a method of interpretation that will provide a ground for the development of a way of reading Chicano literary texts as a group of works that intentionally exploit their peripheral status to and exclusion from the body of works that we might call majority literature. This method of reading obliges us to make connections between the findings of narrative analysis and traditional as well as modern approaches to ideology. Such critical dialectical awareness is crucial in the case of a developing literature like contemporary Chicano literature where literary historians are still involved primarily in the process of establishing the texts in the tradition and resolving questions concerning the issue of canon formation. This work is crucial as a reflection on the primary texts that constitute a tradition, for the dialectical analysis of which I speak both defines the tradition and helps to shape the direction of an art that is, to paraphrase Gates, in the process of "imagining" and "figuring" a world.

Narrative and Dialectics

I begin with the first of my three topics, narrative itself. The problem of narrative structure and of its relationship to the thematic aspects of texts is currently one of the most vital areas of analysis in literary theory. Much contemporary narrative analysis reveals the dialogical nature of meaning.

In *Figural Language in the Novel* (1984) I argued that with its care for authenticating detail and its passion for credibility and intelligibility, the novel especially among narrative forms expresses a continuing desire for types, for monological readings, for an anachronistic mythos of common understanding and a shared universe of meaning. And yet, in the same breath, the novel never ceases to express the conceptual maneuvering that we all must perform in order to conceive reality, indeed to shape reality, in ways that will make sense to the human mind. The novel allows us to seek, to absorb, and to understand new experiences by discovering new forms and rhythms, "grasping and reconstructing the stuff of social change in the living substance of perceptions and relationships" (Eagleton 1976, 34). This conflict between the contrary tendencies toward monological unifications, single voices on the one hand and polyphonic diversity, what Mikhail Bakhtin has called a choir of voices, on the other, all this makes the novel a particularly important Chicano literary genre.

As narrative productions, socially symbolic acts, and not mere reflections of the ideological formations within which they arise, Chicano novels put ideology to work, exposing the framing limits of what we take as self-evident truths, as common sense (Eagleton 1976, 155). These narrative fictions represent that what appears "natural" in the ways individuals live their lives in society is the result of identifiable cultural matrices. These cultural matrices, the truths that we hold to be self-evident, use the signifier to create truths and set them as norms, as coercive texts for meaning, that claim universality. Dialectical readings can point out the reification of these truths from the constructed domains of a specific history and a particular culture. They allow us to see the production of ideology not as a system of formalized ideas, but as ordinary ways of thinking, as common sense. E. P. Thompson puts it very sensibly in these terms. He says that:

Very rarely in history—and then only for short intervals—does any ruling class exercise authority by direct and unmediated military or even economic force. People are born into a society whose forms and relations seem as fixed and immutable as the overarching sky. The "common sense" of the time is saturated with the deafening propaganda of the *status quo;* but the strongest element in this propaganda is simply the fact that what exists exists. (1978, 254)

As narrative representations, these productive processes are necessarily figurative and cannot be abolished because they allow social formations to persist, but they can be articulated and analyzed. That articulation would have as its object what Jameson has called ideological analysis (1981, 12), namely a critical exposition of cultural texts that amounts to a rewriting of the text so that it is seen itself as a rewriting of a prior historical and ideological subtext that is no longer present as such (1981, 81).

Narratives, in sum, are preeminently and rigorously dialectical. Like the ideologies that they articulate, narratives both figure and are determined by their social context (Jameson 1971, 4–10). Read dialectically, narratives indicate that language and discourse do affect human life in determining ways, ways that are themselves shaped by social history. Giving rise to questions concerning language itself, the sovereignty of our identity, and the laws that govern our behavior, narratives reveal the heterogeneous systems that resist the formation of a unitary base of truth.

Ideology and Narrative

Turning now to the second item of my title, the notion of ideology itself, I follow Jameson's claim that narratives in general instantiate ideology as the substance of our collective thinking and collective fantasies about history and reality.

It is sufficient initially, I think, to understand ideology as the ways a culture links social action with fundamental beliefs, a collective identity with the course of history. Basically, ideology functions as a unifying social force (Higham 1974, 10–18). It is, according to Sacvan Bercovitch, "the system of interlinked ideas, symbols, and beliefs by which a culture . . . seeks to justify and perpetuate itself; the web of rhetoric, ritual, and assumption through which society coerces, persuades, and coheres" (Bercovitch 1986, 8). In an essay on American literary history Bercovitch argues that the "network of ideas through which the culture justifies itself is internalized rather than imposed, and embraced by society at large as a system of belief" (Bercovitch 1986, 9). The beauty of the hegemonic power of what Bercovitch calls "the American ideological consensus" (1981, 20–21) is that it has already built into itself a way of dealing with, and neutralizing, "alternative and oppositional forms" of social formation (1986, 9).

In literary and historical terms this American ideological consensus has involved "the legitimation of a certain canon," a canon based on the works of the Puritan forefathers. It has also involved consensus about "the meaning of the term history that was legitimated by a certain vision of America" (Bercovitch, ed., 1986, vii), America as a land of men of independent mind and independent means, developing through "initiative, individualism, self-reliance, and demands for freedom" (Bercovitch 1986, 3). Bercovitch, again, puts it this way:

> An ideology . . . arises out of historical circumstances, and then represents these, symbolically and conceptually, as though they were natural, universal, and right; as if the ideals promulgated by a certain group or class (. . . individualism, mobility, self-reliance, free enterprise) were not the product of history but the expression of self-evident truth. The act of re-presentation thus serves to consecrate a set of cultural limitations, to recast a particular society as Society, a particular way of life as the pursuit of happiness. (Bercovitch 1986, 10)

An ideology as such is not necessarily either good or evil, true or false. We can set aside crude notions of "false consciousness." But an ideology is a system of ideas underlying a certain social order. That is to say, ideology connects what we say and believe with the power structure and power relations of the society we live in (Eagleton 1983, 14). Ideology is thus much more than the unconscious beliefs a people may hold; it is more particularly "those modes of feeling, valuing, perceiving, and believing which have some kind of relation to the maintenance and reproduction of social power" (Eagleton 1983, 15). An ideology will thus repress alternative or oppositional forms when these arise. The ideology of the Puritan colonies, for example, did not simply exclude Native Americans from the colonists' consensus about the new world being fashioned from the wilderness. The native inhabitants were seen as the very embodiments of the evils most threatening to the creation of the new Jerusalem. This ideology of exclusion remained central to the American creed throughout the nineteenth century. And we see its effects in other historical and literary moments.

While I will employ these general senses of "ideology," I begin with Althusser's provisional definition of the ideological as "a 'representation' of the Imaginary relationship of individuals to their real conditions of existence" (Althusser 1971, 162).

For our purposes we need to retain but two features from this somewhat cryptic definition. First, ideology must always be necessarily narrative in its structure because it involves a mapping of the real. That is, it underwrites the stories about what we conceive of as real. Ideology also involves the essentially narrative, or fabulous, attempt of the subject to inscribe a place for itself in a collective and historical process that excludes the subject and that is basically nonnarratable. But as Paul Hirst reminds us, these relations exhibit no necessary homogeneity. This means that the "mapping" of the real cannot exhibit a singular "ideological instance." It must insist on the "heterogeneity of ideological social relations and their effects" (Hirst 1979, 2). Ideology thus refers to "a non-unitary complex of social practices and systems of representations which have political significances and consequences" (Hirst 1979, 54). For Chicano literature this "imaginary relationship" of political significances and consequences is not limited to issues of class ideology. Questions concerning race and gender, for example, are no less important and will not allow us to subordinate them to one single structure. No single map will suffice for an understanding of the "Real," and its features cannot be predicated in advance.

Second, we also need to retain the notion that the "Real" is an outer limit that the subject approaches in the anxiety of moments of truth— moments of personal crisis, of the loss of identity, or of the agonizing political polarizations of revolutionary situations such as those suffered by the characters in much of contemporary Chicano fiction. The makeup of "history" as such, then, is not so much the empirical events of the world as the self-inscription and symbolization in texts of those events and in our thinking about them. In other words our approach to the "Real" must always pass through its textualization, or what Jameson calls its "narrativization in the political unconscious" (1981, 35).

Althusser's notions of ideology offer "a representational structure [that] allows the individual subject to conceive or imagine his or her lived relationship to transpersonal realities, such as the social structure, or the collective logic of History" (Jameson 1981, 30). In this sense the "Real" is not to be considered as a knowable thing in itself. Nor is it a string of facts that one can know directly in the positive form of some "true" representation of consciousness. It is instead a cultural-historical and subjective invention, projected by an ideologically riddled consciousness. The "real" is what "resists symbolization absolutely" (Jameson 1981, 35). According to Terry Eagleton, "The text takes as its object, not the real, but certain significations by which the real lives itself—significations which are themselves the product of its partial abolition" (1976, 72). This narrativized real is not a reproduction, a reflection, or a mirroring of the historical real. Rather than conceiving it as an imaginary transposition or concretization of the historical real, Althusser argues that the textual real is the product of signifying practices whose source is history itself (1971, 222–25). What all this means basically is that reality can be known in experience only if it is first imagined as a formed product of the subjects who recognize it or misrecognize it and express it in symbolic forms. The "imaginary" is thus both an image and a spectral reality through the recognition of which the subject becomes a subject (Hirst 1979, 57). As Paul de Man argues, ideology, like metaphysics, may be conceived preeminently as a precritical stage of knowledge (1984, 132).

And yet, the narrative apparatus that informs ideological representations is not mere "false consciousness." Ideology is much more than that. It is an authentic way of grappling with a Real that must always transcend it, a Real into which the subject seeks to enter, all the while painfully learning the lesson of its own ideological closure and of history's resistance to the fantasy-structures in which it is itself locked. A text can be said to refer not to concrete situations so much as to the ideological formations that concrete situations have produced.

For those of us involved in literary studies, one particularly important result of this way of conceiving the work of ideology is that it allows us to understand the radical "decentering" of the subject, and the consequent emphasis on the collective and the political, that occurs in a contemporary literature like Chicano literature. There are no given, constitutive subjects with an experience of the real. "Subjects are not essential but are constituted" (Hirst 1979, 41). Or, in Althusser's words, "Ideology interpellates individuals as subjects" (Althusser 1971, 170). Appropriating Jacques Lacan's concept of the "mirror phase" (Lacan 1968) as a "speculary, i.e. a mirror-structure" phenomenon (Althusser 1971, 180, 195–219), Althusser argues that the subject exists as a mirror reflection of an *other* subject and becomes a subject itself in its recognition and reflection of and in the other (Hirst 1979, 57). Individuals are always "subjected" to and by certain principles and directives of ideology, so that they will be "happy, useful, and safe subjects, in the political sense of the term" (Lentricchia 1983, 1). To conceive of a text as ideology is thus to focus on the way that it affects the formation and transformation of human subjectivity (Therborn 1980, 2). Ideology is socially conditioned consciousness, allowing men and women to live what Clifford Geertz has called "lives of patterned desperation" (1973, 204). From this perspective human thought thus comes to be seen as a public and not fundamentally a private activity.

To be sure no culture is ideology-free. Chicano narrative fiction presents subjects acting according to variant and competing ideologies, ideologies in opposition to the existing material apparatus of American society. These narratives thus produce clashes or textual aporias that demarcate the limits of ideology itself. Chicano narrative carries out a counterhegemonic resistance to the dominant ideology at the level of various symbolic languages, attempting to figure what we might call, echoing Göran Therborn, an "alter-ideology" (1980, 28). It is worth repeating that the work of this "alter-ideology" is conflictual and oppositional rather than consensual or integrative. The great ethnographic work of Américo Paredes (1958) on turn-of-the-century border ballads can serve as a model for understanding Chicano literature as just such an "alter-ideological" oppositional formation.

From this oppositional perspective the utopian vision of a moment when the individual subject would be completely aware of his or her determination by class ideology, and would be able to step outside of this determination by sheer lucidity and clarity of thought, is a myth (Jameson 1981, 283). But it is precisely at this point that the value of art emerges. If men's and women's conditions of existence cannot be present to them as experience, and if in consequence they live their relation to these conditions in an imaginary mode as if they were given, then art, with its ability to produce the individual's imaginary relationship to conditions of existence, is a vital element of ideological analysis. Great art distances ideology by the way in which, endowing ideology with figurative and narrative articulations, the text frees its ideological content to demonstrate the contradictions within which ideologies are created. Great art is thus speculative in the most fundamental of senses: it allows us to see.

This is not to say that art itself is therefore ideology-free. On the contrary, as Jameson suggests, "ideology is not something that informs or invests symbolic production; rather the aesthetic act is itself ideological, and the production of aesthetic or narrative form is to be seen as an ideological act in its own right, with the function of inventing imaginary or formal 'solutions' to unresolvable social contradictions" (1981, 79). Resorting for the sake of exposition to a Hegelian formulation, we might argue that one rationale for studying "ethnic" literatures as part and parcel of the general problematic of American literature as a whole (rather than seeing them as merely "regional" or "marginal" phenomena of interest only to a specialized literary fringe) is that the masterworks of the dominant literary culture are the dialogical negations of the marginal texts not sanctioned by the hegemonic culture. As the silenced voices of opposition, these other marginal texts serve to highlight the ideological background of the traditional canon, to bring to the surface that repressed formation that Jameson has called the "political unconscious." This is the reason, I think, for the sudden interest on the part of some mainstream scholars in African-American literature, as well as ethnic and feminist literatures in general.

The difficulty of textual interpretation, as of dream interpretation, lies as Jameson claims "in detecting the traces of that uninterrupted narrative [of class struggle and oppression], in restoring to the surface of the text the repressed and buried reality of this fundamental history. . . . The assertion of a political unconscious proposes that we undertake just such a final analysis and explore the multiple paths that lead to the unmasking of cultural artifacts as socially symbolic acts" (1981, 20). Pierre Macherey describes this "unconscious" level as the very site of ideological work. In his own words:

> [T]he ideological background, which constitutes the real support of all forms of expression and all ideological manifestations, is fundamentally silent—one might say unconscious. But it must be emphasized that this unconscious is not a silent knowledge, but a total misrecognition of itself. If it is silent, it is silent on that about which it has nothing to say. We should therefore preserve the expression in all its ambiguity: it refers to that ideological horizon which conceals only because it is interminable, because there is always something more, but it refers also to that abyss over which ideology is built. Like a planet revolving round an absent sun, an ideology is made of what it does not mention; it exists because there are things which must not be spoken of. (1978, 131–32)

What I have in some of my earlier work (1979) called the "difference" of Chicano narrative fiction is precisely a function of its relation to ideology. Ideological analysis of its forms necessarily involves confronting the political consequences of particular social relations and representations. In articulating the space of that "ideological horizon" and the "abyss over which ideology is built," Chicano prose fiction begins to illuminate the gaps and silences that are the limits of the ideological consensus of American literary history.

Reconstructing American Literary History

I conclude with a few words about the third element of my title: the reconstruction of American literary history. This work is being undertaken by a whole new group of Americanists in forthcoming works such as the new edition of the *Cambridge History of American Literature* and in revisionary volumes, such as Bercovitch's recently published *Reconstructing American Literary History* (Bercovitch, ed., 1986) and Werner Sollors's *Beyond Ethnicity* (1986a). Against the power of the old American ideological consensus concerning which texts could be considered literary and historical, this new group of scholars will, according to Bercovitch, make "a virtue of *dissensus*" (Bercovitch, ed., 1986, viii). This dissensus, a dialogue of "conflicting views and interests" (Bercovitch 1986, 5), will serve as the revisionary model for the new American literary history. Against the old consensus, the new dissensus is *integrative:* not "eclectic, synthetic, or indeterminate" but rather "dialogic" (Bercovitch, ed., 1986, ix).

Werner Sollors's enterprise "to look at American culture anew" (1986a, 6) by focusing on the notions of consent and descent as terms which allow us "to approach and question the whole maze of American ethnicity and culture" (1986a, 6) follows very much in the reforming spirit of the new literary history. The conflict in American literature between consent and consensus on the one hand and descent and legitimacy on the other hand, Sollors claims, "can tell us much about the creation of *an* American culture out of diverse pre-American pasts" (1986a, 6; my emphasis).

This sounds wonderful, perhaps even after we notice that both Bercovitch's and Sollors's key words—"consensus" and "consent," "dissensus" and "dissent," "integrative" and "integration," "legitimacy" and "privilege"—themselves ring with the unmistakable clarity of their origins in the liberal-democratic bourgeois political theories that form the foundations of the hegemonic American ideological consensus.

The crucial factor here is that, often, these terms refer to consensus and dissent among the ruling groups themselves and to their legitimacy as members of the state apparatus (Therborn 1980, 109). That is, consensus and dissensus do not apply to those outside the ruling group or the state apparatus: working-class people, people of color, women.

In short, even this new integrative model can in practice turn out to be a counterhegemonic move to renew, defend, and modify, not to undo, the earlier forms of dominance (Williams 1977, 113–14). We might well ask, therefore, how the voices of those traditionally excluded from American literary history are to be "integrated" into that history.

The American ideological consensus that I have referred to takes on a very different quality when we take into account the ways that class origins and racial and gender differences affect literary and social history. At the very least, people of different classes, races, and gender will feel the effects of that consensus and its hegemony differently. And if Jameson's notion of expressive causality is to be taken seriously as a way of regarding history as the "absent cause" accessible to us only through its "narrativization in the political unconscious," then we must not easily dismiss the real power of difference to resist the reifying tendencies of studies such as Sollors's with their presumptuous claims to move "beyond ethnicity" toward the formation of a unitary American culture.

It might be well to notice that one of the things that is usually omitted from such unitary models of an American culture or an American ideological consensus arising from a Puritan, New England, middle-class perspective of the origins of American literary history is the literary tradition of the Southwest. It is a story that tells of the extermination of Native Americans, the enslavement of African-Americans, the subjugation of the Mexican-American people, the oppression of the working class, and the enforcement of the patriarchy.

Because of the decisive connections that are always being made in the writings of Chicano men and women between historical and aesthetic concerns, interest in this marginal group of literary texts is by no means unjustifiable. It is certainly the case that the critical project of many Mexican-American authors has been to offer a different perspective on the volatile configurations of literary and social history that crystallize in twentieth-century American society, in order that we may better understand the workings of that developing postmodern world. This critical understanding takes the form of what I call "the dialectics of difference."

F. O. Mathiessen's great book, *American Renaissance,* set the terms for the study of American literature: according to Mathiessen, his authors "felt that it was incumbent upon their generation to give fulfillment to the potentialities freed by the Revolution, to provide a culture commensurate with America's political opportunity" (1941, Preface). The oppositional literature of twentieth-century Mexican-American men and women is a direct resistance to the ideas inherent in "America's political opportunity," an opportunity that rationalized the colonized oppression of the native people of the Southwest and the exclusion of their writings from the canon of American literature.

An oppositional reconstruction of American literary history would recapture those stories and use them to construct a dialogical system to help us understand both the canonical master works that were sanctioned by the American ideological consensus and the antagonistic works that were not. By placing the masterworks in a framework that includes the voices to which the master texts were covertly opposed, voices that were silenced by the hegemonic culture, we might indeed begin to formulate a *truly* integrated American literary history.

Luis Leal

The Rewriting of American
Literary History

The rewriting of American literary history has been a subject in contemporary critical discourse for at least the last two decades. A short time, indeed, to solve such a controversial problem. One of the latest contributions to the topic is Sacvan Bercovitch's compilation of essays under the title *Reconstructing American Literary History* (1986). As pointed out by Professor Alan Wald in his review of the book, "Most of the important questions about conventional literary history are asked in this book, but no coherent response emerges" (1986, 35).

One of the most important weaknesses of the book, also underscored by Professor Wald, is the fact that, with one exception, all the essays "are wholly Eurocentric. American Indians, Chicanos, Puerto Ricans, and Asian-Americans are as absent from this sketch of a new literary history as they were from Mr. [Robert E.] Spiller's work [*Literary History of the United States*, 1948]. Mr. Bercovitch's 'dissensus' produces some brilliant analytical pyrotechnics, but the result is a very gentle kind of revisionism" (35).

Professor Wald's criticism implies that a true reconstructing of American literary history must take into consideration ethnic writing. In Bercovitch's book the only essay touching upon this aspect of American literature is Robert B. Stepto's contribution, "Distrust of the Reader in Afro-American Narratives." To complicate matters one of the contributors, Werner Sollors, takes the position that single-sex and single-ethnic-group approaches have no place in a reconstructed history of American literature. He goes on to add that "The wide-spread acceptance of the group-by-group approach has not only led to unhistorical accounts held together by static notions of rather abstractly and homogeneously conceived ethnic groups, but has also weakened the comparative and critical skills of increasingly timid interpreters who sometimes choose to speak with the authority of ethnic insiders rather than that of readers of texts" (Sollors 1986b, 256).

The rewriting of American literary history is not a new occurrence; it has been taking place since its first history was written. But it was not until the last three decades that the question about the place of ethnic literatures in that history was raised. The arguments regarding the problems of their inclusion or exclusion in mainstream American literature have not been resolved, some critics thinking that there is no need to consider them as different from mainstream American literature, and others insisting that ethnic literatures are "not quite" American, that they belong to a different type of discourse. Other critics take a neutral position and feel that literary historians should not be overly preoccupied with their inclusion, especially the works of authors writing in a foreign language.

Some critics attribute the exclusion of ethnic writers from the canon not to the fact that these writers are members of ethnic groups, but to other causes, such as well established friendships or tendentiousness. They point out that although the works of some ethnic writers like Joseph Heller and Philip Roth are included within the American literary canon, the works of Hispanics, Afro-Americans, Native Americans, and Asian-Americans are not considered as American in the histories of literature. This inconsistency has been explained by Werner Sollors in his book *Beyond Ethnicity* (1986a) by saying that "writers of national fame or of striking formal accomplishments or of international fame are often categorically excluded from the realm of ethnic writing. This is illustrated by the cases of Nathanael West, Eugene O'Neill, or Vladimir Nabokov and suggests that the limited scope of what we define sometimes quite tautologically—as ethnic literature" (Sollors 1986a, 241–42). He goes on to add the name of Carl Sandburg, a writer he considers to be "an interesting example of a popular ethnic who may be excluded from ethnic definitions because of his very popularity" (242).

Sollors's position would be one more example of those critics who have determined what is and what is not American literature, since only nationally famous authors of ethnic background—or very popular writers like Sandburg—would be included in the canon. However, Sollors goes on to say that "While tautologically narrowing definitions are of little persuasive power, a broader and more inclusive definition of ethnic literature is helpful: works written by, about, or for persons who perceived themselves, or were perceived by others, as members of ethnic groups." But he then contradicts himself by adding, "including even nationally and internationally popular writings of 'major' authors and formally intricate and modernist texts" (1986a, 243). This definition would not exclude, of course, the writers, like Sandburg, listed by Sollors in the preceding page.

Most recently, ethnic critics have attributed the exclusion of minority writers from the history of American literature to a deep-rooted and well-established ideology of exclusion affecting not only literary history but all aspects of American life. To justify the exclusion of ethnic literatures, critics belonging to the majority group proceed from the principle that ethnic literatures are aesthetically inferior. In the article, "An Introduction to Chinese-American and Japanese-American Literatures," which appeared in the volume *Three American Literatures* (1982), the authors, Jeffery Paul Chan and his colleagues, state that "American culture, protecting the sanctity of its whiteness, still patronizes us as foreigners and refuses to recognize Asian-American literature as 'American' literature" (1982, 198).

In one of the two essays on Native American literature appearing in the same volume, Lester A. Standiford traces this patronizing attitude back to the second decade of the century. As early as 1919, he points out, Louis Untermeyer, reviewing a collection of translations from Native American oral poetry, said that the book was a document valuable chiefly for its ethnological interest, adding that "the harsh aborigine can commit poetry as trite and banal as many an overcivilized paleface" (as quoted by Standiford 1982, 169). That review had brought a response from Mary Austin, one of the few critics who at that time found aesthetic values in American Indian poetry. Two months later, in the same publication, *The Dial*, she wrote, "Mr. Untermeyer describes himself as a 'mere man of letters' . . . but it begins to be a question in America whether a man is entitled to describe himself as a man of letters at all who so complacently confesses his ignorance or inability to enter into the vast body of aboriginal literature of his country" (1982, 169). Years later, in her book *The American Rhythm* (1930), Austin accused Americans of refusing to receive anything "from the self-contained culture of the aboriginal" (1930, 42).

It could be said that the ideological background of the traditional canon is not necessarily representative of the nonethnic population. The majority of the works classified as "regional" or "marginal" are those not written by ethnics, but by Euro-Americans. As early as the last decade of the nineteenth century, Charles F. Lummis, in his book *A New Mexico David*, complained of the absence of a history of the United States "not written in a closet," but based on the knowledge that history "began in the great Southwest" (1891, 174). And this complaint, extended to include literary history, was voiced in 1938 by Mabel Major in her book *Southwest Heritage*, where she says, "It is annoying to find American history and letters continually described as a style tradition with its genesis in the *Mayflower* and the Massachusetts Bay Psalm Book" (Major 1938, 33).

Professor A. Owen Aldridge in *Early American Literature: A Comparatist Approach* (1982) attributes the nature of the traditional canon to the narrowness of the British intellectual domination of comparative studies and also to the fact that the earliest compilers of histories of American literature were of New England states and therefore more interested in Puritan New England writers. No less important is the fact that these New England writers gave emphasis to aesthetic values over ideas and historical or political relationships.

It is interesting to observe that for Aldridge the designation "American literature" refers to the literature of the Americas and not only the United States. It is for this reason that he includes such works as Alonso de Ercilla's *La araucana* (1569–89), written in Chile about the Spanish conquest of that region, but not a similar work of 1610 about events that occurred in the Southwest, that is, Gaspar Pérez de Villagrá's *Historia de la Nueva México* (1900), a work similar to Ercilla's in form and content, since both are epic poems about the conquest of native American groups. We don't know why Aldridge excluded this work, but it may be due to the fact that it has never formed part of the canon on aesthetic grounds. This in spite of the fact that Mabel Major had advocated its inclusion in 1938, when she wrote, "Villagrá's account of the heroic capture of Acoma by Zaldívar and seventy men bears comparison with the scaling of the heights outside Quebec by Wolfe if one keeps all the circumstances in mind" (1938, 33). The poem is also excluded from the Mexican literary canon on the same grounds, that is, aesthetic merits.

One of the two references to Mexicano/Chicano literature found in Werner Sollors's book, *Beyond Ethnicity*, is Villagrá's epic poem. The reference, however, appears in a different context. In his chapter on "Ethnicity and Literary Form" Sollors mentions Villagrá's work as an example of the presence of the epic, a form "generally associated with ethnogenesis, the emergence of a people, and can therefore seemingly be appropriated transnationally by all peoples" (1986a, 238). However, he does not mention Ernesto Galarza's autobiography, *Barrio Boy* (1971), when discussing the presence of this genre among immigrants. Why Villagrá? Perhaps because epics produced by members of ethnic groups are few, while autobiographies seem to be plentiful.

Some critics speak about "other American literatures," a designation which implies the existence of more than one American literature. They say that the presence of these "other" literatures is the result of ethnic groups not being fully integrated into American life, as opposed to the conflict of cultures, as proposed by Américo Paredes (1958). If their theory is accepted, then we could say that there will not be a body of homogeneous American literature until these ethnic cultures entirely disappear; in other words until there is total integration or assimilation. There is a strong

sociological reason militating against this ever happening in the near future, since immigration from Latin America and Asia continues, reinforc-
ing and enlarging their ethnic groups in a constant process. As Colin Clarke
and his colleagues state in *Geography and Ethnic Pluralism* (1984):

> Ethnic identities may be more abiding and less superficial than is
> suggested (Jews providing the clearest example among Caucasian mi-
> norities), and racial identity continues to be a major social cleavage;
> moreover, as long as overseas migration exists, ethnic diversity will
> continue to be replenished and sustained. In addition . . . attitudinal
> and life-style diversity appears to be compounding in the advance
> societies with the consolidation and politicisation of life-style groups
> . . . especially in metropolitan areas. In everyday cultural and political
> life this less complete form of pluralism appears far from trivial, if
> largely untheorized. (Clarke, Ley, and Peach 1984, 2)

There are other reasons working for the preservation of a multicultural
society, such as the reluctance of people to give up their culture and of races
to mix freely. As Wayne Charles Miller stated in 1981, "the United States,
considered in a broader cultural perspective, is a composite of peoples . . .
still in the process of self-definition" (1981, 29).

In his defense of the melting pot theory Werner Sollors states that
pluralism equates with unhistorical ethnic persistence and group survival,
while the melting pot equates with historical change and group emergence.
Sollors is obviously thinking about certain Northern European ethnic
groups that have been thoroughly assimilated into American society, while
disregarding the experiences of Afro-Americans, Asian-Americans, Native
Americans, and Hispanic-Americans who, having been here for centuries,
have not yet been assimilated into the mainstream of American society. At
the root of cultural pluralism there may be, as Sollors points out, quoting
the early pluralist Horace M. Kallen, "a notion of the eternal power of
descent, birth, *natio*, and race" (1986b, 260), but to this we need to add that
there are also shared values and traditions, cultural pride, and group solidarity, not to mention the negative factors, such as low educational achievement, economic deprivation, and isolation.

Today, the fact that the fusion of the ethnic cultures into the mainstream has not been achieved gives rise to the presence of literatures written by representatives of these ethnic groups that have not been integrated
into the history of American literature or made an integral part of the
canon. One factor working against this acceptance is that the Chicano
writer can choose his language of expression, or even write in two languages, such as English and Spanish. As Miller says, "the voices of a distinct

Hawaiian culture, the influx of millions of Spanish-speaking people, the continuing insistence by blacks on a discrete African-American consciousness, the resurgence of American Indian cultures, and the phenomena of an ethni-geographical nature all attest to the evolvement of new definitions" (1981, 29). Even supposing that these ethnic groups were to merge, which is quite improbable, there would still be a literature that had to be accepted as American since ethnic literature, according to John M. Reilly "is not so designated because of the authors' race, color, creed, national origin or association. . . . What we designate 'ethnic literature' are the products of authors who choose to feature the significance of ethnicity in their writings" (1978, 4).

There is no unanimity today regarding the form that histories of American literature should take. Sollors rejects the so-called "mosaic" procedure, according to which the history of American literature can best be written by separating the groups that produced such literature in the United States and then writing monographs about them. He believes that the results of this procedure "are the readers and compendiums made up of diverse essays on groups of ethnic writers who may have little in common except so-called ethnic roots while, at the same time, obvious and important literary and cultural connections are obfuscated" (1986b, 255). He documents his assertion by quoting what James Dormon wrote in a review "of such a mosaic collection of essays on ethnic theatre." According to Dormon, "there is little to tie the various essays together other than the shared theme 'ethnic American theatre history'" (1986b, 255).

The theory of unlimited space for other literary traditions, proposed by Marco A. Portales (1984), is also summarily dismissed by Sollors for the reason that "a literary history now could not be more inclusive than those of the past without being explicitly exclusive, too; and it is here that more theoretical statements have to be made to offset the unrealistic combination of pluralist faith and the idea of limitless space" (1986b, 255). At the same time he rejects contemporary literary pluralism because "literary pluralists of our time would like to construct a mosaic of ethnic stories that relies on the supposed permanence, individuality, and homogeneity of each ancestral tradition and has no space for the syncretistic nature of so much of American literature and cultural life" (1986b, 274).

On the other hand, Miller believes in the existence of a multicultural America and suggests that, "While continuing to make use of the tools of close textual analysis, we should seek to 'place' the various American literatures in their cultural contexts. In fact, that process should be our primary work. It may be the key to the next literary history of this nation" (1981, 33).

We can see, then, the complexities facing the independent critic, the academic, and other responsible persons now engaged in the reconstruction of American literary history. Should it be a complete history, with limitless space, or a history with designations for regional or ethnic literatures? As to terminology, should we keep the hyphenated designations or do away with them? Chicanos, of course, have already solved this problem by accepting the term Chicano over Mexican-American. One thing is clear, and that is, the idea—with which even Sollors agrees—that no writer should be excluded from the reconstructed history of American literature by virtue of race, region, or gender.

We must also remember that the problems confronted by critics and literary historians are the same as those found in other countries and other regions. As an example, I quote Wellek and Warren who observed in 1949 that a history of literature in England during the Middle Ages "which neglects the vast amount of writings in Latin and Anglo-Saxon gives a false picture of England's literary situation and general culture" (1949, 40).

Most Chicano literary critics are in agreement that there should be an opening of the definition of American literature to include ethnic literatures, not as separate entities, or marked with hyphenated designations, but as forming an integral and important part of that history. They do not agree, of course, as to the time when that will take place, some thinking that it will be years before that happens, while others assure us that the reconstruction of American literary history is already under way. But even if the rewriting of a new history of American literature has begun, much remains to be done. I believe that for the present at least, Chicano scholars should not be overly concerned with historiographical and canonical problems and should dedicate more of their time to textual and historical Chicano literary studies.

Norma Alarcón

The Theoretical Subject(s) of *This Bridge Called My Back* and Anglo-American Feminism

This Bridge Called My Back: Writings by Radical Women of Color (1983), edited by Chicana writers Cherríe Moraga and Gloria Anzaldúa,[1] was intended as a collection of essays, poems, tales, and testimonials that would give voice to the contradictory experiences of "women of color." To make explicit this end, the editors wrote:

> We are the colored in a white feminist movement.
> We are the feminists among the people of our culture.
> We are often the lesbians among the straight.
> (23)

By giving voice to such experiences, each according to her style, the editors and contributors believed they were developing a theory of subjectivity and culture that would demonstrate the considerable difference between them and Anglo-American women, as well as between Anglo-European men and men of their culture.

As a speaking subject of an emergent discursive formation, the writer in *Bridge* was aware of the displacement of her subjectivity across a multiplicity of discourses: feminist/lesbian, nationalist, racial, and socioeconomic. The peculiarity of her displacement implied a multiplicity of positions from which she was driven to grasp or understand herself and her relations with the real, in the Althusserian sense of the word (Althusser 1971). The writer in *Bridge*, in part, was aware that these positions were often incompatible or contradictory, and problematic, since many readers would not have access to the maze of discourses competing for her body and her voice. This self-conscious effort to reflect on her "flesh and blood experiences to concretize a vision that [could] begin to heal [their] 'wounded knee' " (23) led many a *Bridge* speaker to take up a position in conflict with multiple inter- and intracultural discursive interpretations in an effort to come to grips with "the many-headed demon of oppression" (195).

Since its publication in 1981, *Bridge* has had a diverse impact on feminist writings in the United States. Teresa de Lauretis, for example, claims that *Bridge* has contributed to a "shift in feminist consciousness" (1987, 10), although her explanation fails to clarify what the shift consists of and for whom. There is little doubt, however, that *Bridge* along with eighties writings by many women of color in the United States has problematized many a version of Anglo-American feminism and has helped open the way for alternate feminist discourses and theories.

Presently, however, the impact among most Anglo-American theorists appears to be more cosmetic than not because, as Jane Flax has recently noted, "The modal 'person' in feminist theory still appears to be a self-sufficient individual adult" (1987, 640). This particular "modal person" corresponds to the female subject most admired in Western literature which Gayatri Chakravorty Spivak has characterized as the one who "articulates herself in shifting relationship to . . . the constitution and 'interpellation' of the subject not only as individual but as 'individualist'" (1985, 243–44). Consequently, the "native female" or "woman of color" can be excluded from the discourse of feminist theory. The 'native female,' the object of colonialism and racism, is excluded because, in Flax's terms, white feminists have not "explored how our understanding of gender relations, self, and theory are partially constituted in and through experiences of living in a culture in which asymmetric race relations are a central organizing principle of society" (1987, 640).

It is clear that the most popular subject of Anglo-American feminist theorizing is an autonomous, self-making, self-determining subject who first proceeds according to the *logic of identification* with regard to the subject of consciousness, a notion usually viewed as the purview of man, but now claimed for women (see Kristeva 1981, 19). And believing that in this respect she is the same as man, she now claims the right to pursue her own identity, to name herself, to pursue self-knowledge, and in the words of Adrienne Rich to effect "a change in the concept of sexual identity" (1979, 35).

Though feminism has problematized gender relations as "the single most important advance in feminist theory" (Flax 1987, 627), it has not problematized the subject of knowledge and her complicity with the notion of consciousness as "synthetic unificatory power, the centre and active point of organization of representations determining their concatenation" (Pêcheux 1982, 122). The subject (and object) of knowledge is now a woman, but the inherited view of consciousness has not been questioned at all. As a result some Anglo-American feminist subjects of consciousness have tended to become a parody of the masculine subject of consciousness, thus revealing their ethnocentric liberal underpinnings.

In 1982 Jean Bethke Elshtain noted the "masculine cast" of radical feminist language, specifically citing the terms of "raw power, brute force, martial discipline, law and order with a feminist face—and voice" (611). Also in critiquing liberal feminism and its language, she wrote that "no vision of the political community that might serve as the groundwork of a life in common is possible within a political life dominated by a self-interested, predatory individualism" (617). Althusser has argued that this tradition "has privileged the category of the 'subject' as Origin, Essence and Cause, responsible in its internality for all determinations of the external object. In other words, this tradition has promoted Man, in his ideas and experience, as the source of knowledge, morals and history" (cited by Mac-Donell 1986, 76). By identifying in this way with this tradition, standpoint epistemologists have substituted, ironically, woman for man.

This logic of identification as a first step in constructing the theoretical subject of feminism is often veiled from standpoint epistemologists because greater attention is given to naming female identity and describing women's ways of knowing as being considerably different than men's.[2] By emphasizing 'sexual difference,' a second step takes place, often called oppositional thinking (counteridentifying). However, this gendered standpoint epistemology leads to feminism's bizarre relationship with other liberation movements, working inherently against the interests of non-white women and no one else.

Sandra Harding, for example, argues that oppositional thinking (counteridentification) with white men should be retained even though "There are suggestions in the literature of Native Americans, Africans, and Asians that what feminists call feminine versus masculine personalities, ontologies, ethics, epistemologies, and world views may be what these other liberation movements call non-Western versus Western personalities and world views. . . . I set aside the crucial and fatal complication for this way of thinking—the fact that one half of these people are women and that most women are not Western" (1986, 659). She further suggests that feminists respond by relinquishing the totalizing "master theory" character of our theory making: "This response to the issue (will manage) to retain the categories of feminist theory . . . and simply set them alongside the categories of the theory making of other subjugated groups. . . . Of course, it leaves bifurcated (and perhaps even more finely divided) the identities of all except ruling-class white Western women" (1986, 660). The apperception of this situation is precisely what led to the choice of title for the book *All the*

Blacks are Men, All the Women are White, But some of us are Brave, edited by Gloria T. Hull, Patricia Bell Scott, and Barbara Smith (1982).

Notwithstanding the power of *Bridge* to affect the personal lives of its readers, *Bridge*'s challenge to the Anglo-American subject of feminism has yet to effect a newer discourse. Women of color often recognize themselves in the pages of *Bridge* and write to say "The women writers seemed to be speaking to me, and they actually understood what I was going through. Many of you put into words feelings I have had that I had no way of expressing. . . . The writings justified some of my thoughts telling me I had a right to feel as I did" (Moraga, Foreword to the second edition). However, Anglo feminist readers of *Bridge* tend to appropriate it, cite it as an instance of difference between women, and proceed to negate that difference by subsuming women of color into the unitary category of woman/women. The latter is often viewed as the "common denominator" (De Lauretis 1986, 14), between us, though it is forgotten that it is our "common denominator" in an oppositional (counteridentifying) discourse with some white men that leaves us unable to explore relationships among women.

Bridge's writers did not see the so-called "common denominator" as the solution for the construction of the theoretical feminist subject. In the call for submissions the editors clearly stated: "We want to express to all women—especially to white middle class women—the experiences which divide us as feminists; we want to examine the incidents of intolerance, prejudice and denial of differences within the feminist movement. We intend to explore the causes, and sources of, and solutions to these divisions. We want to create a definition that expands what 'feminist' means to us" (Moraga and Anzaldúa, Introduction to the first edition, xxiii). Thus, the female subject of *Bridge* is highly complex. She is and has been constructed in a crisis-of-meaning situation which includes racial and cultural divisions and conflicts. The psychic and material violence that gives shape to that subjectivity cannot be underestimated nor passed over lightly. The fact that not all of this violence comes from men in general but also from women renders the notion of "common denominator" problematic.

It is clear, however, that even as *Bridge* becomes a resource for the Anglo-American feminist theory of classroom and syllabus, there's a tendency to deny differences if these differences pose a threat to the "common denominator" category. That is, solidarity would be purchased with silence, putting aside the conflictive history of groups' interrelations and interdependence. In the words of Paula Treichler, "How do we address the issues and concerns raised by women of color, who may themselves be even more excluded from theoretical feminist discourse than from the women's studies curriculum? . . . Can we explore our 'common differences' without overemphasizing the division that currently seems to characterize the feminism of the United States and the world?" (1986, 79). Clearly, this exploration appears impossible without a reconfiguration of the subject of feminist theory, and her relational position to a multiplicity of others, not just white men.

Some recent critics of the "exclusionary practices in Women's Studies" have noted that gender standpoint epistemology leads to a 'tacking on' of "Material about minority women" without any note of its "significance for feminist knowledge" (Baca Zinn et al. 1986, 296). The common approaches noted were the tendency to (1) treat race and class as secondary features in social organization (as well as representation) with primacy given to universal female subordination; (2) acknowledge that inequalities of race, class, and gender generate different experiences and then set aside race and class inequalities on the grounds that information was lacking to allow incorporation into an analysis; (3) focus on descriptive aspects of the ways of life, values, customs, and problems of women in subordinate race and class categories with little attempt to explain their source or their broader meaning (Baca Zinn et al. 1986, 296). In fact, it may be impossible for gender standpoint epistemology to ever do more than a "pretheoretical presentation of concrete problems" (Baca Zinn et al. 1986, 297).

Since the subject of feminist theory and its single theme—gender—go largely unquestioned, its point of view tends to suppress and repress voices that question its authority, and as Jane Flax remarks, "The suppression of these voices seems to be a necessary condition for the (apparent) authority, coherence, and universality of our own" (1987, 633). This may account for the inability to include the voices of women of color in feminist discourse, even though they are not necessarily underrepresented in reading lists.

For standpoint epistemologists the desire to construct a feminist theory based solely on gender, on the one hand, and the knowledge or implicit recognition that such an account might distort the representation of many women and/or correspond to that of some men, on the other, gives rise to anxiety and ambivalence with respect to the future of that feminism, especially in Anglo-America. At the core of that attitude is the often unstated recognition that if the pervasiveness of women's oppression is virtually universal on some level, it is also highly diverse from group to group and that women themselves may become complicitous with that oppression. "Complicity arises," says MacDonell, "where through lack of a positive starting point either a practice is driven to make use of prevailing values or a critique becomes the basis for a new theory" (1986, 62).

The inclusion of other analytical categories such as race and class becomes impossible for a subject whose consciousness refuses to acknowledge that "one becomes a woman" in ways that are much more complex than simple opposition to men. In cultures in which asymmetric race and class relations are a central organizing principle of society, one may also "become a woman" in opposition to other women. In other words, the whole category of woman may also need to be problematized, a point that I shall take up below.

Simone de Beauvoir and her key work *The Second Sex* have been most influential in the development of feminist standpoint epistemology. She may even be responsible for the creation of Anglo-American feminist theory's "episteme": a highly self-conscious ruling-class white Western female subject locked in a struggle to the death with "Man." Beauvoir shook the world of women, most especially with the ramifications of her phrase, "One is not born, but rather becomes, a woman" (1974, 301). For over 400 pages of text after that statement, Beauvoir demonstrates how a female is constituted as a "woman" by society as her freedom is curtailed from childhood. The curtailment of freedom incapacitates her from affirming "herself as a subject" (1974, 316). Very few women, indeed, can escape the cycle of indoctrination except perhaps the writer/intellectual because "She knows that she is a conscious being, a subject" (1974, 761). This particular kind of woman can perhaps make of her gender a project and transform her sexual identity.[3]

But what of those women who are not so privileged, who neither have the political freedom nor the education? Do they now, then, occupy the place of the Other (the 'Brave') while some women become subjects? Or do we have to make a subject of the whole world?

Regardless of our point of view in this matter, the way to becoming a female subject has been effected through consciousness raising. In 1982, in a major theoretical essay, "Feminism, Marxism, Method, and the State: An Agenda for Theory," Catherine A. MacKinnon cited *Bridge* as a book that explored the relationship between sex and race and argued that "consciousness-raising" was *the* feminist method (1982, 536–38). The reference to *Bridge* is brief. It served as an example, along with other texts, of the challenge that race and nationalism have posed for Marxism. According to her, Marxism has been unable to account for the appearance of these emancipatory discourses nor has it been able to assimilate them. Nevertheless, MacKinnon's major point was to demonstrate the epistemological challenge that feminism and its primary method, "consciousness-raising," posed for Marxism. Within Marxism class as a method of analysis had failed to reckon with the historical force of sexism. Through "consciousness-raising" (from women's point of view) women are led to know the world in a different way. Women's experience of politics, of life as sex objects, gives rise to its own method of appropriating that reality: feminist method (Mac-Kinnon 1982, 536). It challenges the objectivity of the "empirical gaze" and "rejects the distinction between knowing subject and known object" (1982, 536). By having women be the subject of knowledge, the so-called "objectivity" of men is brought into question. Often this leads to privileging women's way of knowing in opposition to men's way of knowing, thus sustaining the very binary opposition that feminism would like to change or transform. Admittedly, this is only one of the many paradoxical procedures in feminist thinking as Nancy Cott confirms, "It acknowledges diversity among women while positing that women recognize their unity. It requires gender consciousness for its basis, yet calls for the elimination of prescribed gender roles" (1986, 49).

However, I suspect that these contradictions or paradoxes have more profound implications than is readily apparent. Part of the problem may be that as feminist practice and theory recuperate their sexual differential through "consciousness-raising," women reinscribe such a differential as feminist epistemology or theory. With gender as the central concept in feminist thinking, epistemology is flattened out in such a way that we lose sight of the complex and multiple ways in which the subject and object of possible experience are constituted. The flattening effect is multiplied when one considers that gender is often solely related to white men. There's no inquiry into the knowing subject beyond the fact of being a "woman." But what is a "woman" or a "man" for that matter? If we refuse to define either term according to some "essence," then we are left with having to specify their conventional significance in time and space, which is liable to change as knowledge increases or interests change.

The fact that Anglo-American feminism has appropriated the generic term for itself, leaves many a woman in this country having to call herself otherwise, that is, "women of color," which is equally "meaningless" without further specification. It also gives rise to the tautology, Chicana women.

Needless to say, the requirement of gender consciousness only in relationship to man leaves us in the dark about a good many things, including interracial and intercultural relations. It may well be that the only purpose this type of differential has is as a political strategy. It does not help us envision a world beyond binary restrictions, nor does it help us reconfigure feminist theory to include the "native female." It does, however, help us grasp the paradox that within this cultural context one cannot be a feminist without becoming a gendered subject of knowledge which makes it very difficult to transcend gender at all and to imagine relations between women.

In *Feminist Politics and Human Nature* (1983), Alison M. Jaggar, speaking as a socialist feminist, refers repeatedly to *Bridge* and other works by women of color unrepresented in feminist theory. Jaggar claims that socialist feminism is inspired by Marxist and radical feminist politics though the latter has failed to be scientific about its insights. *Bridge* is cited various times to counter the racist and classist position of radical feminists (1983, 249–50, 295–96). Jaggar charges that "Radical feminism has encouraged women to name their own experience but it has not recognized explicitly that this experience must be analyzed, explained and theoretically transcended" (381). In a sense Jaggar's charge amounts to the notion that radical feminists were flattening out their knowledge by an inadequate methodology, that is, gender consciousness-raising.

Many of Jaggar's observations are a restatement of *Bridge*'s challenge to Anglo-American feminists of all political persuasions, be it liberal, radical, Marxist, or socialist, the types sketched out by Jaggar. For example, Jaggar's "A representation of reality from the standpoint of women must draw on the variety of all women's experience" (386) may be compared to Barbara Smith's view in *Bridge* that "Feminism is the political theory and practice to free *all* women: women of color, working-class women, poor women, physically challenged women, lesbians, old women, as well as white economically privileged heterosexual women" (61). Jaggar continues, "Since historically diverse groups of women, such as working-class women, women of color, and others have been excluded from intellectual work, they somehow must be enabled to participate as subjects as well as objects of feminist theorizing" (386). Similarly, writers in *Bridge* appear to think that "consciousness-raising" and the naming of one's experience would deliver some theory and yield a notion of "what feminist means to us" (xxiii). However, except for Smith's statement, there is no overarching view that would guide us as to "what feminist means to us." Though there is a tacit political identity—gender/class/race—encapsulated in the phrase "women of color" that connects the pieces, they tend to split apart into "vertical relations" between "culture of resistance" and the "culture resisted or from which excluded." Thus, the binary restrictions become as prevalent between race/ethnicity of oppressed versus oppressor as that between the sexes.

The problems inherent to Anglo-American feminism and race relations are so locked into the "Self-Other" theme that it is no surprise that *Bridge*'s coeditor Moraga would remark, "In the last three years I have learned that Third World feminism does not provide the kind of easy political framework that women of color are running to in droves. The *idea* of Third World feminism has proved to be much easier between the covers of a book than between real live women" (Moraga, foreword to the second edition). She refers to the United States, of course, because feminism is alive and well throughout the Third World largely within the purview of women's rights or as a class struggle.[4]

The appropriation of *Bridge*'s observations in Jaggar's work differs slightly from the others in its view of linguistic usage implying to a limited extent that language is also reflective of material existence. The crucial question is how indeed can women of color be subjects as well as objects of feminist theorizing? Jaggar cites María Lugones's doubts, "We cannot talk to you in our language because you do not understand it. . . . The power of white Anglo women vis-à-vis Hispanas and African-American women is in inverse proportion to their working knowledge of each other. . . . Because of their ignorance, white Anglo women who try to do theory with women of color inevitably disrupt the dialogue. Before they can contribute to collective dialogue, they need to 'know the text,' to have become familiar with an alternative way of viewing the world. . . . You need to learn to become unintrusive, unimportant, patient to the point of tears, while at the same time open to learning any possible lessons. You will have to come to terms with the sense of alienation, of not belonging, of having your world thoroughly disrupted, having it criticized and scrutinized from the point of view of those who have been harmed by it, having important concepts central to it dismissed, being viewed with mistrust" (1983, 386). Lugones's advice to Anglo women to listen was post-*Bridge*. But we should recall that one of *Bridge*'s breaks with prevailing conventions was, of course, linguistic. If prevailing conventions of speaking/writing had been observed many a contributor would have been censored or silenced. So would have many a major document or writing by minorities. *Bridge* leads us to understand that the silence and silencing of people begins with the dominating enforcement of linguistic conventions, the resistance to relational dialogues, as well as the disenablement of peoples by outlawing their forms of speech.

As already noted, Anglo-American feminist theory has assumed a speaking subject who is an autonomous, self-conscious individual woman; yet, it has also taken for granted the linguistic status which founds subjectivity. In this way it appropriates woman/women for itself and turns its work into a theoretical project within which the rest of us are compelled to fit. By forgetting or refusing to take into account that we are culturally constituted in and through language in complex ways and not just engendered in a homogeneous situation, the Anglo-American subject of consciousness cannot come to terms with her (his) own class-biased ethnocentrism. She is blinded to her own construction not just as woman but as an Anglo-American one. Such a subject creates a theoretical subject that could not possibly include all women just because we are women.

Against this feminist backdrop many "women of color" have struggled to give voice to their subjectivity, as evidenced in the publication of the writings collected in *Bridge*. However, the freedom of women of color to posit themselves as multiple-voiced subjects is constantly in peril of repression precisely at that point where our constituted contradictions put them at odds with women different from themselves.

The pursuit of a "politics of unity" solely based on gender forecloses the "pursuit of solidarity" through different political formations and the exploration of alternative theories of the subject of consciousness. There is a tendency in more sophisticated and elaborate gender standpoint epistemologists to affirm "an identity made up of heterogeneous and heteronomous representations of gender, race, and class, and often indeed across languages and cultures" (De Lauretis 1986, 9) with one breath and with the next to refuse to explore how that identity may be theorized or analyzed, by reconfirming a unified subjectivity or "shared consciousness" through gender. The difference is handed over with one hand and taken away with the other. If it were true as Teresa de Lauretis has observed that "Self and identity, . . . are always grasped and understood within particular discursive configurations" (1986, 8), it does not necessarily follow that one can easily and self-consciously decide "to reclaim (an identity) from a history of multiple assimilations" (1986, 9) and still retain a "shared consciousness." Such a practice goes counter to the homogenizing tendency of the subject of consciousness in the United States. To be oppressed means to be disenabled not only from grasping an "identity," but also from reclaiming it.

To grasp or reclaim an identity in this culture means always already to have become a subject of consciousness. The theory of the subject of consciousness as a unitary and synthesizing agent of knowledge is always already a posture of domination. One only has to think of Gloria Anzaldúa's essay in *Bridge*, "Speaking in Tongues: A Letter to Third World Women Writers" (165–74). Though De Lauretis concedes that a racial "shared consciousness" may have prior claims than gender, she still insists on unity through gender, "the female subject is always constructed and defined in gender, starting from gender" (1986, 19). One is interested in having more than an account of gender; there are other relations to be accounted for. De Lauretis still insists, in most of her work, that "the differences among women may be better understood as differences within women" (1986, 14). This position returns us all to our solitary, though different, consciousness, without noting that some differences are (have been) a result of relations of domination of women by women, that differences may be purposefully constituted for the purpose of domination or exclusion, especially in oppositional thinking.

Some of the writers in *Bridge* thought at some point in the seventies that feminism could have been the ideal answer to their hope for liberation. Chrystos, for example, states her disillusionment as follows, "I no longer believe that feminism is a tool which can eliminate racism or even promote better understanding between different races & kinds of women" (69). The disillusionment is eloquently reformulated in the theme poem by Donna Kate Rushin, "The Bridge Poem" (xxi–xxii). The dream of helping the people who surround her to reach an interconnectedness that would change society is given up in favor of self-translation into a "true self." In my view the speaker's refusal to play "bridge," an enablement to others as well as self, is the acceptance of defeat at the hands of political groups whose self-definition follows the view of self as unitary, capable of being defined by a single "theme." The speaker's perception that the "self" is multiple ("I'm sick of mediating with your worst self / On behalf of your better selves" [xxii]) and its reduction harmful gives emphasis to the relationality between one's selves and those of others as an ongoing process of struggle, effort, and tension. Indeed, in this poem the better "Bridging self" of the speaker is defeated by the overriding notion of the unitary subject of knowledge and consciousness so prevalent in Anglo-American culture.

Difference, whether it be sexual, racial, or social, has to be conceptualized within a political and an ideological domain.[5] In *Bridge*, for example, Mirtha Quintanales points out that "in this country, in this world, racism is used *both* to create false differences among us *and* to mask very significant ones—cultural, economic, political" (153).

Consciousness as a site of multiple voicings is the theoretical subject, par excellence, of *Bridge*. These voicings (or thematic threads) are not viewed as necessarily originating with the subject, but as discourses that transverse consciousness and which the subject must struggle with constantly. Rosario Morales, for example, says "I want to be whole. I want to claim myself to be Puerto Rican, and U.S. American, working class & middle class, housewife and intellectual, feminist, marxist and anti-imperialist" (91). Gloria Anzaldúa observes, "What am I? *A third world lesbian feminist with Marxist and mystic leanings.* They would chop me up into little fragments and tag each piece with a label" (205). The need to assign multiple registers of existence is an effect of the belief that knowledge of one's subjectivity cannot be arrived at through a single "theme." Indeed the multiple-voiced subjectivity is lived in resistance to competing notions for one's allegiance or self-identification. It is a process of disidentification (Pêcheux 1982, 158–59) with prevalent formulations of the most forcefully theoretical subject of feminism.

The choice of one or many themes is both a theoretical and a political decision. Like gender epistemologists and other emancipatory movements, the theoretical subject of *Bridge* gives credit to the subject of consciousness as the site of knowledge but problematizes it by representing it as a weave. In Anzaldúa's terms the woman of color has a "plural personality." Speaking of the new *mestiza* in *Borderlands/La Frontera*, she says, "She learns to juggle cultures. The juncture where the mestiza stands, is where phenomena tend to collide" (1987, 79). As an object of multiple indoctrinations that heretofore have collided upon her, their new recognition as products of the oppositional thinking of others can help her come to terms with the politics of varied discourses and their antagonistic relations.

The most remarkable tendency in the work reviewed in this essay is the implicit or explicit acknowledgment that, on the one hand, women of color are excluded from feminist theorizing on the subject of consciousness and, on the other, that though excluded from theory, their books are read in the classroom and/or duly (foot)noted. Given these current institutional and political practices in the United States, it is almost impossible to go beyond an oppositional theory of the subject. However, it is not the theory that will help us grasp the subjectivity of women of color. Socially and historically, women of color have been now central, now outside antagonistic relations among races, classes, and genders. It is this struggle of multiple antagonisms, almost always in relation to culturally different groups, and not just genders, that gives configuration to the theoretical subject of *Bridge.* It must be noted, however, that each woman of color cited here, even in her positing of a "plurality of self," is already privileged enough to reach the moment of cognition of a situation for herself. This should suggest that to privilege the subject, even if multiple-voiced, is not enough.

Notes

1. Hereinafter cited as *Bridge,* the book has had two editions. I use the second edition published by Kitchen Table Press, 1983. The first edition was published by Persephone Press, 1981.

2. For an intriguing demonstration of these operations, see Seyla Benhabib, "The Generalized and the Concrete Other: The Kohlberg-Gilligan Controversy and Feminist Theory" (1987, 77–95).

3. For a detailed discussion of this theme, see Judith Butler, "Variations on Sex and Gender: Beauvoir, Wittig, and Foucault" (1987, 128–42).

4. See Miranda Davies 1987.

5. Monique Wittig cited in Elizabeth Meese 1986, 74.

Part II

Representations of

the Chicana/o Subject:

Race, Class, and Gender

Genaro Padilla

Imprisoned Narrative? Or Lies, Secrets, and Silence in New Mexico Women's Autobiography

Prefigurations

What I wish to consider in this essay is the formation of imprisoned autobiographic discourse. What happens when the autobiographic impulse finds its self-constitutive means undermined by the very discursive practices that make autobiographic textualization possible? What happens when an individual finds herself in a situation where memory is encouraged to imprint itself upon the page, but only in a language and idiom of cultural otherness that mark its boundaries of permissible autobiographic utterance? Given the discursive domination to which the subordinate cultural self must make supplication if it wishes to survive in any form, the imprinted self is likely to be a representation that discloses intense cultural self-deceit, political fear, and masked and self-divided identity. The "I" is made alien to itself, existing as it does deeply embedded in a discursive world outside of its own making or control. We discover an "I" that reveals its incarceration within a network of discursive practices invented by cultural imperialists whose goal has been and still is to lock it into a cell of alien linguistic culture and ideology, into a consciousness that participates in its own submission, transformation, and erasure.

To begin let us contextualize Fabiola Cabeza de Baca's and Cleofas M. Jaramillo's neocolonial situation in New Mexico by recalling the rupture effected by a war of conquest, in this case the Mexican-American War of 1846–48, in which the entire national apparatus of the United States was overlaid upon that of northern Mexico. Militaristic domination was only the initial blow that gave way to various forms of coercion through which the conquest sought to complete itself. As in all wars of conquest, the dominating culture, from the moment it has forced another group supine, must subvert the structure of the group's ideological consciousness as much as possible. It must make the subjected culture forget the details of its domination and make it believe that it has not surrendered so much as availed itself of a more progressive sociocultural national experience. In short, it seeks to bring the subjected group to consent.

Where there is dissension from sectors of the subjected group, perhaps from those who occupy the lower social strata, the dominating culture must bring the precolonial elites into closer proximity with its structures of power, must make these dispossessed elites deceive themselves into thinking they occupy positions of authority, and must turn that carefully monitored authority against those individuals who openly resist. The dispossessed elite, in addition to the modicum of political power they are granted, are also fitted with a socioideological discourse that not only accedes to their dispossession, but actually becomes the official cultural discourse through which the subjected group makes sufferable its subordination. Domination and suppression, the locus of its historical-cultural identity, is somehow, incredibly, transformed into a fabulous domain of cultural romance, aristocratic pretense, lies, and self-deceit.

What residue of self and culture can we look for in autobiographic narrative that has been denatured, robbed of its content, and made a prisoner of an illusory and idyllic past? Since cultural hegemony is seldom complete, that is to say, since every subject, or prisoner, wishes to be free, we must search for those moments where dissent discloses itself in even the most acquiescent discourse. We must look therefore for momentary struggles in the narrative, revealed perhaps only in whispers of resistance, quelled immediately but signaling like a flash through the dense texture of language and reified memory. In such whispers we discover those gaps in the narrative where the native cultural "I" voices itself against the imperial "Other" to speak through the bars of the ideological prison in which it is confined.

I

The present is a husk—the past was a
romance and a glory.
—The Land of Poco Tiempo, *Charles F. Lummis*

The site of this particular discursive struggle for ideological domination is found in what I call folkloric autobiographies composed by Hispanos in the first half of the twentieth century in New Mexico. I wish to argue that the composition of these autobiographies find their generative will in folklore and historical society development in the Southwest from the turn of the century to a pitch of activity in the thirties during the Work Projects Administration (WPA) programs, especially the Federal Writer's Program. Moreover, I argue that Anglo-American intellectuals, writers, and artists who came to New Mexico at the beginning of the twentieth century invented an aesthetic discourse of myth and romance that deeply inscribed itself upon the popular consciousness and provided one of the few forms through which Hispanos could compose their lives for public view. Along with the discursive form came an entire structure of troubling assumptions about native Hispano culture, history, language, and the self.

There are other texts with which one might begin tracing this discursive formation, but Charles F. Lummis's widely read *The Land of Poco Tiempo* (1893a, 1921, 1952, 1973) may be identified as a significantly generative text and Lummis himself as a central agent of cultural invention. Focusing on the landscape at great length, as well as on the physiognomy and cultural practices of "the Mexican," "the Pueblo," and "the Apache," Lummis's book was a combination of sensational ethnography, impressionistic history, and amateur archaeology. His lyrical romance of the Southwest opens thus:

> Sun, silence, and adobe—that is New Mexico in three words. Here is the land of *poco tiempo*—the home of "Pretty Soon." Why hurry with the hurrying world? The "Pretty Soon" of New Spain is better than the "Now! Now!" of the haggard States. The opiate sun soothes to rest, the adobe is made to lean against, the hush of day-long noon would not be broken. Let us not hasten—*mañana* will do. Better still, *pasado mañana*. (1893, 1)

The influence of Lummis's book was extraordinarily wide. As Paul Walter comments in the "Foreword" to the 1952 fourth edition of the text: "*The Land of Poco Tiempo*, when it first appeared . . . aroused the interest not only of the traveling public, but also writers, painters, scientists, to whom the volume disclosed an inexhaustible vein of subjects for pen, brush, and research" (1952, xi). Lummis, possessed of a huge ego, placed himself at the center of this circle and was enormously influential in directing novelists and poets, ethnographers, historians, and artists to settle in New Mexico where, once arrived, they participated in the "preservation" of Indian and Mexican cultural practices.

The textual production of this intellectual emigration from 1900 to 1940, to choose an important enclosure, consisted of scores of novels, volumes of poetry, plays, literary magazines, not to mention professional and amateur ethnographic narratives that as the WPA Writer's Program publication, *New Mexico: A Guide to the Colorful State*, pointed out: "began to appear, first slowly and then with an accelerated pace, until their number now [1940] is almost bewildering" (1940, 134). A short list of some of the books published during the decades of the twenties and thirties, by their very titles, suggests the formation of a certain discursive concentration upon the landscape and the exoticism of native New Mexican cultures: *Red Earth* (1920), Alice Corbin; *Caravan* (1922), Witter Bynner; *Horizontal Yellow* (1935), Spud Johnson; *Blood of the Conquerors* (1921) and *Wolf Song* (1927), Harvey Fergusson; *Death Comes for the Archbishop* (1927), Willa Cather; *The American Rhythm* (1923), *The Land of Journey's Ending* (1924), *Starry Adventure* (1931), and *One Smoke Stories* (1934), Mary Austin; *The Royal City of the Holy Faith* (1936), Paul Horgan; *Miguel of the Bright Mountain* (1936) and *The Little Valley* (1937), Raymond Otis; *Laughing Boy: A Navajo Romance* (1929), Oliver La Farge; *Desert Drums* (1928), Leo Crane; *Dancing Gods* (1931), Erna Fergusson; *Native Tales of New Mexico* (1932), Frank G. Applegate; *Coronado's Children* (1930), J. Frank Dobie; and *The Burro of Angelitos* (1937), Peggy Pond Church.

And then, of course, there was D. H. Lawrence who Mabel Dodge Luhan had lured to her desert mountain home in 1922 to interpret "the true, primordial, undiscovered America that was preserved, living, in the Indian bloodstream" (Sagar 1982, 6). Lawrence never wrote the "magnificent creation" Dodge Luhan had in mind, but there are a scattering of widely disseminated impressionistic essays, a parcel of very bad poems, and even a fragment of a drama—a kitchen piece set in Taos. However, as some Southwestern scholars won't let anyone forget, D. H. Lawrence's spirit hovers over the New Mexico landscape in which, like all the rest of these Anglo *estranjeros,* he apparently discovered the primitive blood consciousness for which the disaffected aesthetes of Western culture longed. In one piece called "Taos," for instance, he wrote: "Places can lose their living nodality. Rome, to me, has lost hers. In Venice one feels the magic of the glamourous old node that once united East and West, but it is the beauty of an after-life. Taos pueblo still retains its old nodality . . . the old nodality of the pueblo still holding, like a dark ganglion spinning invisible threads of consciousness" (Sagar 1982, 11).

However spiritually high-minded they may have considered themselves, these artists and intellectuals who retreated to the Southwest to escape the dehumanizing effects of a modern, increasingly technological society, often participated in the dehumanization of their subjects, or better put, their objects—Mexicans and Indians. The *estranjero* artists were more sympathetic than usual, not marking native people negatively, that had been thoroughly enough done in the nineteenth century (see Robinson *With the Ears of Strangers* 1963), but nevertheless essentializing them, setting them into the sediment of the earth instead of relating to them as social subjects, mystifying and mythifying their cultural practices, reducing their social history, ignoring their individuality. The result was a form of negative anthropomorphizing.

Should a native New Mexican wish to write about native culture during the first half of the twentieth century, she or he would be coerced (perhaps without anyone verbally or otherwise directly coercing) into composing a text—ethnographic, fictive, or autobiographic—determined by the overwhelmingly nonnative discursive world through which one moved. Nina Otero de Warren, for example, was one native whose folkloric reminiscence, *Old Spain in Our Southwest* (1936), slotted itself comfortably, title and nostalgic contents, into our representative shelf of New Mexican exotica. There were others—Cleofas Jaramillo, Aurora Lucero-White, Fabiola Cabeza de Baca—whose memories were arrogated, whose voices were blended into this mass mythifying (socializing) project, whose texts were, in their structural essentials, preformed. When, in the act of remembering their own history and the cultural practices that identify them, they confront the unpleasant residue of their own conquest, they often retreat into whispers of discomfort, confused historiography, muted social criticism, and silence.

For example, while describing the decline of her family ranch in *We Fed Them Cactus* (1954), Fabiola Cabeza de Baca makes pointed social commentary on the subject of land grant fraud in New Mexico and then abruptly silences herself. She writes:

> When General Kearny talked to the citizens of Las Vegas on August 15, 1846, he promised protection for the New Mexicans and their property. . . . He also promised that the Spanish and Mexican land grants would be respected. But New Mexico, isolated for so many centuries, did not have enough lawyers to plead the cause for its own people. The owners of the grants and other lands were unable to pay for the surveying and gradually most of the land became public domain. Unaccustomed to technicalities, the native New Mexicans later lost even their homesteads because of ignorance of the homestead laws, but all this belongs to a subject too vast to discuss in this history of the Llano. (1954, 176)

On the one hand, Cabeza de Baca is precise on the date and content of Kearny's statement; on the other, she lapses into the historically facile tale of New Mexico's "centuries of isolation." And, given the topic of the chapter, the loss of her father's land to swarms of homesteaders, it should be clear that at the center of the "history of the Llano" is the very subject of legal fraud that she dismisses as inappropriate to her narrative.

Much of the native New Mexican literature of this period reads like Cabeza de Baca's diffident, abruptly self-censoring, and sentimental narrative. One cannot but agree with Raymund Paredes who contends that there is "something profoundly disturbing about this body of work [Mexican-American literature in English that emerged from New Mexico during the thirties]. It seems a literature created out of fear and intimidation, a defensive response to racial prejudice, particularly the Anglo distaste for miscegenation" (1982, 56). His concern is legitimate. It is difficult to read a literature that "described a culture seemingly locked in time and barricaded against outside forces . . . confronting the harsh environment with a religiosity and resolve reminiscent of the conquistadors themselves" without feeling some aversion for the historical amnesia and delusive class pretenses displayed by many of these native writers. Before derogating these writers to the political rubbish heap to which we have often consigned our acquiescent, ideologically imprisoned *antepasados*, what I wish to consider more closely are the socioliterary exertions that account for conceptualizations of the self that seek a unifying center in an uncontaminated Spanish past and, where there is an uncontaminated past, a present absolved of its social reality. Paredes's unsparing reading of this "defensive" literature opens space for a critically reaccentuated reading if it encourages us to consider the forces at work in shaping just such "defensive" strategies. Hence, as "profoundly disturbing" as this literature may be, we must not dismiss it before engaging in a more thorough analysis of the ideological and discursive exertions at work in its formation.

Consider, again, the case of Cabeza de Baca. Situating *We Fed Them Cactus* within the context of her folkloristic activities at the time of its composition must alter our ideological take on its "disturbing" contents. Cabeza de Baca was a prominent member of the New Mexico Folklore Society during the fifties; she was elected second vice-president in 1952, first vice-president in 1954, and state president in 1955, the year her book appeared. In the 1955 issue of the *New Mexico Folklore Record* there is notice of a reception in her honor:

On January 29, 1955, the Santa Fe Group of the New Mexico Folklore Society, led by Ina Sizer Cassidy, gave a merienda and autograph party in honor of our State President, Fabiola Cabeza de Baca Gilbert, whose book, *We Fed Them Cactus* was published by the University of New Mexico Press . . . a social occasion was held . . . at the home of Mrs. John A. Lowe. At four o'clock, Mrs. Gilbert gave a short resume of her book and related some of the memories from her childhood on a New Mexico hacienda. (1955, 3)

When one reads this kind of "merienda" review together with the editorial notes, the list of contributors, most of whom were nonnatives (Cassidy, E. W. Baughman, T. M. Pearce, Julia Keleher, Mary Wheelwright) and the contents (a compilation of folk tales and ballads, Indian myths, ghost town stories, local outlaw legends), it becomes rather apparent that the society was both folkloristically and ideologically conservative. No need for historical or cultural tendentiousness when one could be quaint.

So, the company in and for which Cabeza de Baca's narrative was written may be said to mediate her memoirs, laying a romanticizing folk-loristic discourse upon it through which it can hardly speak for itself. The narrative, however, does here and again disclose fissures of duplicity that we must consider closely. Even her abrupt self-silencing may be read as strategic: what she says about land fraud opens an issue that the form and audience do not admit, but, like a person muttering under her breath, gets said just enough to raise an eyebrow. Hence, in this and other similar narratives, where there is silence we must look for the facial gesture, where secrets the nuance of the whisper, where lies the listener who is being lied to.

II

Under the apparent deadness of our New Mexico villages there runs a roman-tic current invisible to the stranger and understood only by their inhabitants. This quiet romance I will try to describe in the following pages of my auto-biography, although I feel an appalling shortage of words, not being a writer, and writing in a language almost foreign to me.—Romance of a Little Village Girl

In the thirties a diminutive woman residing in Santa Fe, after having as she writes, "caught the fever from our famous 'cinco pintores' and author Mary Austin," began writing about her own Nuevomexicano culture. She first published *Cuentos del Hogar* (1939a), a collection of twenty-five tales her mother had related when she was a child; she then compiled a cookbook called *The Genuine New Mexico Tasty Recipes* (1939b). Encouraged by the success of those two books, she completed another, a folkloristic narrative that combined reminiscence and ethnographic description. Some twenty years later in her autobiography, she remembered this period, the difficulty she found in forcing language onto the page, especially a language in which she did not feel comfortable, the sense she had that people outside of the culture were literally trying to steal her writing:

I tried sending my manuscript to some of our Western universities. After holding it for several months, they would return it, saying they

did not have the funds with which to publish it. One professor said he
was writing a book. Would I permit him to use two or three of my
stories in his book? I then understood. All they wanted was to read my
manuscript and get ideas from it, so I decided to have it published by a
small private press here in my city. (1955, 168)

That nearly pirated book was a folkloristic narrative called *Shadows of the
Past* (1941) and the autobiography in which she more expansively remembers herself in the last quarter of the nineteenth and first half of the twentieth century is a belated product of the thirties and forties titled *Romance
of a Little Village Girl* (1955).

Cleofas Martínez-Jaramillo was this woman. The autochthonous imperative that underlay her folkloric organizing and her folkloristic autobiography should be reconsidered as an activity that was invented for her
and yet reappropriated by her. What is at stake is not only determining the
ownership of a text, but marking off the ways in which such ownership
constructs the "I" in both its cultural and personal configuration. Given her
simultaneous sense of ethnographic responsibility to the community from
which she springs and her desire to inscribe her own experience, *Shadows
of the Past* and *Romance of a Little Village Girl* collapse the lines between
cultural history and autobiography. Both texts raise questions about the
proximity between cultural and self representation; both are texts in which
the "I" and culture identify each other, at least insofar as lived experience
intersects with cultural practice. The enfolding of these two forms results
in texts that are problematically transilient; the narrative is a rather sim-
plistic cultural description and yet an increasingly complex personal history. This is especially the case in *Romance of a Little Village Girl* where
memory of day-to-day and year-by-year complications in the personal life
overtakes the facile narration of ethnohistorical events. Before the personal
life assumes proprietary demand in the narrative, however, Jaramillo works
through a romance of the cultural self.

Jaramillo's desire for an original simplicity and purity is marked out in
the Preface of *Romance of a Little Village Girl*. The prefatory remarks
disclose Jaramillo's wish to return to a harmonious and ahistoric plane of
edenic cultural experience. Jaramillo figures herself as an Eve who once
lived in an isolated valley, a veritable edenic locale: "In this little valley of
the Arroyo Hondo, situated in the northern part of the state of New Mexico,
hemmed in by high mountains and hills, sheltered from the contamination
of the outside world, the inhabitants lived peacefully, preserving the customs and traditions of their ancestors" (1955, vii). The autobiographical act
is itself an edenic enterprise. She wishes to "live again in memory the

girlhood years that were enriched with comfort and love, innocent of any wickedness, sheltered from all care and grief" (1955, vii).

As aged narrator, as the woman who moved away from innocence into the contaminated world of experience, she wishes to retrieve a coherence that may be traced, as she believes, to a cultural locale still in force "under the apparent deadness" of village life; the "romantic current," moreover, remains "invisible to the stranger and understood only by their inhabitants." Sprung from native soil, she is still secretly connected with this romantic current and therefore authorizes herself to restore the cultural meanings that motivate her people. Here and elsewhere she will insist that despite all of the cultural ethnography recorded by nonnative observers, the true current of cultural meanings remains invisible, except to the native inhabitants themselves. What is set at odds with this deep romantic current, however, is the entire surface of historical events that are killing village life. Yet, this immediate historical surface is outside of the legitimate literary discourse prevailing during the moment she composed her life; hence, reaching for what she apparently believes to be a deep spiritual well of cultural meaning replaces a narrative that should exercise its right to describe those hard surfaces of reality—land usurpation, banking practices, taxation, probate laws—that underlie the "deadness" of village life.

Northrop Frye's comments on the social motive underlying the romance are directive here (on Chicano romance, see Calderón 1983, 9–11, and 1986). Jaramillo's "quiet romance" constitutes a nostalgic mythos that effaces historical surface. As Frye suggests in *Anatomy of Criticism*:

> The romance is nearest of all literary forms to the wish-fulfillment dream, and for that reason it has socially a curiously paradoxical role. In every age the ruling social or intellectual class tends to project its ideals in some form of romance. . . . Yet there is a genuinely 'proletarian' element in romance too which is never satisfied with its various incarnations, and in fact the incarnations themselves indicate that no matter how great a change may take place in society, romance will turn up again, as hungry as ever, looking for new hopes and desires to feed on. The perennially childlike quality of romance is marked by its extraordinarily persistent nostalgia, its search for some kind of imaginative golden age in time or space. (1957, 186)

This nostalgia for an imaginative golden age functions to repress harsh social transformation throughout much of Jaramillo's narrative. The initial utterance of the opening historico-genealogical chapter, "The New Spanish Province," is an epigraphic lyric that discloses the romantic desire out of which Cleofas Jaramillo constructs her autobiographical identity. The self recedes into a distant past existing at the precise juncture between the old world and the new. The "I" recalls itself in the "first white speck on the Western sea" made by a "Spanish sail." Here is what in New Mexico has become the reductive story of sixteenth-century Spain brought uncontaminated to the verdant little valley where she was born some 400 years later; her people's historical configuration, her own evolution through time and space, collapses into a string of historical non sequiturs that celebrate the "romance and adventure [that] have always ridden hand in hand with the Spanish race":

> Intrepid Cortez, Coronado and Oñate and brave De Vargas, and many other explorers and colonizers followed after him ['wise Columbus'], with the same urge. They brought with them colonists and missionary priests. Toiling and suffering untold hardships, they penetrated through mountain passes, across vast prairies, conquering savage Indian tribes and establishing settlements in the wilderness. Developing farms, they raised scant crops for their maintenance. The missionaries built churches appalling in their construction. They helped carry the faith and culture of old Spain into these remote worlds. Hardships only meant exciting adventure: they did not discourage the Spaniards' desire to discover and conquer. (1955, 2)

Within a few paragraphs she has moved from the "first white speck on the Western sea" to sometime in the nineteenth century where her family, having traversed the centuries in an unspoiled genetic and cultural line from De Vargas (1692), situate themselves in northern New Mexico. Such history spares itself of the complexities of sociohistorical process, geographic exigency, profound Native American influences, and cultural evolution consequent to the long migrations into the far northern provinces of Mexico. History is reified out of the need for a simpler story of Spanish adventure, conquest, settlement, isolation (especially isolation) and its adjunct "purity"—uncontaminated sixteenth-century Spain propagating itself even anew in an insulated corner of the world. Where cultural history is concerned, here or anywhere else in the narrative, one discovers little more than just such romance, a wish-fulfillment narrative that sets history into relation with a cultural unity she believes underlies the "melting ruins" of traditional Nuevomexicano life. As it turns out, historical romance is better than no history, even if it is a masquerade.

Yet, this historical masquerade is grounded in the consciousness and cultural production of the nonnative Other. Inventing an uncontaminated Spanish past came rather easily given the prevailing discourse at work in New Mexico, perhaps especially in Santa Fe during the thirties when Jaramillo was helping Anglo-Americans organize the annual fiesta and participating in various cultural preservation activities. Mary Austin, mentioned as a vital inspiration to Jaramillo, was one cultural outsider who during the twenties was largely responsible for shoring up the residue of the Spanish past, embellishing Spanish cultural fragments where necessary and inventing Spanish cultural practices where there were visible gaps. Consider Austin's autobiography, *Earth Horizon*, published in 1932, years before Jaramillo's: "The colonists who came here originally came direct from Spain; they had not much tarrying in Mexico. They brought with them what they remembered, and as soon as they began to create, they made things in the likeness of old Spain. . . . They made *santos* and *bultos* [church altar statues carved in wood] in the pattern of the holy images of sixteenth-century Spain" (1932, 358). As for what had once been a local religious ritual fiesta, Austin recalls:

> There was an annual fiesta at Santa Fe which was attended by the natives, but not very successfully. There was a tendency to divert it to tourist uses. This grew to be an offense to the artists, so that Witter Bynner, John Sloan, Gus Bauman, Will Shuster, and a dozen other artists set out to create a fiesta that should be Spanish; they persuaded the natives and finally the rest of the community. It has grown to be notable, and thoroughly, alively native. (1932, 358)

Never mind that significant elements of this "thoroughly, alively native" fiesta were invented by Anglo-American artists before consulting with those natives. Perhaps it was enough that the natives were persuaded somewhere along the way that they should follow their Anglo-American benefactors in recovering purer Spanish traditions than they alone maintained. As Jaramillo herself wrote in her *Romance:* "Many additions have lately been brought about to make it a genuine Spanish fiesta. It now starts with the burning of *Zozobra,* the Spanish effigy of gloom" (1955, 170). Yet, this entirely nonnative *Zozobra* was the creation in 1926 of Will Shuster who took the idea, not from Spain, but from someone else who had seen something of the sort in Mexico.

Precisely such discursive and extracultural intercessions in both recovering and purifying the region's *true* cultural past are superimposed upon Jaramillo's autobiography to such an extent that she mimics the romanticizing discourse provided by non-Hispanos: "The glamour and beauty which appeals to the senses of the artists and the writers who have come into our country should appeal more forcefully to us, the heirs of the artistic culture and of the poetry and the religious traditions which our Spanish ancestors left to crystallize on the crests of our New Mexico mountains"

(1955, 183). Jaramillo's narrative of the crystallized Spanish self is incarcerated within a language and a discursive form that impedes the self's capacity to distinguish itself from that image invented by the cultural *estranjero*. It is through external categories of cultural definition that she sees herself. What we see, of course, is that the image assigned by the cultural Other to the Hispano/Mexicano "I" is one predetermined by its own just-so story of what took place in the West in a remote locale of history. The intellectuals, writers, and painters who came to the West, and whose discursive power held sway in places like Santa Fe and Taos, were less interested (in some cases not at all interested) in the lived history and culture of the people settled there than in their own romance about the Western space.

But our *antepasados* were not fools. They had moments of clarity, I believe, in which they knew they were lying to themselves, and they certainly knew they were engaged in a battle in which lies were crucial to survival. In intercultural discourse between a dominant and subject group, survival is predicated upon strategically voicing one's presence. Often, simply being able to open one's mouth signals a moment of affirmation. Uncertainty, hesitance, nostalgic sentiment often belie a certain unclarified resentment and opposition. Hegemonic exertion had the effect of lulling the Nuevomexicano into a realm of fantasy that *was* just fantasy, self-conceit, illusion, but *also* a way of saying "No!" to cultural effacement. The discourse of the Spanish past provided a way of being more "native" even though the authenticating apparatus was a parcel of historical distortions. Yet it was also a duplicitous discourse that served the simultaneous purpose of making New Mexico safe for the *estranjeros* and providing a socially symbolic form of control for Nuevomexicanos whose world was dissolving like the adobe structures to which Cleofas Jaramillo more than once refers.

Jaramillo may be considered a Hispanophile, but it would be a mistake to think Jaramillo therefore passive. She recognized the exploitative motive in the behavior of those newcomers who were infatuated with Nuevo-mexicano culture. Her almost single-handed organization of La Sociedad Folklórica in the thirties must be regarded as a gesture of resistance to Anglo domination of cultural preservation activities in Santa Fe. Although the idea for La Sociedad was influenced by similar Anglo-American folklore preservation projects (specifically J. Frank Dobie's Texas Folklore Society), there was a crucial cultural turn in forming the group. Jaramillo writes: "the first rules which I drafted still govern the organization. These rules were that the society should be composed of only thirty members, all of whom must be of Spanish descent, and that the meetings must be conducted in the Spanish language, with the aim of preserving our language, customs and traditions" (1955, 176). Such rules, clearly a form of ethno-codifying, effectively excluded the likes of Mary Austin, Will Shuster, Witter Bynner, and other "writers and artists who have come into our country."

In the same chapter where she describes her efforts to organize La Sociedad Folklórica she makes a number of comments that mark resistance to various forms of cultural hegemony: her efforts to "arouse more interest amongst our Spanish-speaking population in taking part in the fiesta" is described as a direct response to cultural activities controlled by Anglo-Americans, she says, because, "so far we have been seeing mostly what Americans have arranged" (174); she remembers that the "Fiesta Council, having heard about my activities, elected me to be a member and sent me an invitation to attend the weekly meetings" (174), asked her group to elect the fiesta queen and then, for "political reasons" told the group "we would have to choose another" (175) which they refused to do. Jaramillo also shows that she is quite capable of the art of subtle sarcasm when she refers to an article published in *Holland Magazine* about New Mexican cooking by a "Mrs. D." The article she remembers was "nicely written and illustrated, but very deficient as to the knowledge of our Spanish cooking. In giving the recipe for making tortillas it read, 'Mix bread flour with water, add salt.' How nice and light these must be without yeast or shortening! And still these smart Americans make money with their writing, and we who know the correct way, sit back and listen" (173).

Quibbling over the fiesta queen and the ingredients in tortillas seem small enough gestures of resistance, but, taken together with other articulations of resistance in Jaramillo, just such voicings add up to *coraje*. Such *coraje*, or anger, has to alter our reading of something as simple and apparently harmless, for instance, as *The Genuine New Mexico Tasty Recipes*. We no longer have a recipe book of quaint "Spanish" dishes, but a gesture of cultural assertion. As Tey Diana Rebolledo has pointed out, a "sense of place and belonging can be connoted by such mundane activities as regional food traditions. . . . The Cookbook . . . preserves these traditions" (1987, 102). Interspersed between the recipes, Jaramillo remembers familial and community occasions that contextualize the very preparation and consumption of food. On the one hand, *Tasty Recipes* represents the popularization of ethnic cuisine and, in that respect, represents a desire to cater to members of the dominant culture. On the other, Jaramillo contextualizes consumption in an explicitly cultural manner and, therefore, suggests how intimately food is related to lived cultural experience. Hence, we discover a form of culinary resistance—Anglo-Americans can follow the recipe and still not eat Nuevomexicano cooking.

I'm being somewhat facetious, of course, but Jaramillo wasn't when referring to Americans making "money with their writings" while the natives, who live the culture, "sit back and listen." She didn't. *The Genuine New Mexico Tasty Recipes* opens an interstice for counterhegemonic expression at a level that is all but overlooked, unless one is listening for just such whispers of opposition. In this case, what seems the ideologically neutral compilation of a cookbook becomes an "embryonic" site of contention of the kind that Antonio Gramsci (who I name for the first time but who has been with me throughout the essay) identifies in his comments on folkloric expressions of counterhegemony (see "The Study of Philosophy," *Prison Notebooks* 1971). What at first seems acquiescence, upon closer reading reveals verbal gestures of discontent and anger that fail to smother themselves. Jaramillo may open her mouth initially to share a recipe, but that she has opened her mouth to correct the recipe is the beginning of assertion.

Likewise her *Romance* may begin in apology and verbal hesitance but it opens to a life disclosed within a troubling context of social transformation that refutes its own sentimentality. In fact, the prefatory hesitance Jaramillo discloses about writing the "quiet romance" turns out to be a crucial site of negotiation for control of the text given its projected readership. "I will try to describe [this quiet romance] in the following pages of my autobiography, although I feel an appalling shortage of words, not being a writer, and writing in a language almost foreign to me. May I offer an apology for my want of continued expression to some parts of my story," Jaramillo writes in the Preface. To whom is she explaining if not to an Anglo-American readership? She is apologizing for writing haltingly, perhaps inaccurately, crudely, in a foreign literary idiom. On the one hand, she desires to inscribe her experience, to utter herself into permanence; on the other, she concedes her relative inability to do so in the form determined by that brood of Anglo writers in Santa Fe and their readership. As later in the narrative she explains, she began writing about her culture and herself because "writing and painting are contagious in this old town" (Santa Fe in the thirties). One might speculate that being a writer of the sort typified by Mary Austin, Alice Corbin, and Peggy Pond Church would not, under native circumstances, have appealed to Jaramillo. Not that Nuevomexicanos didn't write, but the forms Nuevomexicano writing took were not ethnographic and even more certainly not self-ethnographic. And I haven't even mentioned her apology for writing in English—"almost a foreign language." Jaramillo's admission is appalling if one considers that she is saying here (without saying) that she is thinking herself in Spanish, remembering herself in her native tongue, but reaching for herself textually in a foreign language.

That she wrote in English is a troubling but necessary contradiction.

She authors her own cultural preservation activities, in English, for an Anglo-American readership in order to forestall another Anglo from describing her people's cultural history. On this issue Jaramillo is strategically ethnocentric if one recalls her claim that the cultural life "of New Mexico villages" appears dead only because it is "invisible to the stranger" and, where apparent in any guise, is nevertheless misread because the cultural codes can be "understood only by their inhabitants." Jaramillo's renunciation of nonnative ethnographic discourse is here doubled, complete. Whereas she altogether refuses to authorize nonnative discourse—however eloquent, she authorizes herself to speak in a "foreign language"—however awkwardly. Hence, Cleofas Jaramillo may apologize for her "want of continued expression," yet she expropriates the discourse of the Other as a resistive gesture against another Anglo-American legitimizing the wrong ingredients for making tortillas, so to speak, and in the process of being appropriated by, actually appropriates, the discourse of the Other.

In the closing chapter, "Rhythm in Adobe," Jaramillo remarks that writing has increasingly taken on a life sustaining significance for her. Along with reading, the "work of writing" keeps her from "becoming too lonely and discouraged" now that she is living alone in her seventy-fifth year. Fragments of cultural history remain to be contributed to Dr. Reginald Fisher, who asked if "we [La Sociedad Folklórica] would write and give him the genealogy of our families for a book, which he is compiling on the history of the early Spanish families in the state" (196). She is still being encouraged (or cajoled) by external cultural agents to continue her writing; nevertheless, it is clear that the act of writing itself has become a life-extending activity. Or, rather, it has become her life. Like the hot mineral spring of Ojo Caliente to which she refers in the chapter, writing renews the "spirit and mind." The book must close but the final chapter echoes with reasons not to: "Each time I come to the end of my story, something happens to incite me to continue writing a little longer" (198).

In this final chapter Cleofas Jaramillo discloses an uncanny sense of the textuality—and intertextuality—of her life: "I must try to put this little work on the market and, also, the two plays I 'snitched' from my first book. For now at this book's close, I am also coming to the close of my seventy-fifth year of my life" (199). She and the book have become coterminous. She must finish the story because she senses the end, but to stop writing is to come to the end. It would appear, then, that despite an "appalling shortage of words" and "want of continued expression," even despite her discomfort with English, Cleofas Jaramillo has, by the end of *Romance of a Little Village Girl*, seized the discourse of the nonnative Other as a palliative against death—her own and that of the culture from which she springs.

III

What I have proposed is a contextually reaccentuated reading of Cleofas Jaramillo's autobiographical narrative that restores the discursive network out of which a subordinate text appears and in so doing discovers the socioliterary forces that conspire to control the text, encouraging its cultural romanticizing and historical conceit, reminding it of its formal duties as cultural history, muting it where it raises troublesome questions, and eliding unpleasant socio-ideological issues. As I have shown, the proliferation of nonnative, Anglo-American cultural discourse in New Mexico between 1900–1940 led to what Michel Foucault identifies as "systems of exclusion" for the "control and delimitation of discourse" that, in effect, exercised a "power of constraint upon other forms of discourse" (1972, 219–20). This "system of exclusion," I contend, was so powerful that the literary activity of an entire generation of Nuevomexicanos was "at once controlled, selected, organized" by a powerful nonnative discursive agency that dulled its ability to see straight to the heart of its own experience or, to the extent that it did, disrupted its capacity to express itself fearlessly.

Even George I. Sánchez's classic *Forgotten People: A Study of New Mexicans* (1940), a politically progressive critique of the social and cultural policies which dispossessed and impoverished Hispanos, surrenders itself at significant junctures to reductive ethnohistoricism, cultural ambivalence, and ideological contradictions. The narrative is generally characterized by a judicious social voice that, in deflating the "pomp and splendor" which "cloak the Spaniard colonial endeavor" (1940, 3), exposes the political and economic policies that systematically dispossessed New Mexicans. Yet, Sánchez's reasoned social critique ends up repeatedly qualifying itself in ways that are conspicuously at cross purposes. It is not unusual to find Sánchez, in one paragraph, commenting upon the Nuevomexicano's rugged struggle and cultural synthesis ("The colony gave birth to a new people, people whose mode of life tempered their Spanish heritage and caused them to create social and economic patterns that fitted their environment" [13]) and, in a following paragraph, bemoaning the damaging effects of cultural isolation ("Their struggle is, in reality, not one against material factors. They battle their own cultural inadequacy. They are unprepared to act in their new environment—unprepared because of centuries of isolation. They have no tradition of competition, of education, or of Western civilization beyond the sixteenth century" [13]). And throughout the study Sánchez's vigorous opposition to the socioeconomic consequences of the American "march of imperialism" ends up, as on the last page, recontained by assimilationist rhetoric: "the ultimate goal that underlies the thesis of the study is the proper incorporation of the New Mexican into the American fold. That incorporation requires that the New Mexican be fitted to make his contributions to the American civilization" (97).

Hence, the ideological configuration of Sánchez's narrative, notwithstanding its progressive intention, reveals numerous contradictions that are the effect of the "power of constraint" at work in discursive practice, as well as the hegemonic exertions of the dominant culture toward consensus. Together with Michel Foucault, Antonio Gramsci has taught me that these *antepasados* participated in their own submission in ways that they didn't clearly understand given their ambiguous relations with the dominant Anglo-American culture. Sánchez himself opposes the cultural deracination of his people and yet acts as an agent in such a process when he writes: "Almost a hundred years after becoming American citizens, a broad gap still separates them from the culture which surrounds them. In lieu of adequate instruction, they have clung to their language, their customs, their agricultural practices. Though no fault can be found with a society because it seeks to perpetuate worthy elements of its culture, it is to be regretted that, in this instance, the process has not been accompanied by suitable adaptations" (28).

Such marks of contradictory consciousness are all too common in this and other narratives of the period—whether sociological, ethnographic, or autobiographic. Hispanos celebrate their customs and traditions, yet blame themselves for failing to adapt to the dictates of the dominant culture. Historical memory evokes articulations of resistance and within the same breath gestures of retraction. Those Hispano writers to whom I refer voice their resentment and even anger at moments and then, as though surprised by the harsh sound of their own words, placate their audience, take back the moment in an effort to *explain* themselves more clearly.

Apprehending such discursive and hegemonic exertions forces me to reconsider my initial disaffection from these my cultural kin and ultimately provides understanding and re-filiation. That is to say, like Paredes and other critics of my generation, I am troubled, and in no small manner alienated, by the aristocratic pretense and social elitism Jaramillo, Cabeza de Baca, Lucero-White, and others often display in their work of half-a-century ago. After all, my own family's experience in New Mexico can hardly be considered an aristocratic romance. My mother's family, like those described by Sánchez, was a displaced Nuevomexicano migrant group of the twenties and thirties who cut sugar beets and harvested potatoes in Colorado, and my father only went to the sixth grade before he joined his brothers laboring in the railroad shops. Nevertheless, reading autobiographical and ethnohistorical narratives provides filiative traces of my own cultural "I," the self that discovers its genealogical sources in the lives of my parents, as well as in those narratives that are my textual parents. It may be that I voice more clearly than they, the socioliterary effects of cultural subordination and class stratification, but it is they whose lived and textual experience, however mediated, wedged the opening for wider resistance in another time and place.

To raise troubling antecedent texts to inclusion within the Chicano literary tradition requires more than summarily, if not begrudgingly, recognizing their presence within the chronology of our literary production. The textual exhibition of what Gramsci refers to as subordinate, or "subaltern" consciousness, is an embarrassment only when we do not fully unravel the extraordinary nexus of domination and control that our *antepasados* experienced. We must account for the complex textual voicings of socially subordinate writers without losing ourselves to a form of progressive intellectual snobbery that overlooks or ignores those flashes in imprisoned discourse that are a textual signal of embryonic consciousness, whispers of antecedent resistance that have provided us the opening for clearly revisionary and resistive utterance.

Elizabeth J. Ordóñez

Body, Spirit, and the Text:
Alma Villanueva's *Life Span*

Western philosophical tradition has consistently organized our conception of the world into binary oppositions, polarities such as light/dark, culture/nature, man/woman, logos/body, or spirit/body. This systematization of reality into neatly ordered categories might at first glance seem a cleverly convenient and practical way of reckoning with an otherwise chaotic array of phenomena. However, its function within patriarchal culture has often resulted in the inordinate privileging of one side of the oppositions—the rational—and in a consequent alienation and marginalization of the feminine or corporeal side of the polarity. These oppositions also produce metaphors of creativity which similarly privilege the masculine, such as the linking of pen with penis and the female body with text to be deciphered or blank page to be inscribed (Gubar 1981). Even Derrida, whose theories playfully challenge phallocentrism, speaks of writing as a scattering of seed upon the hymeneal blank page (1976).

Recent feminist theory, however, has questioned this hierarchical ordering in our culture. Above all, by questioning our uncritical complicity with the classifications of phallocentric discourse, it has sought to subvert the latter's assumptions and ultimately dismantle its oppositions. Rather than leaving their pages blank for the writings of others, many recent writers are instead seeking to redefine themselves and their bodies as splendidly fertile sources of their own creativity. Even more, as Julia Kristeva proposes, the feminine is being advanced as the space not only of art and writing but of truth, "le vréel" (the "trureal"), the "unrepresentable truth that lies beyond and subverts the male order of logic, mastery, and verisimilitude" (Kristeva 1979, 11; Culler 1982, 173). In American culture the poet Adrienne Rich has advised: "we must touch the unity of resonance of our physicality, the corporeal ground of our intelligence" (1977, 62). Rich's point of view and program for her poetics is not unique in our culture, for Alicia Ostriker has discovered that "during the last two decades, American women poets have been employing anatomical imagery both more frequently and more intimately than their male counterparts" (1980, 248). Most important in this observation is Ostriker's discovery that in the work of these poets "body is not assumed to be inferior to some higher principle" (1980, 248). Instead, traditional oppositions are deconstructed and reintegrated into something at once transformative and transcendent.

The recent writings of Chicana poet Alma Villanueva are aptly read and interpreted in light of these current European and American theories of feminine textuality. Villanueva has consistently affirmed the natural and physical power of woman in her work. Her earlier collections, *Bloodroot* (1977) and *Mother, May I?* (1978) repeatedly challenge the assumptions of a polarized culture in which the overly technological and the rational are privileged. To this end they affirm the interconnectedness of all living things; the self as an integrated union of opposites; metamorphosis and transformation; rebirthing and renaming. Many of her poems dismantle patriarchal oppositions in their insistence on redefining the nature of female and male, body and spirit, experience and its inscription into the poetic text. Through essay as well as poetry, Villanueva continues to explore the indissoluble connections between woman's body and spirit. She reaffirms the Jungian theories of psychic integration, the need for woman to synthesize her intuitive and bodily aspects with her Logos or masculine side. But most central to Villanueva's thesis is her discovery of how the female protagonist of contemporary literature by woman often synthesizes feminine and masculine, sexuality and spirituality "by a means not usually respected: her body" (Villanueva n.d., 4). In various examples Villanueva finds that "sexuality is . . . woman's center of spirituality" (Villanueva n.d., 5), and she concludes her own survey by citing the Jungian Irene Claremont de Castillejo, who maintains "that for the whole woman there is no possible cleavage between spirit and body" (1974, 108). Many roads thus lead to the same conclusion: that the traditional split between body and soul is no longer viable and that its pernicious legacy for women is being erased by today's woman, writing affirmatively and with a common purpose across the boundaries of nationality and ethnicity.

In *Life Span* (1985) Villanueva once again fuses and synthesizes sexuality (or the female body), spirituality, and the poetic text. As I have described in the collection's introduction, "the life force which infuses *Life Span* is born of an alchemical blending of opposites, the simple complexity of the wholeness of life. The poet blends the ethereal and the earthy to create a magical balance of the miraculous and the mundane" (1985, v). The collection's opening poem, "Communion," establishes the work's characteristic longing for transcendence through the integration of opposites:

I would wish life to
be simple—to

be complex as air—
as still as roots—
quiet as vision—
sound as love—
pregnant with words
or babies—
growth as natural
as death—
life follows breath,
dreams—

I would wish life to
lay itself on my
tongue like a wafer of
living flesh in
the folds of absolute
silence.
(Villanueva 1985, 1)

By employing a metaphor of compensatory communion or a female revision of orthodox transubstantiation, the poet implicitly draws male spirituality down from its empyrean heights and relocates her own life, her own spirit in the living flesh. Her ideal life would have the tongue (woman's poetry) to welcome the living body (the center of female spirituality), while silence (the unconscious wellspring of the poet's text) would receive the blessing of its corporeal inspiration. Through this metaphor of communion, body and spirit are united, and the poetic text implicitly skirts the undesirable polar alternatives, the either/or of traditional culture: what might be labeled (male) discourse in opposition to (female) silence. The poem suggests, rather, something analogous to the Lutheran consubstantiation of both/and (simple/complex, air/roots, words/babies, growth/death), and as did Luther's theology, it signals a break from established orthodoxy and authority.

What to do with this self-proclaimed freedom becomes the challenge of "The Labor of Buscando La Forma" ("The Labor of Searching for the Form").

The poem's code-switched title already draws the reader's attention to the potential for crossing and mixing. In fact, the title and the poem's central metaphor—dishes—function also as metonymies marking the poem's double play with doubleness. On one level the entire poem articulates a blending of national cultures, as the Chicana voice juxtaposes her own quest for identity and aesthetic form with that of her Mexican sisters: "In the Yucatan, a woman in labor / must find her own form to give birth" (12). On another level the dish functions as a metonymy for women's culture everywhere ("The woman in England uses / dishes. The woman in / France. The woman in / Cuba. The woman in / Japan. The woman in / Persia. The woman in / Kansas. The woman in / Moscow, Tiajuana, Baghdad / and Stockton" [11]), while particular versions of the dish serve also as metaphors for the duality of each woman's experience in her respective culture. The glass dish thus becomes a metaphor for inspiration and discovery ("at / the bottom there's / always something / left" [9]); later a repetitive litany of dishes evokes woman's anger and rage ("Dishes, dishes: / she / remembers her mother / throwing dishes. . . . She herself, once / turned an entire table / over" [9–10]). But the dish, or the sign for woman's conflictive experience within advanced culture, does not entirely satisfy this poet as the absolute range of her possibilities; she longs for some form beyond the confines of cultural familiarity: "There must be a / woman, somewhere, that rolls / her food in tender leaves, then / eats them, / too" (11). Nature, as somehow beyond all cultural constructs, seems to offer the promise that even multiple cultural codes cannot: "The leaves welcome us / in greenery. They / rustle hello. The / forest is a silence / and dwarfs you / properly, invites / you to sit / and listen, open / your pores, open / your mouth to / sing and eat" (11–12). Once again, silence works through the body to emerge as another discourse linking creative to bodily imperatives ("sing and eat"). Furthermore, in the forest one can eat without dishes, and thereby transcend those mediating artifacts which signal the division between culture and nature. Most importantly, nature, as the space where body and spirit find unity, allows woman to recreate the sources of her inspiration and mold them into shapes that she alone may choose: "shape the earth into the / plates of nourishment: Her / own form" (12).

The poet is not always entirely certain if she should venture into that subversive, even shocking territory of corporeal language which French feminist Chantal Chawaf has said "stirs up our sensuality, wakes it up, pulls it away from indifferent inertia" (177). But in "The Words" she does decide to dare, to affirm the vitality of her body and desire in her verse:

Dare I say the
words that keep
new life, growing,
in the old life of
the flesh . . . ?

Dare I lay my
legs open to
the tongue of
desire, . . . ?

Dare I give my
body to this
sweet service—?
(13)

Here Villanueva successfully forges another double-edged metaphor—"the tongue of desire." On a more obvious, literal level it articulates a shameless affirmation of female sexual desire and anticipates maternal instinct ("the sucking / lips of babies" [13]); as a biological metaphor for discourse, it summons up a more inclusive concept of the text, one which surrenders to corporeal utterances as does the body lost in sexual passion ("my moaning / throat / you . . . forget / my name" [14]), a text made up of words and sounds signifying potential sources of renewed vitality and spirituality ("new life, sweet service"). Unlike Eliot's Prufrock, who also asks if he dare let his hair down ("Do I dare to eat a peach?") but then cedes, finally, to fear, this female poetic voice still has time to change the language of her life. She ends with an affirmation of desire ("I want you"); he is overcome by waves of aged disillusionment ("and we drown") (Eliot 1962, 8–9).

"Revelation" speaks of a subsequent moment in the life of the body and the spirit: what happens when "romance is gone." Without man, woman looks beyond the sexual act for poetic sources. In the multiplicity of her maternal body and in the presence of her child, she finds a fount of words:

when I left you, the romance
was gone—but
something remained like an
internal poetry that
would not stop—
that demanded its own
conclusion. The
romance leaves when

the baby is three
months old; they

are vocal, demanding,
ever-present, as
the word presents
itself, again and
again. The love
of listening, the
need to endure,
the cyclic joy . . .

When the center is revealed,
a poetry is burning, so
clear and so bright,
it blinds us . . .

When romance is gone
there is the sun,
the rainbow, the warmth
that is real.
(23–24)

When the discourse of romance is gone, another language surfaces: the sensuality of maternal communication which seems to turn conventional expectations about language acquisition on their head. Here the mother relearns to speak from the cyclic, nonlinear chatter of the babe. There is something here, too, which evokes Julia Kristeva's theory of the semiotic, that "more archaic dimension of language, pre-discursive, pre-verbal, which has to do with rhythm, tone, colour, . . . and is linked to the bodily contact with the mother before the paternal order of language comes to separate subject from mother" (Gallop 1982, 124). When the paternal signature is erased from the poet's text with the passing of romance, she is left, paradoxically, with not less but more, something potentially unlimited and highly desirable ("internal poetry that / would not stop- / . . . and what is left / is what I want—[23]). The fertile residue of the semiotic reemerges after layers of encrusted impediments between woman and the clarity of her poetic voice are stripped away. Villanueva's poetic source ("cyclic joy") and Kristeva's privileging of the language of "la jouissance maternelle" are thus strikingly congruent: both can be seen to embrace a simultaneity of the "spiritual, physical, [and] conceptual at one and the same time" (Roudiez 1980, 16). As "Revelation" finally "discloses / what we refused to see" (24), its movement from heterosexuality through "jouissance maternelle," reveals a textual and spiritual source of unparalleled brilliance ("a poetry . . . so / clear and so bright / it blinds us").

A recurrent image emblematic of Villanueva's quest for a wholeness and a transcendence rooted in nature is that of the winged woman. Appearing in "Wonder" and "Winged Woman," this figure who skirts more zones of heat and brilliance (the edge of the sun and the moon), whose heart dwells in the mountains, and whose name is blessed by the sea is a key metaphor personifying the poet's awakening self-integration—as balanced and symmetrical as the verses and images of "Wonder":

> In the crack of dawn, I
> perceive my wings lifting—, . . .
> Now I skirt the edge of dawn.
> Now my wings drip
> blood, blending
> with dawn, that
> burning source.
>
> Now I skirt the edge of
> the moon, its razor
> sharp edge, in
> half, I
> feel its
> wholeness; in
> darkness and
> light.
> (47–48)

French feminist Hélène Cixous has linked her theory of the "feminine text" to woman's irrepressible penchant toward flight. Cixous's paean to flying as distinctly "woman's gesture" provides another striking theoretical parallel to Villanueva's poem "Winged Woman." First, consider Cixous:

> Flying is woman's gesture—flying in language and making it fly. We have all learned the art of flying and its numerous techniques; for centuries we've been able to possess anything only by flying; we've lived in flight, stealing away, finding, when desired, narrow passageways, hidden crossovers. . . . It's no accident: women take after birds and robbers just as robbers take after women and birds. They go by, fly the coop, take pleasure in jumbling the order of space, in disorienting it, in changing around the furniture, dislocating things and values, breaking them all up, emptying structures, and turning propriety upside down.

What woman hasn't flown / stolen? Who hasn't felt, dreamt, performed the gesture that jams sociality? . . . Who hasn't inscribed with
her body the differential, punctured the systems of couples and opposition? (Cixous 1980, 258)

Analogously, Villanueva's "Winged Woman" echoes Cixous's affirmative
escape from constrictions with its references to flying and stealing, its
images signifying a transcendence of opposites through dislocation and
diffusion:

Winged woman, feathers
of the peacock your
stole: you stole

the rainbow—your
wings, at once,
everywhere—your

gaze before you—
your wings shaded
with light—the

sea purifies
your name
again and again—

the mountains,
proud mothers,
hold your
heart—
(51)

Not insignificantly Cixous, as does Villanueva, associates female cor-
poreality, experience, and the text with the sea; indeed, with the whole of
nature: "our seas are what we make of them, full of fish or not, opaque or
transparent, red or black, high or smooth, narrow or bankless; and we are
ourselves sea, sand, coral, seaweed, beaches, tides, swimmers, children,
waves. . . . More or less wavily sea, earth, sky—what matter would rebuff
us? We know how to speak them all" (1980, 260).

In like manner Villanueva's winged woman enjoys a symbiotic link
with the sea ("the sea remembers / well your labor" [51]) and with its
creatures ("the whales / remember" [51]); and this woman who is at one
with nature is one and the same as the poet herself: "Winged / woman, my /
self" (52). Villanueva's winged woman is a poet who can "speak them all,"

an inclusive cosmic discourse "at once, / everywhere": in water, on earth, atop mountains, in air (or as Cixous celebrates: "more or less wavily sea, earth, sky").

In no other poem is the woman poet's limitless, flowing, utterly effusive capacity for both corporeal and textual generation more forcefully stated than in "Siren." This poem stirringly achieves that synthesis of body, spirit, and the text toward which the entire collection moves:

Who is this woman with
words dangling from
the ends of her
hair? leaping
out from her
eyes? dripping
from her breasts? seeping
from her hands? Her

left foot, a
question mark.
Her right
foot, an
exclamation.
Her body, a
dictionary dying
to define life,
growth, a
yearning. Her

love as constant
as the sea—
tangy as salt—
dangerous (even
        to her
self); her heart ruptures,
mends with each
new poem, word,
breath—but
she'll never
stop questioning,
begging, answering
herself (the word
        is constant now

in her
ears). She is a woman
singing to her
death, the
bone's still
marrow, the
womb's fluttering
flesh, love's
lost beauty
always found
at the edge of silence.
She is a
woman singing
in the snow.
(64–65)

Again, the theories of Cixous help place Villanueva's poetic voice within a framework of "feminine writing" as cultural transgression. Clearly the siren, as a woman singing for her life in a frozen landscape, participates in the same differential realm as Cixous's hypothetical feminine writer: she inhabits a text which privileges the voice, one in which "writing and voice are entwined and interwoven" (Cixous and Clément 1986, 92). But what can the voice say for which words—written words alone—will not suffice? Once more Cixous suggests an answer: "The voice sings from a time before law, before the Symbolic took one's breath away and reappropriated it into language under its authority of separation. . . . With each woman the first, nameless love is singing" (Cixous and Clément 1986, 93). The singing voice of the siren harkens, then, back to that—perhaps mythical—time before the law (that is, before paternal or phallocentric law), when women's voices were not yet relegated to hierarchical separation or (to borrow from the poem's own conceptual implications) to "the edge[s] of [imposed] silence." The siren's voice reappropriates a dynamic, self-defined discourse emanating from all regions of woman's body and soul (hair, eyes, breasts, hands, feet, heart, womb); its lexicon is nothing less than the entire body which becomes the source of wisdom and desire. Further, as the siren / poet's heart ruptures, she metonymically breaks apart that system of phallocentric oppositions which structures our culture, and when the heart mends, new poems, words, and songs implicitly rearrange those oppositional relationships. The "Siren" thus embodies and sings with the same heterogeneity and unbounded expression which characterize Cixous's ideal feminine writer: "Heterogeneous, yes. For her joyous benefits she is erogenous; she is the erotogeneity of the heterogeneous: airborne swimmer, in flight, she does not cling to herself; she is dispersible, prodigious, stunning, desirous and capable" (Cixous 1980, 260). The Siren / poet's discourse is grounded on the same paradox as the feminine writer's: in her prodigious dispersal she becomes not less but more, an eminently capacious articulator of her own desire ("she'll never / stop questioning, begging, / answering").

As I have written in the Introduction to *Life Span*, "poetic expression and self-development are inseparable" in this collection (v). Yet though the poetic voice is often cast as a loner in the wilderness, it echoes inside an implicitly alien cultural construct ("I never have put much stock / in pyramids and such / they / leave me cold" [6]). As opposed to soaring stone monuments to "man's brilliance," this female voice prefers to "believe in heat" (6) and accept nothing less than life. Similarly, the poet's voice settles for nothing but its "own form," and by opening itself to its "tongue of desire," it reacts implicitly with other cultural forms and tongues which might oppress or restrict it. It journeys to its own mecca in "My Mecca" (41) and speaks "too much, too loudly" in "Escandalosa" (30); it asserts its own feminine and Chicana authority within the overarching cultural framework of different—even alien and oppressive—beliefs and modes of articulation. The voices of *Life Span* thus slip and escape from polarized modes of expression to achieve a balanced melding of corporeal life, spiritual flight, and poetic language. This integrated textuality situates itself beyond the limits of hierarchical oppositions and eludes the traditional positioning of woman's discourse upon that order's lowermost rungs.

Alvina E. Quintana

Ana Castillo's *The Mixquiahuala Letters:* The Novelist as Ethnographer

Personal narrative mediates this contradiction between the engagement called for in fieldwork and the self-effacement called for in formal ethnographic description, or at least mediates some of its anguish, by inserting into the ethnographic text the authority of the personal experience out of which the ethnography is made.—Mary Louise Pratt (1986)

In recent years the academy has been shaken by a significant shift in scholarly concerns which raises provocative questions regarding the politics of representation. By addressing problems in the Western intellectual tradition, cultural critics have uncovered what has come to be thought of as a crisis in representation. Giving rise to such subjects as the objectification of women and other minorities, their debates challenged theories of interpretation. Mary Louise Pratt's quote resonates with a self-critical mode characteristic of the present moment in history, a moment in which dominant ideas and assumptions are problematized because of their ideological implications. While illustrating how questions raised in this time of reassessment have been appropriated by modern anthropological discourse, Pratt also reveals how some anthropologists have begun to question their own practices. She is, in fact with her treatise, deconstructing the ethnographic process, as she sharpens her focus on the concept of ethnographic authority, questioning the notion of objectivity. When we consider Pratt's assertions concerning personal narrative and formal ethnographic description, it becomes evident that we must also reevaluate the authority of personal experience. For in classical anthropological terms:

Ethnography is a research process in which the anthropologist closely observes, records, and engages in the daily life of another culture—an experience labeled as the fieldwork method—and then writes accounts of this culture, emphasizing descriptive detail. These accounts are the primary form in which fieldwork procedures, the other culture, and the ethnographer's personal and theoretical reflections are accessible to professionals and other readerships. (Marcus and Fischer 1986, 18)

Pratt's voice is but one of many which have begun to question ethnographic authority, reflecting on the relationship between personal narrative and "formal ethnographic description." We can view her approach as one which developed in dialectical relationship to a re-envisioning process that was initiated by Clifford Geertz's *The Interpretation of Cultures* (1973). What Geertz called for in his text was a reassessment of the ethnographic field-work process—a process he still thinks of as objective, though symbolic and interpretive in nature. Pratt, on the other hand, suggests that the representation of culture involves a creative and interpretive mode of writing which reflects the subjective experiences of the ethnographer.

Although Geertz and Pratt connect the symbolic and interpretive quality of ethnographic writing, it is Pratt who implies that ethnographies are never simply ethnographies but rather "ethnographies for," written in the interest of the dominant culture. But as dominant culture is a value-laden term which signifies a point of view that has been traditionally dominated by a male perspective, as both the tradition of novel writing by men and traditional ethnography have functioned to systematically marginalize or "other" women, we begin to see the ideological limitations of both of these narrative forms. And once we apprehend that ethnographies are merely interpretations, we must determine the extent to which these interpretations or detailed descriptions can qualify as factual and objective documentations. Following this line of inquiry brings forth an interesting paradox concerning the creative, interpretive process. Is it possible to develop a discourse that is both interpretive and objective? Because the relationship between interpretation and subjectivity is a blurred one, it would seem that the anthropologist's method for observing and documenting the "daily life of another culture" could easily be viewed as subjective literary production. In George Marcus's and Michael Fischer's terms (1986) ethnography becomes a personal and imaginative vehicle by which anthropologists provide cultural critiques rather than objective representations.

What becomes evident at this point in our inquiry is the relationship between imaginary writing and ethnography as a written product. Both forms of writing reflect limited ways of seeing the world; both are influenced by social conditions and the ideology of a particular historical moment. In this light it is interesting to think about feminist writers of fiction, who, much like an anthropologist, might focus on microcosms within a culture, unpacking rituals in the context of traditional symbolic and social structures of subjugation. Yet unlike both the conventional anthropologist and the classical Chicano writer of fiction, the Chicana feminist is also interested in scrutinizing the assumptions that root her own cultural influences, unpacking so-called tradition and political institutions that shape patriarchal ways of seeing. Even though the Chicano narrative has always had some cultural context, focusing on the ethnic identification process by redefining past traditions as the work of Tomás Rivera, Américo Paredes, and Oscar Zeta Acosta illustrates, it has for the most part overlooked issues that revolve around female gender identification.

The Mixquiahuala Letters (1986) is a postmodernist, Chicana feminist novel that reflects the historical forces of the eighties, as well as an incredible diversity of concerns, literary and otherwise, from what has been previously recognized and legitimized by canonical structures. What I want to explore is not so much the pervasive ramifications of an American literary canon, which serves to reify social injustice and inequality as it suppresses the nature and development of the experiences of people of color, but rather how a close reading of The Mixquiahuala Letters reveals Ana Castillo's attempt to retaliate, by striking out against the limitations created by canonical structures. Castillo's novel functions as an oppositional feminist discourse that challenges the limitations inherent in both Anglo-American and Mexican culture. Certainly, feminist literary criticism has helped to expose the limitations of a canon which fails to equitably represent the nature and development of "white" women in America. But when we consider how mainstream feminist theory has likewise, because of its failure to appraise race and class oppression, helped to perpetuate white middle-class values, it seems to me that we can deem Chicana feminist creative writings as emancipatory cultural formations, that are either in alternative or oppositional relationship to Anglo-American feminist discourse.

Chicano culture draws on two external forces and has been labelled by anthropologists as a "creole culture" because it is one which draws on two or more origins: (1) a long-standing culture one is born into, and (2) a culture in terms of its social and political forces in the immediate environment. Both of these points of origin are limiting for Chicanas in that neither addresses gender issues. The Chicana writer is thus engaged in mediating and negotiating between two cultural systems, constructing a cultural and feminist identity as she works to deconstruct the predominantly male cultural paradigms that have worked to suppress a female perspective. Following this train of thought, Chicana literature functions as a bold cultural intervention, which ironically enough resembles what we have come to respect as interpretive or experimental ethnography. I want to begin my study by juxtaposing the words of two cultural critics, Clifford Geertz and Ana Castillo:

> There is no such thing as human nature independent of culture. (Geertz 1973)

> There was a definite call to find a place to satisfy my yearning spirit, the Indian in me that had begun to cure the ails of humble folk distrustful of modern medicine; a need for the sapling woman for the fertile earth that nurtured her growth. (Castillo 1986)

Geertz and Castillo, though utilizing different discourses directed to different audiences, raise similar issues concerning culture and human nature. Geertz's comments are drawn from his rather elaborate discussion on culture in chapter 1 of *The Interpretation of Cultures*. He contends that humans are like animals suspended in the "webs of significance" they themselves have spun. An analysis of these webs should not be viewed as an experimental science in search of law but rather as an interpretative search for meaning. If humans are suspended within cultural webs, it seems obvious that "there can be no such thing as human nature independent of culture." Geertz's ideas, taken out of their anthropological context, seem innocent enough, but we must remember that he is speaking as an ethnographer, speaking in terms of "the Other" and so-called "primitive culture." If we consciously avoid the subtle trappings of this hierarchical way of seeing, his metaphor can also be used to describe the self-fashioning process marginal ethnic groups undertake in the United States, as they attempt to create an existence, drawing from not one but two distinct cultural systems. It is important to note that Geertz's views on culture and his notion of interpretive analysis (thick description as he calls it) have been appropriated by many feminist scholars, since the feminist analysis of women's culture also involves decoding and interpreting many of the same systems with which traditional anthropologists are concerned (i.e., gender relations, kinship, sexuality, taboos, etc.).

Castillo's words are different than Geertz's in that they are taken from a work of fiction—*The Mixquiahuala Letters*. She makes no claims of factualism, but states rather explicitly early on that her text is fiction, and that "Any resemblance it may have to actual persons or incidents is coincidental" (Introduction, n.p.). Even so, it is clear in the above passage that as a creative writer, she, like Geertz, is grappling with the influence of an elusive, but powerful, cultural force. It becomes clear to Castillo's readers that her protagonist's existential well-being is dependent on culture. When we carry forward Geertz's semiotic concept of culture and evaluate the ethnographic writings of traditional anthropologists as representations based on individual interpretations, it becomes difficult to qualify them as objective, factual accounts of reality. Once we admit that these cultural representations should also be viewed as a mixture of descriptive and inter-pretive modes of discourse, the gap between imaginary and ethnographic writing shrinks before our eyes as both forms of writing are reduced to a particular way of seeing the world. And as such, we can see that Castillo, like Geertz, is involved in the process of describing and interpreting culture.

But aside from what appears to be a somewhat natural affinity, these two quotes are also interesting because on a broader level, they illus-trate the vast difference in objective and subjective writing. Geertz, in the straightforward language of an "authority," states that all human nature is influenced by culture. In contrast, Castillo's language, more personal in tone, elaborates on Geertz's comments regarding the significance of cul-ture. As they bring to life a rather academic yet direct observation, her words seem to embroider Geertz's by illustrating why or how his thoughts might be applied in the real world of subjective experiences. With her words she has in effect grounded his theory in practice. In the final analysis it is evident that each quote seems to grow in insight when juxtaposed to the other. This grounding of theory with practice becomes relevant when we begin to consider the rather abstract subject: the Chicana writers' quest for self-definition.

Put simply, the process of fashioning any kind of marginal identity (whether it be Chicana, feminist, or hyphenated American) involves a series of negotiations and mediations between the past and the future—a past and a future which for the Chicana is culturally explosive in terms of women's experiences and historical implications because, at this point in history, she attempts to define herself as she maneuvers between two opposing realities that fail to acknowledge her existence. Chicanas are not represented, but instead fall into the category of structured absences in both Chicano and Anglo feminist ideologies. Because of the Chicana's positioning between the Chicano and Anglo feminist postures, she is faced with the task of formulat-ing an ideology, an identity out of two plans: the nostalgic plan of the past and the stereotypical Anglo feminist plan for the future. The nostalgic past refers to the idealization of old customs, largely a patriarchal interpretation of Mexican cultural traditions and history. The limitations of this plan are obvious when compared to the barriers created by an Anglo-American feminist movement which has, for the most part, failed to acknowledge female differences based on culture and ethnicity. It is because of this movement's failure to acknowledge differences that Anglo-American feminist theory has provided Chicanas with more of a mirage than a vehicle for understanding or change. *The Mixquiahuala Letters* illustrates Chicanas caught between these two polarities, moving closer to self-discovery by drawing and synthesizing usable aspects from both Anglo and Mexican cultures, weaving a complicated present out of the past and future options. The novel centers on the marginal experiences of two friends, Teresa and Alicia, as they live and travel through Mexico and the United States. By representing the daily activities of these two women, Castillo is able to reveal exactly what is at risk when an invisible entity attempts to define itself out of the structured omissions of two oppositional ideologies.

Stephen Greenblatt's *Renaissance Self-Fashioning* (1980) is useful for conceptualizing the Chicana's self-definition process. Although his discussion focuses on self-fashioning in Renaissance literature, it provides a workable method for analyzing the Chicana's struggle for self-identification. It is because of the clear distinctions he makes between self-fashioning in upper and marginal classes that his approach becomes useful to our inquiry. He states that for marginal classes:

> Self-fashioning is achieved in relation to something perceived as alien, strange, or hostile . . . ; self-fashioning always involves some experience of threat some effacement or undermining, some loss of self . . . ; we may say that self-fashioning occurs at the point of encounter between an authority and an alien, that what is produced in this encounter partakes of both the authority and the alien that is marked for attack, and hence that way achieved identity always contains within itself the signs of its own subversion or loss. (1980, 9)

Greenblatt's discourse emphasizes the issues involved when marginals ("aliens" as he calls them) seek to obtain an autonomous status created by self-identification. When we consider Greenblatt's analysis, we can see how the Chicanas' self-fashioning "always involves some experience of threat" or "some loss of self." Castillo's protagonist, Teresa, speaks of such a loss when she reflects on her relationship to Mexico in letter number nineteen: "Mexico. Melancholy, profoundly right and wrong, it embraces as it strangulates. Destiny is not a metaphysical confrontation with one's self rather, society has knit its pattern so tight that a confrontation with it is inevitable" (59). Teresa's words reveal that she understands that her destiny as a woman is not determined through a confrontation with herself, but rather through a confrontation with a society that holds the very real threat of restricting, silencing, and marginalizing women. In letter number thirteen, Teresa refers to another threat, while at the same time revealing her attitudes about Anglo women. She writes to Alicia:

why i hated white women and sometimes didn't like you:
Society had made them above all possessions
the most desired. And they believed it.
My husband admitted feeling inferior to them. . . .
i hated
white women who took black pimps
everyone knows savages have bestial members
i hated
white women who preferred Latins and Mediterraneans because of the
fusion of hot and cold blood running through the very core of their
erections and nineteenth-century romanticism that makes going to
bed with them much more challenging than with wasp men who are
only good for making money and marrying. (43)

Teresa's thoughts communicate how she, as an individual, perceives white
women as a threat. But when we consider this letter as a symbolic representation of cultural attitudes, it tells us something basic about the Chicana
woman's experience. Yet her reference to her husband's admission of feeling
inferior to them illustrates how the threat created by white women moves
beyond gender distinctions. With this letter Castillo has unmasked one of
the ideological limitations of Anglo feminist theory, a feminism with little
concern for issues of race, class, or culture. It becomes apparent in Teresa's
letter that the subordination and control of "women of color" is further
complicated when white women are elevated to the status of "most desirable": as a backlash to this white privilege, women of color, regardless of
their gender, are relegated to a subordinate position with respect to white
women, simply because the standards for desirability are based on light
skin beauty. And once we consider the structured absences in feminist
theory, Chicana autonomy becomes a critical issue that cannot be overlooked.

For Greenblatt autonomy, though important, does not represent the
central issue. What is crucial here is the power one has to impose a shape
upon oneself, a power to control one's identity. He, like Geertz and, for that
matter, many Chicano writers, argues that the interplay between external
forces is what determines self-fashioning. His discussion reinforces the
need to understand the external forces that will ultimately affect the Chicana's self-fashioning process. If we are to carry this discussion further, then
we must consider these "external forces" and the implications involved
whenever Chicanas attempt to define themselves in cultural and feminist
terms. The issues I wish to address, therefore, focus specifically on how *The
Mixquiahuala Letters* negotiates and mediates between the external forces
which encompass time and space as well as the past and future.

Chicana critic Norma Alarcón conceives of Chicana poets as "umpires" mediating between a past Chicano patriarchal interpretation of culture, which holds the potential for locking them into "crippling traditional stereotypes," and a future that can be equally limiting within an "Anglo-American feminist promise" (1985). In *The Mixquiahuala Letters*, Ana Castillo has moved beyond her role as poet "umpire" into the position of modern (experimental) ethnographer, as she has produced a personal narrative which mediates between objective and subjective narratives, thereby overcoming what James Clifford has identified as anthropology's "impossible attempt to fuse objective and subjective practices" (1986, 109). The significance of Clifford's point becomes clearer when we consider Eric Wolf's thoughts on fieldwork in *Europe and the People Without History* (1982):

> Fieldwork—direct communication with people and participant observation of their on-going activities . . . became a hallmark of anthropological method. Fieldwork has proved enormously fruitful in laying bare and correcting false assumptions and erroneous descriptions. It has also revealed hitherto unsuspected connections among sets of social activities and cultural forms. Yet the very success of the method lulled its users into a false confidence. It became easy for them to convert merely heuristic considerations of method into theoretical postulates about society and culture. (13)

Indeed, if we consider *The Mixquiahuala Letters* as a personal narrative that mediates between objective and subjective practices, we can envision—as I have argued elsewhere (1988)—examining the social sciences and literature together to set the stage for a more inclusive type of theorizing. In other words, once we make one minor adjustment and move toward an interdisciplinary approach, anthropology's impossibilities appear to become possibilities. Likewise, when we consider Castillo's text as a mediation between objective and subjective practices, the imaginary, fictive content of this novel seems to transcend its form. Once we are able to make this leap in consciousness, opening rather than closing our respective discourses, the limitations created by our fragmented visions quickly begin to dissipate.

Because Castillo's epistolary novel consists of letters that systematically observe, record and describe experiences that take place in the daily life of Mexican and American culture—a process we have previously described as the fieldwork method—we can read it as a parody of modern ethnographic and travel writing. It is interesting to note that Castillo's process of textual production is somewhat suggestive of Linda Hutcheon's *A Theory of Parody* (1985). Drawing from the double etymology of the prefix *para* she concludes: "on a pragmatic level parody was not limited to producing a ridiculous effect [para as 'counter' or against], but that the equally strong suggestion of complicity and accord [para as 'beside'] allowed for an opening up of the range of parody. This distinction between prefix meaning, has been used to argue for the existence of both comic and serious types of parody" (53).

As a parody of modern ethnography, Castillo's text becomes an enterprise that provides the voices and experiences involved in growing up Chicana, revealing in Wolf's words "unsuspected connections among sets of social activities and cultural forms." Like an ethnographer, Castillo uses the voice of her informant, Teresa, to focus on what is at risk when a Chicana attempts to fashion an identity in response to two opposing cultures. In letter number four, Teresa foregrounds the Catholic church's enormous influence on young women as the institution molds individual Mexican/Chicana identity into a cultural model that promotes women's passivity and guilt. She writes:

> Alicia,
> Do you know the *smell* of a church? Not a storefront, praise the Lord, hallelujah church, or a modest frame building with a simple steeple projecting to the all heavens, but a CATHEDRAL, with doors the height of two very tall men and so heavy that when you pull one open to enter you feel as small as you are destined.
> You were never led by the hand as a little girl by a godmother, or tugged by the ear by a nun whose dogmatic instruction initiated you into humility which is quite different from baptism when you were anointed with water as a squirming baby in the event that you should die and never see God face-to-face because you had not been cleansed of the sin of your parents' copulation.
> It smells of incense, hot oils, the wax of constant burning candles, melting at a vigilant pace, the plaster of an army of saints watching with fixed glass eyes, revered in exchange for being mediators and delivering your feeble prayers. It smells of flowers and palms that precede Easter. It smells of death. The last time i went to CHURCH, genuflecting my way to the confessional, i was eighteen years old.
> i was a virgin, technically speaking, a decent girl, having been conditioned to put my self-respect before curiosity. This did not satisfy the priest, or should i say, stimulate his stagnant duty in that dark closet of anonymity and appointed judgement.
> He began to probe. When that got him no titillating results, he suggested, or more precisely, led an interrogation founded on gestapo technique. When i didn't waiver under the torment, although feeling

my knees raw, air spare, he accused outright: *"Are you going to tell me you haven't wanted to be with a man? You must have let one do more than . . . than what?*

i ran out of the booth in tears and in a rage, left the CHURCH without waiting to hear my penance for absolution of my unforgivable sins. (24–25)

Her emotional narrative describes religious rituals that have limited the development of a feminist political consciousness. Her thoughts on religion also resonate with the powerful words of Chicana feminist and social activist Cherríe Moraga:

Women of color have always known, although we have not always wanted to look at it, that our sexuality is not merely a physical response or drive, but holds a crucial relationship to our entire spiritual capacity. Patriarchal religions—whether brought to us by the colonizer's cross and gun or emerging from our own people—have always known this. Why else would the female body be so associated with sin and disobedience? Simply put, if the spirit and sex have been linked in our oppression, then they must also be linked in the strategy toward our liberation. (1983, 132)

Castillo uses the epistolary form as a vehicle, enabling her to move freely from one issue to another, from one country to another as she describes the relationship between the sexes. But more importantly, it is the epistolary from which gives her the flexibility to describe the differences between the way women are viewed in the United States and Mexico. In an entry devoted to recollections about her experiences in Veracruz, Teresa recalls a conversation she had with Ponce, a Mexican engineer:

He began, "I think you are a 'liberal woman.' Am I correct?" His expression meant to persuade me that it didn't matter what I replied. In the end he would win. He would systematically strip away all my pretexts, reservations, and defenses, and end up in bed with me.

In that country, the term "liberated woman" meant something other than what we had strived for back in the United States. In this case it simply meant a woman who would sleep nondiscriminately with any man who came along. I inhaled deeply from the strong cigarette he had given me and released the smoke in the direction of his face which diminished the sarcastic expression. (73)

In postmodernist fashion Castillo provides her readers with a pastiche of what has been a nearly invisible section of Chicano culture. Her fragmented approach is a powerful tool that enables her to negotiate and mediate as she probes the female psyche. Her style reflects the influence and power of many of Latin America's greatest writers. And because of this it comes as no surprise that she dedicates her novel "in memory of the master of the game, Julio Cortázar" (Introduction, n. p.).

Following Cortázar, Castillo is also a mistress of play, an author who seems to intuitively understand the issues at stake when providing a puzzlelike narrative. The text comes to life as a series of games revolving around courtship, wit, and women. In the opening letter to the reader, Castillo playfully suggests three proposed readings of her novel: "It is the author's duty to alert the reader that this is not a book to be read in the usual sequence. All letters are numbered to aid in following any one of the author's proposed options: For the Conformist; For the Cynic; For the Quixotic" ("Dear Reader," n. p.). She closes by including a message "For the reader committed to nothing but short fiction, all the letters read as separate entities. Good luck whichever journey you choose!" Castillo forces her readers to select a sequence; the interpretation of an itinerary through her text is in fact left open to them. By taking this step she has managed to release her readers from what could be referred to as her personal biases or subjective interpretations. Castillo's narrative strategy aimed at releasing her readers from a prescribed reading, encourages them to become active participants in her text. Umberto Eco's concept of the "open work" is reminiscent of Castillo's process of textual production.

> [i] "open works," insofar as they are in movement, are characterized by the invitation to make the work together with the author and [ii] on a wider level [as a subgenus in the species "work in movement"] there exist works, which though organically completed, are "open" to a continuous generation of internal relations which the addressee must uncover and select in his act of perceiving the totality of incoming stimuli. [iii] Every work of art, even though it is produced by following an explicit poetics of necessity, is effectively open to a virtually unlimited range of possible readings, each of which causes the work to acquire a new vitality in terms of one particular taste, or perspective, or personal performance. (1979, 63)

Castillo's use of the "open work" structure allows her to become an active participant in her own novel. She is in this way not only mediating between "personal narrative" and "objective description," but also between her role as author and her role as reader. It is through this mediation process, as an aside to the reader, that she raises questions regarding the issue of authority and interpretation, an issue which has become problematic in the disciplines of history and anthropology. We could very easily think of Castillo's text as meta-ethnography.

Thus Castillo's novel functions as a linguistic artifact that does more to inform readers about the Chicana's struggle for self-definition than many of the contemporary theoretical efforts, which because of their failure to consider race, ethnicity, and class as variables have produced ineffective, one-dimensional paradigms. In *The Mixquiahuala Letters* Castillo attempts to retaliate against social injustice and inequality by documenting what is at risk when the Chicana defies authority in order to break away from the stagnant traditions and ideals that smother and suppress female desire. She explores the female psyche—the unspeakable, unveiling secrets and taboos in language that are profound and whimsical, perverse and waggish. Ultimately, the text can be read as a revolt against order, which eloquently illustrates why it is essential for feminists to expose and thereby destroy the power of any outside or foreign "authority" by creating a space for themselves. The novel reveals how subjective experiences provide relevant strands of information, which are essential to creating a space that is fundamental to the Chicana's self-definition process. In this way Castillo's epistolary novel (like mainstream feminist theory) is effective in simultaneously marking out women as special selves and claiming, in Marilyn Strathern's words, "that knowledge of the self as such can come only from acknowledging this special nature" (1984, 22).

Renato Rosaldo

Fables of the Fallen Guy

In English my name means hope. In Spanish it means too many letters. It means sadness, it means waiting. It is like the number nine. A muddy color. It is the Mexican records my father plays on Sunday mornings when he is shaving, songs like sobbing.

It was my great grandmother's name and now it is mine. She was a horse woman too, born like me in the Chinese year of the horse—which is supposed to be bad luck if you're born female—but I think this is a Chinese lie because the Chinese, like the Mexicans, don't like their women strong.

My great-grandmother. I would've liked to have known her, a wild horse of a woman, so wild she wouldn't marry until my great grandfather threw a sack over her head and carried her off just like that, as if she were a fancy chandelier. That's the way he did it.

And the story goes she never forgave him. She looked out the window all her life, the way so many women sit their sadness on an elbow. I wonder if she made the best with what she got or was she sorry because she couldn't be all the things she wanted to be. Esperanza. I have inherited her name, but I don't want to inherit her place by the window.

At school they say my name funny as if the syllables were made out of tin and hurt the roof of your mouth. But in Spanish my name is made out of a softer something like silver, not quite as thick as sister's name Magdalena which is uglier than mine. Magdalena who at least can come home and become Nenny. But I am always Esperanza.

I would like to baptize myself under a new name, a name more like the real me, the one nobody sees. Esperanza as Lisandra or Maritza or Zeze the X. Yes. Something like Zeze the X will do.—(Cisneros 1988, 12–13)

I am indebted to the Stanford Humanities Center for providing support during the period when this essay was written. José David Saldívar encouraged my project and initially suggested that I read Sandra Cisneros, Denise Chávez, and Alberto Ríos. Kathleen Newman and Mary Louise Pratt also offered helpful comments on the essay.

"My Name," from Sandra Cisneros's short story cycle *The House on Mango Street* exemplifies the experimentation and achievement of recent Chicana narrative. In trying new forms Chicana writers have developed a fresh vision of self and society; they have opened an alternative cultural space, a heterogeneous world, within which their protagonists no longer act as "unified subjects," yet remain confident of their identities. In moving through a world laced with poverty, violence, and danger, Esperanza acts assertive and playful. She thrives, not just survives, as she virtually dances through her life with grace and wit.

Esperanza tells a gendered coming of age story that picks upon a distinct strand of a Chicano heritage. More matriarchal than patriarchal, her vision reaches back to her great-grandmother and forward to Zeze the X. Yet her constant play, her deceptively childlike patter, subverts oppressive patriarchal points of cultural coherence and fixity.

Esperanza inhabits a border zone peopled with multiple subjectivities and a plurality of languages and cultures. Moving between English and Spanish, her name shifts in length (from four letters to nine), in meaning (from hope to sadness and waiting), and in sound (from being as cutting as tin to being as soft as silver). Initially accepting her matrimony, her name, Esperanza then refuses to assume her great-grandmother's place by the window. In concluding her story, she yet again turns things topsy-turvy by baptizing her invisible, real self: Zeze the X.

Like her grandmother, Esperanza is a horse woman, but not a female counterpart of the male warrior horseman, the *jinete* or the *hidalgo.* No, she was born, of all things, in the Chinese year of the horse; in her heterogeneous cultural world, the Chinese and the Chicano readily come into play together. Both Chinese and Mexicans agree, she says, because neither culture likes its women strong. Her narrative moves, as if along links in a chain of free associations, and great-grandmother Esperanza undergoes a metamorphosis from a presumed rider, the horse woman, to the beast itself, a wild horse of a woman.

Patriarchal Precedents and "Authentic" Culture

The Chicana vision of Cisneros has been written against earlier, but still vital, narratives of cultural authenticity. Such narratives hold up an ideal of *"pureza,"* one in which culture is autonomous, homogeneous, and coherent. The *"pureza"* ethic often derives enduring cultural forms from a primal patriarchal order.

Consider a half-playful, half-serious epic version of a coming of age ritual under the primordial patriarchal order. In those days of high mimetic solemnity, a young man was chosen to acquire spiritual and physical potency from an ancestral figure. During a prophetic dream, with its atmosphere of culturally undeniable truth, the founding patriarch listed his successors in a dynastic lineage which culminated with the "chosen" young man (compare Rosaldo 1978). Thus, in the mythic past the young man received his patrimony, his name and his "sacred objects" consisting of a regal sword and shield.

Alternatively, consider a patriarchal precedent more closely linked with the present, such as José Antonio Villarreal's *Pocho* (1959). Not unlike Ernesto Galarza's *Barrio Boy* (1971), this is a story about moving "north from Mexico." Among other things the novel plays with the dilemmas of resistance and assimilation. The main character, Richard Rubio, appears caught in the irresolvable tension between what he perceives as the three available ways of being in the world: that of warrior hero inherited from the irretrievable past, the absolute loss represented by assimilation, and the corruption of pachuquismo. The ambiguity of his perceived situation prevents Richard Rubio from either settling unequivocally on any single possibility or developing his own alternative vision.

Richard presents his father, Juan Rubio, as the warrior hero from the irretrievable past. In a parodic scene evocative of a clichéd Mexican movie, Juan enters a *cantina*, picks up a teenage woman, and deliberately insults, then guns down her lover. After the soldiers who arrest him discover his identity as a revolutionary hero, they take him to their general. When the two old soldiers converse, Juan speaks of dignity, manhood, and honor:

> "If a man has been a man, he will always be a man. I know I will be. I will never forget that which I believe is right. There must be a sense of honor or a man will have no dignity, and without the dignity a man is incomplete. I will always be a man."
>
> "Ojalá," said the General.
>
> "For the present," said Juan Rubio, "I will run cattle for your gringo, but only because I would rather do that than work as a farmhand. After all, I am a jinete." (Villarreal 1959, 15)

By insisting on his identity as a horseman, a *jinete* or an *hidalgo*, Juan Rubio actually assumes the masculine identity so artfully played upon by the horsewoman Esperanza. His diction like a bad translation from the Spanish, he enters the world of textbook Castilian history inhabited, for example, by Américo Castro's epic Spaniards who above all else value their honor and dignity. Villarreal thus projects the warrior hero Juan Rubio into the irretrievable past. For Richard, his father appears to be a peculiarly unattainable standard for conduct.

Similarly, another pioneering work from the late fifties, Américo Paredes's *"With His Pistol in His Hand"* (1958), imaginatively creates an "authentic" patriarchal culture. His work has a warrior hero at its center. In its opening poetic vision, south Texas-Mexican society from 1750 until the Anglo-Texan invasion after 1848 appears pastoral, egalitarian, and patriarchal. Yet this version of early south Texas-Mexican society appears too harmonious to be true. Even if it were true, however, its patriarchal order should, after more than fifteen years of recent feminist scholarship, be critiqued. The notion of a just and stable patriarchal order papers over internal conflicts and contradictions brought about by the inequalities among men (see Montejano 1987).

Lest there be any confusion, my purpose in underscoring the mythic quality of Paredes's poetic characterization of early south Texas-Mexican society is not to demean his work. Gregorio Cortez was a crucial figure of resistance for the south Texas-Mexican imagination through the late fifties and into the sixties. At the time Anglo-Texan white supremacy was even more virulent than today, and the Chicano movement had not yet appeared on the horizon. Indeed, if I were to have a patron saint for these intellectual labors (which I am not about to do) it would be Américo Paredes, not, for example, Fredric Jameson.

His poetic vision of early south Texas society aside, Paredes has developed a sophisticated conception of culture that attends to history, politics, and relations of inequality (see Rosaldo 1985). He sees culture as bound by circumstances, constantly changing, and internally diverse. His goal is, not totalizing, but contextualist. Rather than delineate a static pattern, he shows the interplay of culture, power, and history. When one asks, for example, about so-called ethnic labels of self-identification (Mexican, Chicano, and so on), Paredes counters like a fox, not with a single "self-designation," but with myriad names. It all depends, he says, on who is speaking to whom under what circumstances. Are they distant or intimate? Is their relationship egalitarian or one of dominance and subordination?

The Fading of the Warrior Hero

The change from the warrior hero to other forms and figures of resistance has evolved a good deal since the late fifties. Consider, for example, Edward James Olmos's portrayal of Gregorio Cortez in the cinematic version of Paredes's book, *The Ballad of Gregorio Cortez*. As we know from *Zoot Suit* and *Miami Vice*, Olmos can play either the flamboyant or the tight-lipped tough guy, but in the film he played Cortez as a humble peasant who happened to be in the wrong place at the wrong time. His resistance was thrust upon him by a mistranslation. He was made, not born, a hero.

Similarly, the warrior hero has faded away in the following passage from Reyes Cárdenas's recent poem "I never was a militant Chicano":

> I never shot up
> a federal courthouse
> like Reies Tijerina
> but I know
> that the frustrations
> won't stay
> locked up forever.
> I was never
> really a pachuco
> but I saw then what I still see now—
> that we're
> getting nowhere,
> that things
> are worse
> than they were
> in the forties
> and fifties.
> (1987, 43–44)

Cárdenas supports the Chicano movement's goals, but deliberately distances himself from its earlier and not altogether moribund masculine heroics. He has cleared the ground for new figures and modes of resistance, yet to be defined. What follows will explore an emergent politics of culture inscribed, among other places, in the works of Denise Chávez, Alberto Ríos, and Sandra Cisneros.

The Mirror and the Dance

In seeking fresh definitions of the culture of resistance, let us consider, not the novel, but its poor relation, the short story cycle. In a pertinent essay Mary Louise Pratt (1981) has suggested that the formal marginality of such cycles enables them to become arenas for experimentation, the development of alternative visions, and the introduction of women and teenagers as protagonists. Marginal genres thus are often the site of political innovation and cultural creativity. Such has been the precedent, for example, in the work of Tomás Rivera.

The following discussion of Chávez, Ríos, and Cisneros will extend the playfully serious paradigm already introduced in its first phase: the passing down of the patrimony (or, as in the following cases, the matrimony), often occurring during dreamlike states and made concrete in culturally appropriate "sacred objects." The second phase is the awakening of adolescent sexuality, with both its promise and its dangers. How do protagonists find ways to survive as they confront a threatening world? The third phase resides in the discovery of the grace or the potency that enable the protagonists to thrive in dangerous worlds.

Denise Chávez's *The Last of the Menu Girls* (1986) consists of seven stories which vary greatly in length, from seven to fifty-one pages. In one case Chávez experimentally "crosses over" by using two narrators, one of whom is an Anglo-American. Throughout, she plays with diction and voice in a manner that makes her stories near dramas. Her tales follow a central protagonist, Rocío Esquibel, who appears in the mundane world of work, as a nurse's aid, a teacher, and a writer.

Matrimony. Rocío Esquibel's lineage goes back to a matriarch. As she is in a dreamlike state, waking up from a nap, she sees a strong, beautiful, articulate woman's face:

> Who was that woman?
> Myself.
> I thought about *loving* women. Their beauty and their doubts, their sure sweet clarity. Their unfathomable depths, their flesh and souls aligned in mystery.
> I got up, looked in the mirror and thought of Ronelia, my older sister, who was always the older woman to me. It was she whom I monitored last. It was she whose life I inspected, absorbed into my own.
> It was my sister's pores, her postures that were my teachers, her flesh, with and without clothes, that was my awakening, and her face that was the mirror image of my growing older. To see her, was to see my mother and my grandmother, and now myself. (63)

The lineage goes back, through women, to her grandmother. Her matrimony consists of neither objects nor names, but rather of her own body, its flesh, soul, pores, and postures. All becomes visible in the mirror where Esquibel sees herself, and in herself she finds her older sister, her mother, and her grandmother.

Sexuality and danger. Confronted with danger, the death of her Great Aunt Eutilia, the thirteen-year-old Rocío dances her adolescent sexuality. While Great Aunt Eutilia smells and oozes with death, Rocío responds with dance and song:

> Down the steps I leaped into Eutilia's faded and foggy consciousness where I whirled and danced and sang: I am your flesh and my mother's flesh and you are . . . are . . .

Eutilia stared at me. I turned away.

I danced around Eutilia's bed. I hugged the screen door, my breasts indented in the meshed wire. In the darkness Eutilia moaned, my body wet, her body dry. Steamy we were, and full of prayers. (14–15)

Rocío's matrimony provides a bodily, sexual connection with her great aunt whose death threatens her very person.

Grace. Rocío's body and her being are one with her mother's, her grandmother's, and her grandmother's sister's. She steamily dances her emerging sexuality in response to the certain danger of devastating loss. Her best resource for confronting danger is her bodily grace. Rather than using denial or retreating from death, Rocío finds her way through whirling movements and the erotic embrace that leaves its mark in the screen door.

Pedo *Power*

The remaking of manhood is thematized in Alberto Ríos's short story cycle *The Iguana Killer: Twelve Stories of the Heart* (1984). If Chávez experiments by introducing an Anglo narrator, Ríos does so in one story by making his narrator a teenage girl. Each story has a different narrator and a different cast of characters. This narrative dispersal contrasts with the "unified subject" who organizes sagas of masculine heroics. Ríos's short story cycle instead is unified, among other ways, by the classic tale of moving north from Mexico and an exploration of awakening of adolescent sexuality.

Ranging from ten to twenty pages in length, the short stories have resonance with fables whose central characters are animals. Sapito or "frog" is the first story's protagonist, and Pato or "duck" is a later story's central figure. The animal realm appears close to the surface in the initial fable set in Mexico and grows more attenuated as the cycle proceeds.

Matrimony. Not unlike Esperanza in Cisneros's story, Sapito, who lives in Tabasco, Villahermosa, traces his descent from a matriarch, his grandmother, who lives in Nogales, Arizona. His descent from the matriarch becomes ritually real through the conferral of "sacred objects," not a regal sword and shield, but a more parodic, if equally phallic pair: a baseball and a bat. The sacred objects arrive in the mail as gifts for the *Día de los Reyes Magos*, the Day of the Wise Kings:

He opened the two packages from Nogales, finding a baseball and a baseball bat. Sapito held both gifts and smiled, though he wasn't clearly sure what the things were. Sapito had not been born in nor ever visited the United States, and he had no idea of what baseball was. He was sure he recognized and admired the ball and knew what it was for. He could certainly use that. But he looked at the baseball bat and was puzzled for some seconds.

It was an iguana-killer. "*¡Mira, mamá! un palo para matar iguanas!*" It was beautiful, a dream. It was perfect. His grandmother always knew what he would like. (2)

This description mockingly alludes to more elevated ritual dreams during which people, in an atmosphere of culturally undeniable truth, receive their sacred patrimony.

Shortly after Sapito's reception of the sacred objects from the matriarch he involves himself in the mock beheading of a patriarch. Sapito and his friends find a *cahuama*, a giant sea turtle, which the narrator describes as follows: "The *cahuama* had seemed huge as the boys were pulling it, fighting so strong in the water, but it was only about three feet long when they finally took a breath and looked. Yet, they all agreed, this *cahuama* was very fat. It must have been a grandfather" (9). Shortly afterward, a man cuts off the head of the *cahuama*. So much for the patriarch.

Sexuality and danger. The story of sexual awakening ranges through adolescent possibilities. At one extreme, preadolescent boys cannot imagine having anything to do with girls. When Joey, for example, hears about intercourse, he knows it can't be true because it doesn't feel good: "It's kinda like school. Just like school" (35). In another case, Ríos experiments by making his narrator-protagonist a girl who conducts a romance with an unknown boy by receiving and sending notes attached to a cow. In this tenderly parodic pastoral, the cows smell: "Like when you smell a skunk—you certainly know you're alive" (61). For Ríos's adolescent protagonists, the dangers to their emerging sexual personas become evident more through labored acts of suppression than artful moments of explicit expression.

Potency. The potency in the protagonists' budding sexuality emerges from the body. It is "bio-power." Sapito has bulging eyes. Pato is fat and sweaty: he stinks. Tonio epitomizes these corporal potencies with his *pedos*, his farts:

It was a good lunch. It must have been, because he exploded. Loud.

"*¿Otro pedo?*" yelled his father from the living room. "At least get out of the kitchen, Tonio, *por favor!*" He was not asking nicely but it didn't matter to Tonio. Not any more, not when he finally realized. This farting was a power, "*pedo* power" his brother Jaime called it, and it was a very worthwhile thing to do. (85)

The power leaves Tonio embarrassed, but it gives him something no other kid in town has: a room of his own. It protects him from certain dangers.

Sexuality, Danger, Grace

In Sandra Cisneros's *The House on Mango Street* one finds no movement "north from Mexico," nothing like the plot line of such works as Ernesto Galarza's *Barrio Boy* (1971). Instead the protagonist remains stationary in a Chicago neighborhood which itself changes around her as she comes of age. Cisneros's short story cycle contains forty-five tales which range from one to five pages in length.

Matrimony. "My Name," the story where this essay began, told of Esperanza's reception and playful redefinition of her matrimony as a horsewoman, but not a woman looking out the window all her life. She even played on her name, its sound and meaning in English and Spanish, until she baptized herself, "Zeze the X." Esperanza made herself, through imagination and whimsy, from within a living, changing tradition.

Sexuality and danger. If Chávez wrote near dramas, the stories in *The House on Mango Street* are near poems. Their play on themes of sexuality and danger occurs within the patter of precise and "childlike" diction which often imitates nursery rhymes:

> Across the street in front of the tavern a bum man on the stoop.
> Do you like these shoes?
> Bum man says, Yes, little girl. Your little lemon shoes are so beautiful. But come closer. I can't see very well. Come closer. Please.
> You are a pretty girl, bum man continues. What's your name, pretty girl?
> And Rachel says Rachel, just like that.
> Now you know to talk to drunks is crazy and to tell them your name is worse, but who can blame her. She is young and dizzy to hear so many sweet things in one day, even if it is a bum man's whiskey words saying them.
> Rachel, you are prettier than a yellow taxi cab. You know that. (39)

The resonance with "Little Red Riding Hood" becomes evident as the bum man asks her to draw nearer, virtually saying, "The better to see you my dear." His threatening presence echoes the clichéd warning of parents to their children: "Don't take candy from strangers." Instead of candy, the bum man offers saccharine words and calls her a pretty girl with beautiful shoes. In time he offers her a dollar for a kiss.

The protagonist Esperanza tells the story of her sexual awakening, a process at once sensuous and dangerous. "Hips" thus begins: "One day you wake up and there they (your hips) are. Ready and waiting like a new Buick with the keys in the ignition. Ready to take you where?" (47). In a later story

Esperanza is bursting: "Everything is holding its breath inside me. Everything is waiting to explode like Christmas. I want to be all new and shiny. I want to sit out bad at night, a boy around my neck and the wind under my skirt" (70). In describing her coming of age Esperanza interweaves her sexuality, her rounding hips, and automobiles. Not unlike a car, she is polished and ready to go (where?). In being "bad" she moves toward the sensuous, threatening edges of the world.

In this play of desire and danger Esperanza meets dangers by gracefully moving on. If her sexuality resembles a new car, her shoes and dancing stand for her grace: "And uncle spins me and my skinny arms bend the way he taught me and my mother watches and my little cousins watch the boy who is my cousin by first communion watches and everyone says, wow, who are those two who dance like in the movies, until I forget that I am wearing only ordinary shoes, brown and white, the kind my mother buys each year for school" (46). The threats she counters with grace most often involve male violence and both literal and figurative efforts to confine and subordinate women.

Remaking Cultures of Resistance

The short story cycles of Chávez, Ríos, and Cisneros have opened fresh vistas in what Américo Paredes saw so clearly as the inextricably intertwined realms of culture and politics. What culture is losing in coherence and "*pureza*" it is gaining in range and engagement. The politics of culture found in these recent short story cycles moves toward terrain of borders, spaces that readily include African-Americans, Anglos, schools, workplaces, and heterogeneous changing neighborhoods.

The protagonists of Chávez, Ríos, and Cisneros live with grace, by their wits, through improvisation. Their worlds are fraught with unpredictability and dangers, yet their central figures have enormous capacities for responding to the unexpected. Death occasions erotic dance, a baseball bat becomes an iguana killer, and a name twists and twirls until it reaches the end of its alphabet, "Zeze the X." In time no doubt the protagonists of such tales will age and move from adolescent sexual awakenings to adult worlds with their fabric of enduring forms of intimacy, friendship, and enmity, where sexual relations are both heterosexual and homosexual.

Part III

Genre, Ideology,

and History

Héctor Calderón

The Novel and the Community of Readers: Rereading Tomás Rivera's *Y no se lo tragó la tierra*

I

Although the study of narrative structures—both oral and written, Western and non-Western—had a significant role to play within what is now termed the boom in literary theory of the seventies, within Chicano critical discourse this area, until recently, had merited little scrutiny. My "To Read Chicano Narrative: Commentary and Metacommentary" (1983) was a first attempt at working out on theoretical and performative levels the interrelationships among narrative, politics, and history, with particular attention to the ideological underpinnings of Chicano romance and satire. Although my essay drew on the cultural and genre criticism of Northrop Frye (1957, 1976) and on the role of the reader in narrative in the work of Wolfgang Iser (1974, 1978), it owed much of its overall theoretical framework to Fredric Jameson's statement that the "strategic value of generic concepts for Marxism lies in the mediatory function of the notion of a genre, which allows the coordination of immanent formal analysis of the individual text with the twin diachronic perspective of the history of forms and the evolution of social life" (1981, 105) or, in other words, that genres are useful only as they relate to the social worlds that give rise to them.

Though I was unable to clearly articulate it in that 1983 article, what troubled me about criticism on Chicano narrative was its reliance on reified notions of both genre and history. I had chosen the term "narrative" for my title to distinguish the array of storytelling models available to Chicano and

An early version of this essay was presented as "Literatura chicana como comunicación," Mesa Redonda: Problemas y Perspectivas de la Literatura Chicana, Department of Spanish and Portuguese, UCLA, November 22, 1981.

Chicana writers from the term "novel" which had become all-encompassing and normative in the Chicano critical vocabulary. This term "novel"
was used in an unhistorical way, oftentimes, showing up the prejudices of
each critic. Some early works were negatively and superficially evaluated
because they were fragmentary sketches and did not comply with the
novel's orderly development of plot and character; others, because they did
not conform to the realism of the novel, were easily classified as examples
of Latin American magical realism. This monolithic classification of the
novel, employed by almost every critic, had not only done little to advance
the study of the wide variety of Chicano narrative structures, it also had led
to serious misunderstandings and misleading classifications. And although
literary history did play an important role in now classic essays (Leal 1973,
R. Paredes 1978), it was used to legitimate an autonomous self-sufficient
Chicano tradition, an unbroken evolutionary line of Chicano narrative that
descended from sixteenth-century Spanish chronicles of the Southwest
without any serious study of the national, institutional, ideological, or
artistic affiliations of each writer. However, because of wide-ranging yet
rigorous readings of a single text, the work of Américo Paredes (1958) in the
pre-Chicano period and that of Joseph Sommers (1977) and Ramón Saldívar
(1979) after the Chicano movement stands out in sharp relief against these
studies.

These problems of mediating between genre and history have now been
superseded by scholars who have elaborated further on such different forms
as oral tales, the *corrido*, romance, satire, chronicle, sketch, biography, and
autobiography (Calderón 1985, 1986; Limón 1978, 1986a and 1986b, and his
essay in this volume; J. D. Saldívar 1985; R. Saldívar 1979, 1985, 1990;
R. Sánchez 1985a and 1985b). As for the future of this area of research, we
can anticipate a more dialectical understanding of the transformation from
the nineteenth-century Mexican and Mexican-American period to our present Chicano moment.

II

A wide cultural and critical horizon informs my view of narrative,
shaped by the affiliations with the institutions of learning in this country as
well as by my own Mexican border experience in Calexico, California. To be
sure an early interest in folklore and later my scholarly interest in Spanish-
American narrative derived from my own culture and the cultural role of
storytelling in my Mexican-*mestizo* family. I am referring to the *cuentos*,
proverbs and sayings, myths, *corridos* and songs, historical and personal
anecdotes, and religious tales used for recording and organizing knowledge

in daily activities. But that world of the late forties and fifties in which I grew up literally within view of the border is not the Chicano world of the nineties. My research on Chicano literature is now informed by recent theory, and this includes the incorporation of work by progressive critics as well as reacting to many principles of the popular but conservative brand of deconstruction and poststructuralism of the seventies and eighties. As in the critical sphere a similar situation obtains in literature, and I have been exploring this dual nature of the Chicano experience in the ideological and artistic connections between the Western tradition and Chicano literature, which is to say, the formal or technical manipulations and transformations of the dominant literary tradition that must be worked out in order to represent a specific Chicano cultural content, which until very recently was limited to a working-class, Third World type.

Thus while our literature may inform the dominant culture with an alternative view of the world filtered through myth and oral storytelling or offer an oppositional political perspective, this is done so from within educational institutions. Almost all Chicana and Chicano writers of fiction have earned advanced degrees in the United States. And when we think of contemporary Chicano print culture and list the objects of critical attention for both critics and writers, such as the strategies of the point of view, the romantic or legal identification of author with his or her own creation, the conceptual apparatus unifying thought and discourse, the question of sympathy of readers for characters, the interaction between writer and readership, then we realize how institutionally Western our literature is. Yet, we cannot deny that until very recently Chicanas and Chicanos as critics and writers were very marginal to this artistic discourse. We should then say that within the present historical conjuncture Chicano narrative is the product of recent literate elites who are reworking artistic forms to reconcile Native American, *mestizo*, Spanish, Mexican, and Chicano realities with present social contradictions. The Chicano narratives that I know, especially those written in the seventies, represent the vast transformations that "el norte de México" or the American West has undergone from Native American nomadic life, to Spanish and Mexican agricultural and ranching stages, to migrant worker culture of this century. Viewed from this dual perspective, Chicano literature is not simply a "minority" or marginal literature, it is one of the latest chapters of the Western tradition, or, perhaps, with an eye to the future of the Americas, it is indicative of new, alternative cultural traditions.

Needless to say, for me, Tomás Rivera's *"Y no se lo tragó la tierra"*/ *"And the Earth Did Not Part"* (1971), performs such a mediatory function; it was a reformulation of the Mexican-*mestizo* cultural world into the beginning of a Chicano narrative tradition. And despite recent formal experimentation by younger Chicana and Chicano writers, they have continued in the prenovelistic mode of the short story cycle or the novel-as-tales established by Rivera (see Rosaldo's essay in this volume). It had such a strong impact on me both personally and critically that reading it altered my view of the origins of the form that almost defines modern European narrative. While working on my dissertation, *Self and Language in the Novel* (Calderón 1987), Rivera's book returned me to that prenovelistic moment of the novel, before it became the bourgeois literary monument that it is today.

Instead of reading the *Quijote* on a grand scale in opposition to Greek epic à la Lukács, I looked to Cervantes's late sixteenth- and early seventeenth-century cultural context which resembled Rivera's own. Cervantes belonged to the first generation of professional writers in Spain coinciding with the flourishing of literary academies, the publication of aesthetic treatises, and the emergence of a popular readership; however, Cervantes also lived in a world that still relied largely on the oral tradition. Although *Don Quijote* appeared at the dawn of European modernity, although it incorporated the new emergent scientific discourses of psychology and linguistics, it also owed much to the didacticism of traditional storytelling of ballads, legends, popular tales, sayings, and proverbs. Almost all the central characters of Part I are storytellers, and, of course Sancho is a *campesino.* A similar case can be made for Rivera's situation and the publication of his book which appears as Chicano culture becomes an object of institutionalized knowledge. I am still amazed at the pace with which our literature evolved from the first publications of Quinto Sol with a literary history, a canon, critical principles and professional critics in place in the academy almost overnight.

Tierra and *Don Quijote* also have striking formal similarities. It will serve us well to recall that *Don Quijote* I (1605), like Rivera's book, was an experimental event with the short story form. In the first *Quijote*, Cervantes was reworking the epic (narrative) principle of maintaining the reader's interest through variety of incident without sacrificing formal unity. The first *Quijote* can be considered a string of interpolated exemplary tales unified by its fully psychologized characters. And such is the case, for its composition can be dated around the time that Cervantes hit upon psychological realism with his first exemplary tales, such as "El Licenciado Vidriera" ("The Glass Licentiate") (see El Saffar 1974, 13–19). Rivera's parting reference to orality, writing, and print culture in his last interpolated vignette concerning Bartolo, the "poeta del pueblo," refocused my attention to the worldly site of Cervantes's formal experimentation with the shorter tales in *Quijote* I, leading me from Quijote's private library to Palomeque's inn where illiterate farm workers would gather at harvest time to listen to literature. At this narrative crossroads a Spanish community in miniature, a group that includes an illiterate audience as well as educated readers, will enjoy and profit from Cervantes's handwritten copy of "Novela del curioso impertinente" ("The Meddlesome Curiosity"), which the absent writer has left in a bag at the inn. The bag, the writer's private literary laboratory, also contains "Novela de Rinconete y Cortadillo," two romances, and biographies of two historical figures.

This realistic form, as yet unnamed, therefore, also developed out of the shorter *novela* combining the contrary impulses of empirical and imaginative writing and structured as a series of interpolated tales designed to allow audience and readers profit and pleasure during times of leisure. These public situational elements of the novel invoked by Cervantes in the Prologue to his *Novelas ejemplares* (1613) and by Rivera within his own text are in line with the communal and social function of oral storytelling. Yet Cervantes was fully aware that in his *república* reading was fast becoming a critical activity designed for isolated individuals. When in the words of the Canon of Toledo, Cervantes states that the reader's understanding should be wed to plot, he is saying, among other things, that formal unity is also the critical reader's duty. To be sure, in Cervantes's novel the ideology of the individual rational subject as the locus of signification will unite the different tales, determine characterization and structure the participatory role of the reader. Given these similar revolutionary cultural contexts and the need to address emergent readerships, Rivera's exemplary novel-as-tales, as I will demonstrate below, should be read as a reinvention of the formal and ideological possibilities of the novel to represent a Third World Chicano culture.

III

Since its invention in Europe in the seventeenth and eighteenth centuries, the modern realistic novel has been in the hands of writers a means of self-expression, and the genre's fluid narrative structure and psychological characterization have served novelists to dramatize the search for personal identity. With its emphasis on the individual self, its secularization of human experience, its critical rendering of popular beliefs, Rivera's *Tierra* is no exception to the conceptual framework of the novel. Like Cervantes's *Don Quijote*, Rivera's book begins with a scene of nomination: from an unknown source the young protagonist is trying to answer to his name. This division in the character between self and other could lead through traditional transformations in the plot to the affirmation of individual identity. However, in a departure from the standard characterizations of this genre, the protagonist's desire for completeness is artistically solved through a nonindividualistic form of narration which culminates with the recognition of both personal and collective identity. In the final frame section of the novel, third-person omniscient and first-person, eyewitness narrators unite with the voices of many other characters through an impersonal, stream-of-consciousness technique that recalls the relationship of oral storytellers to their audience.

Despite the presentation of Chicano cultural norms held up for scrutiny and negation, the nameless protagonist finds his group identity through the memory of the people that have made his story. This solution is all the more ideologically and rhetorically effective when we consider that readers must assist in reconstructing two frame pieces, twelve brief tales, and thirteen interpolated fragments into a unified plot.

A decade after the publication of *Tierra*, Rivera writes: "Perhaps the most important element of Chicano literature is that it was able to capture from the beginning of the decade this very wisdom of a very disparate and amorphous nation or kindred group. It was able to do that because there was a hunger not only in the community but in the Chicano writer to create a community. Up to the present time, one of the most positive things that the Chicano writer and Chicano literature have conveyed to our people is the development of such a community" (1982, 17). *Tierra* should hold special significance not just because in 1971 it was the first novel published by Quinto Sol Publications; more importantly, the book parallels the Chicano movement of the late sixties and early seventies through its reassessment of traditional culture, its historical self-consciousness, and, specially, through its developing sense of group solidarity.

From hindsight, contemporary readers may be deceived by the apparent transparency of Rivera's novel. We should realize that being in the vanguard of contemporary Chicano fiction, Rivera and the Quinto Sol editors were working under new artistic and political assumptions. Because of the exigencies of the moment, the need to maintain cultural autonomy, Chicano literature was marked by a strong didactic and reformist character (see Ybarra-Frausto 1978). This social function of art was an important consideration as was the representation of Chicano subjects as literary characters acceptable to his readership. Much of the artistic success of *Tierra*, therefore, depended upon how well Rivera imagined his future Chicano audience, on his ability to judge what kind of rhetorical strategies were readers able to accept. To his credit (and with the aid of Quinto Sol) Rivera was able to modify the literary strategies of individualistic narrative to meet the needs of his community.

I do not want to dismiss writers previous to the tradition established by Quinto Sol. That Spanish and Mexican literary traditions existed in Spanish language journals and newspapers of the West and Southwest is a historical fact that has been documented by Luis Leal (1973, 1980, 1982), Francisco Lomelí (1980), Doris Meyer (1978), and Juan Rodríguez (1982), among others. Equally important is the English language tradition described by Raymund Paredes (1978, 1982) and Genaro Padilla (1984), the one which, it seems to me, culminates with José Antonio Villarreal's *Pocho* (1959). My argument is simply that these writers did not have at their disposal the potential popular and academic readers that the movements of the sixties and the institutionalization of the Chicano experience had made available for Rivera and those who were to follow after him. Ramón Saldívar (1979) is correct in pointing out the interesting relationship between *Pocho* and *Tierra;* there are some striking conceptual similarities which Saldívar describes. In terms of the Chicano literary tradition Rivera's work can be read as an intertextual response to the negative attitudes toward public involvement of the omniscient narrator, Villarreal, and character, Richard Rubio, in *Pocho.* To be sure the cultural ambiguities of not being an authentic Mexican or "American" that lead to the sudden Joycean ending of Villarreal's novel (recalling Stephen's escape in *A Portrait of the Artist*) are solved by Rivera at the end of the sixties precisely because of the ideology of the Chicano movement.

Here, I am arguing against the view of Chicano narrative as a ready-made object to be defined, studied, and historicized in evolutionary terms as was the case with the first writings about this literature. Are the chronicles of the Southwest written by Spaniards of the sixteenth and seventeenth centuries part of Chicano literature? Are Mexican writers and expatriates traveling through or living in Texas and California to be included among Chicano writers? These questions are not easy to answer. My solution is to pose them in another form. If we are to radically historicize Chicano literature, shouldn't we study, instead, how the forces of change have formed Chicanos and their literature in the twentieth century? *Tierra's* narrative structure, it seems to me, allows us to see these historical transformations and the emergence of a new group identity.

Since it is my contention that *Tierra* is directed toward a particular group of readers that will actively participate in the development of the plot, it will serve us well to interpret this novel stressing its dual dimensions. It is a structure of signs informed by ideological and historical contexts. As is well known, Rivera, who was born in Crystal City, Texas, in 1935, wanted to capture through their own Spanish voices the experiences of Texas farm workers in the forties and fifties in their travels throughout the Southwest and Midwest (the migrant worker population of Crystal City is the object of study in Menefee [1941] 1974). But as I will emphasize, the novel is more than a denotative or literal representation of a period, for through the fragmentary plot readers are forced into reconstructing an historical logic and producing for themselves situations in which choices and judgments have to be made about traditional Chicano culture. The performative working out of possibilities and alternatives make this novel both exemplary with reference to the individual reader and utopian in relation to the historical moment.

Although the many plots of the book are proffered by a combination of third-person and first-person narrators in fragmentary installments with each section complete in itself, the book has a clear formal design. Two pieces dealing with the young male protagonist, "El año perdido" ("The Lost Year") and "Debajo de la casa" ("Under the House"), frame the twelve tales and thirteen untitled interpolated fragments. The tales concerning the many anonymous characters have an impression of formal unity and de-velopment among them emphasized by the first story, "Los niños no se aguantaron" ("The Children Were Victims"), followed by the central story, literally and figuratively, "Y no se lo tragó la tierra" ("And the Earth Did Not Part"), and concluding with "Cuando lleguemos" ("When We Arrive"). All three focus specifically on the plight of farm workers in their work associ-ated settings. The opening death in the fields of the farm worker child must be read against the awakening consciousness of the adolescent farm worker in the central piece. In turn, this individual act of rebellion should be interpreted in relation to the unspoken expression of hope by a truckload of farm workers in the concluding tale.

In addition, the inner core of the plot, the three tales, "La noche estaba plateada" ("It Was a Silvery Night"), "Y no se lo tragó la tierra," and "Pri-mera comunión" ("First Communion"), recount crucial moments of private rebellion and cultural transgression in the life of a young boy of varying ages. With their theme of personal identity these radiate back to the initial frame tale and forward to the concluding section of the novel when all characters, tales, and fragments are united in a vast narrative moment. Moreover, as if to circumscribe the novel, the beginning and ending frame pieces can be read as a complete ironic statement, "El año perdido debajo de la casa," which is the case because the young protagonist had been recalling the incidents within the cycle of a year which he thought had been lost to him; from hindsight, however, he discovers that he had gained the experi-ence of one year.

In sum, this novel-in-pieces encourages the reader to conceive of it as a legible whole through an intertwined plot that is both linear and circular, static yet changing. And just as the concept of the frame in communication theory gives instructions or aids in understanding the message within the frame (see Bateson 1972, 188), the readers of *Tierra* can discern the overall frame of reference, which is to say, the concern for individual identity within group collectivity that structures the beginning and ending pieces as well as the reader's participation. And because all twelve tales are framed for analysis by a pair of interpolated fragments, the role of the reader emerges from the gaps that must be filled in order to insure structural and thematic continuity. Thus the developing plot is explicitly based on a series of changing relationships. That the narrative supplies instructions for this process of understanding can be grasped from the last interpolated fragment and the final collective moment in which Rivera delivers his views on the social function of art as these inform the act of reading.

In the last interpolated fragment Rivera describes the artist's responsibility toward his public as one of binding together. Every year the itinerant folk-poet Bartolo would come around the last month of the year when the farm workers had returned from northern states. His poems would sell quickly because they contained the townspeople and affected the audience in a way that was both emotional and serious, "emocionante y serio." Moreover, Bartolo tells his audience to read his poems aloud because the voice was the seed of love in the dark. Rivera's portrait of the artist contains the social function of storytelling which is to bind the culture together by representing human experience and providing both pleasure and instruction during times of leisure. And the suggestion to read aloud is Rivera's reference to an oral-aural context in which the human voice memorializes the culture. There are interesting points of coincidence between Chicano culture and sixteenth- and seventeenth-century Spain in which the emergence of writing and print media existed within a culture that was largely oral. Renaissance chapbooks, the *pliegos sueltos*, the *romancero*, even the "reading performances" of the chivalric romances (recalling the illiterate audience at Palomeque's inn in *Don Quijote* I), like Bartolo's poems and Rivera's text combine both traditions. Rivera was a writer who lived in a world of specialization: he had academic and institutional affiliations. Yet he also participated in a culture that was only partially literate and a strong storytelling tradition from his youth was crucial for the composition of his book (Rivera 1975). Rivera's Spanish vernacular patterns (what the unnamed narrator of the beginning and ending frames remembers seeing and hearing) which imitate the simple and direct, face-to-face style of the Mexican-*mestizo* speech community are, therefore, a means of working out of individualistic writing toward an imagined social whole or group in which a high degree of literacy is not crucial for communicating. This ending fragment in the novel is a strong self-referential moment through which the individual Chicano reader can be made aware of his or her own cultural experience represented through the voices of the many nameless characters. That this artistic and social context should also provide instructions for the interaction between text and reader is clearly evident from the concluding narrative of the many voices delivered by the young protagonist from beneath the house. And as the boy emerges from the darkness to the clarity of thought, he discovers that the solution to the problem of identity is one of understanding his changing relationship to his people:

> Se fue sonriente por la calle llena de pozos que conducía a su casa. Se sintió contento de pronto porque al pensar sobre lo que había dicho la señora se dio cuenta de que en realidad no había perdido nada. Había encontrado. Encontrar y reencontrar y juntar. Relacionar esto con esto, eso con aquello, todo con todo. Eso era. Eso era todo. Y le dio más gusto.

> He went smiling through the street full of mud holes that led to his house. Suddenly he felt happy because, when he thought about what the lady had said, he realized that he hadn't lost anything. He had found. To find and find again and join. To relate this to this, that to that, all to all. That was it. That was all he had to do. And he became even happier. (169, my translation)

While most critics have correctly interpreted this conclusion as part of the process of maturation of the central character, this ending frame in which the voices of the characters reappear through the consciousness of the narrator also offers explicit instructions to readers to mirror the character's sense of memory and discernment by relating the twelve tales and thirteen fragments one to another and bind together the many plots into a meaningful whole, "un todo." Through its structure and with the assistance of the reader, Rivera's novel reinforces the thematic constant of the individual's relationship to her or his community.

Given Rivera's performative strategies, given that crucial tales repeat the overall plot of discovery and understanding, *Tierra* should be placed within the tradition of realist exemplary fiction established by Cervantes with *Don Quijote* and the *Novelas ejemplares*, a tradition which was bequeathed to eighteenth-century European novelists. Even though literature in the sixteenth and early seventeenth centuries reflected public moral and didactic concerns, the act of reading was fast developing within a situational context which reflected the unique talents of the writer and the individuality of the reader. Cervantes's personal concern for prose fiction allowed him to transform into an ideological precondition for the novel, in its first historical phase, the aesthetic norm which dictated that serious poetry should be both pleasing and instructional. Cervantes steered a middle course between these Horatian precepts allowing readers to receive pleasure and profit from their own rational souls, from their own capacity to make judgments. His characters display a sense of discernment which is also indicative of the reader's own transformation which he or she undergoes during the reading process. By exemplary literature, therefore, I mean writing whose aims are epistemological rather than openly didactic because readers are encouraged by literary strategies to make their own judgments which then stimulate a process of learning (Iser 1974, 34–35). And while both Cervantes and Rivera write in Spanish and, in a sense, invent or imagine a "nation" of readers, Rivera reminds the reader that she or he is part of a larger social whole.

In Rivera's transactive approach to reading, anonymous characterization, widely acknowledged folk and religious beliefs, typical cultural situations serve as mirrors for Chicano readers. In addition the transformation of the unnamed central protagonist through the two frame pieces and the three central tales should be reflective of the reader's capacity for making judgments about his or her own Chicano experience. This participatory phenomenon is all the more evident in the design of the book. Although it is fragmentary, it is not, as I argue, a pastiche nor chaotic or self-destructive as are other Western modernist and postmodernist texts. On the contrary, care is taken to involve readers in an orderly plot and encourage construction of meaning through interpolations. Cervantes used a somewhat similar technique with his interpolated tales which transform the main plot into its very opposite in order to give the reader a clear view of what she or he is supposed to understand (Iser 1974, 50). However, in the absence of an omniscient narrator aiding in the necessary connections, the reader of *Tierra* is called upon to take a more active role, to retrace the mapped-out strategies.

In general, the discerning reader of *Tierra* is challenged by Rivera's oppositional strategies to project alternative social possibilities. The reader is forced to evoke traditional norms and examine them critically. These strategies are also ideological in the sense that Chicano readers are made aware of the structural and conceptual limits of their own class and cultural situation. Through the first half the novel's changing structure calls into question commonly held beliefs. And the direction of the plot is toward a rationalization of the landscape and a more worldly interpretation of the Chicano experience. This movement in the plot is well within the novel's secularization of thought, which is to say, the conception of a psychological subject no longer totally immersed in a natural world of spiritual forces or ruled over by myth, religion, and abstract notions of fortune. From the initial fragment readers should distinguish a series of contrasts between, on one hand, ignorance, superstitions, and religious beliefs and, on the other, the oppressive material conditions experienced by farm workers. The interrelation between these two poles is that these beliefs blind Chicanos to the real causes and conditions of their existence. For example, the young boy of the first interpolated fragment who drinks the glass of water that his mother placed underneath the bed for the spirits establishes an opposition between metaphysical agency versus human action. The negation of this residual popular belief from the Mexican Southwest should be compared and read against the (1) repressive conditions and the natural elements of sun and heat that weigh heavily upon the thirsty children of "Los niños no se aguantaron," (2) the exploitative and falsely reassuring spiritualist of the second fragment who communicates with the missing soldier, (3) and the mother of "Un rezo" ("A Prayer") who relies on the will of God to return her son from Korea. Through the first fragments and tales the novel is punctuated with examples of racism, exploitation, and fatalism whose causes are not supernatural but social and historical.

Mexican or *mestizo* is the name for the world of these farm workers who live in poverty and ignorance and whose conduct is almost totally controlled by the institution of the Church. One cannot deny that the historical forces that gave rise to this social group were set in motion with the colonization of the New World. Although these people live in the twentieth century, from the thirties through the fifties, their group consciousness has its origins in the feudal-like organization of life in which Native Americans, blacks, *mestizos,* and mulattos formed the bottom tier of a peonage and caste system. Rivera, who had been a farm worker and became a professor of Spanish, was not ignorant of the colonized mind, and he spoke to this fact in an essay on Richard Rodriguez's subaltern relationship to the dominant culture (Rivera 1984). And to Juan Bruce-Novoa's question on the distinctive perspective on life that Chicano literature offered, Rivera responded: "But I don't think Chicano literature necessarily has a different perspective. If it does, it's in the area of looking at the world through the eyes of the oppressed, something like a Third World type. That would be an element of distinctiveness" (Bruce-Novoa 1980, 156).

Rivera's oral style has often been compared to Juan Rulfo's (Sommers 1977). This is a valid comparison. Although there is no hint of Rulfo's magical realism in *Tierra,* Rivera learned much from Rulfo, especially from his *El llano en llamas* (1953). But we should also understand that both were acutely aware of the forces of colonial feudalism and gave voice in their writings to a group—peasants, *peones* and *campesinos*—whose discourse has always been marginal to power. Rulfo knew rural Mexico well and worked for the Instituto Indigenista. He also commented that his tales of rural Jalisco owed much to a ruthless patriarchal structure established by the *encomenderos, caciques,* and the Church (see Harss and Dohmann 1967, 265–67, and Roffé 1973, 64–66). Despite the changes brought about by the Mexican Revolution, Rulfo's literary characters, like Rivera's, live in a "timeless" world beset by sin and an unyielding fatalism. Within Chicano historical scholarship, on the question of colonization, Tomás Almaguer (1974) among others has adequately shown that migrant farm workers as a seasonal labor force within the capitalist economy of the United States have their origins in another mode of production, the *repartimientos, enco-* ———, and *cuadrillas* of the Spanish colonial empire. And we should add that those structures of religious thought that Rivera foregrounds originated with the evangelizing zeal of the Church. Given this context, Rivera is formulating a version of the Chicano subject as socially situational and historical in opposition to subjectivity based on the religious soul.

This opposition is crucial to the understanding of the three central tales in which a younger generation's questioning of religious orthodoxy points toward a major turning point in the world of farm workers. In these tales Rivera is repeating an important moment which Spanish Americans had experienced in the nineteenth century when governments stripped, with a vengeance, all secular power from the Church. This seems to be the first major political move in postcolonial societies ruled almost totally by the Church. This a juncture in the plot of *Tierra* to which Chicanos, especially young ones, cannot remain indifferent. In these tales Rivera foregrounds the importance of traditional Catholic values for an older generation. Yet, what gives hope and consolation to farm worker parents against the insecurities of existence becomes conservative, static, and unyielding for the young protagonist. This is a significant historical moment of change precisely because traditional values are emptied of their pragmatic content and, instead of confirming reality, express the limits of a repressive hegemony (Williams 1977, 110). The tensions between metaphysical agency and the oppressive conditions of existence—the elements of sun, heat, and thirst of the first fragment and tale—finally come to a climax in the central tale, "Y no se lo tragó la tierra," when the young protagonist violates his parents' ultimate cultural taboo and blasphemes against divine will. With this act of rebellion against fatalism, the central character simultaneously acknowledges the materiality of space (the earth does not part) and affirms his own reason and freedom. As an individual subject, he feels capable of doing whatever he desires:

Tenía una paz que nunca había tenido antes. Le parecía que se había separado de todo. Ya no le preocupaba ni su papá ni su hermanito. Todo lo que esperaba era el nuevo día, la frescura de la mañana. . . .
Salió para el trabajo y se encontró con la mañana bien fresca. Había

nubes y por primera vez se sentía capaz de hacer y deshacer cualquier cosa que él quisiera.

He experienced a peace that he had never felt before. He felt that he had separated himself from everything. He was no longer worried about his father nor his younger brother. All that he looked forward to was the new day, the coolness of the morning. . . .

He left for work and he encountered a very cool morning. There were clouds and for the first time he felt capable of doing and undoing whatever he desired. (70, my translation)

The emotional state of the character foreshadows the comic ending of the final frame. And the thematic direction of the plot toward personal responsibility and self-determination is previewed in various ways by the preceding fragment in which a group of farm workers is left without hope of breaking its ties to the soil. Nothing was realized by the well-intentioned motives of the Protestant minister who wanted to teach them carpentry. For the reader, however, the adolescent farm worker's cool detachment from everything, including his family, that results from his successful private act of rebellion must be weighed against the concern for the group.

This central tale is flanked by two other interlocking ones that examine from a secular perspective abstract or religious notions of good and evil; the first is derived from the folk tradition concerning the appearance of the devil, the other from a Catholic rite of passage. The inquisitive boy of "La noche estaba plateada," who after calling forth the devil by his name comes to the awareness that all remained the same, all was peaceful: "Todo estaba igual. Todo estaba en paz." (56). Although evil is personified by the figure of the devil in a *pastorela* (religious drama), it does not exist as a spiritual entity directly affecting human lives as Catholic doctrine teaches. On the contrary, evil can be all too human and social, as the boy, the victim of racism, in the preceding fragment understands completely well after he is refused a haircut: "Entonces comprendió todo" (Then he understood everything.) (53). The last story in the central triad, "La primera comunión," injects humor into these otherwise serious narratives. Rivera pokes fun at the institution of catechism which forces children into manufacturing sins of the flesh although they haven't committed such wrongdoing and don't fully understand the concept of the body as the temple of evil. On the way to confession the young character witnesses a couple copulating, what he imagines in his own way to be a sin of the flesh. Like the other rebellious characters, he refuses to admit to his sin during confession and imagines the pleasure one gains from such sins of the flesh to be like the good feeling one receives from God's grace. In fact, he concludes by stating that he desired to know more about everything: "Tenía ganas de saber más de todo"

(85). That humankind has an important physical nature that can be pleasurable is implied by the grandfather of the preceding fragment who is paralyzed from the neck down. He realizes the foolishness of his grandson who wants to dismiss his youthful years and rush in an instant of time to his thirtieth birthday.

Taking into account the development of the plot through the reinterpretation of these notions of good and evil, readers can detect an important historical conjuncture, a break with the past in the sense that an alternative mode of consciousness, inconceivable to an older generation, is emerging from the "medievalism" of traditional Chicano culture. The secretive acts of rebellion—the characters do not reveal their thoughts and actions to others—overturn deeply ingrained beliefs that date back to the early Church fathers. While at the same time collapsing stages in the development of Western thought, Rivera leads the reader away from traditional Mexican culture; the overarching theological/mythological narrative that should never be questioned is transformed into secular literature wherein the human understanding is the locus of signification. Thus through its developing plot the narrative demonstrates that individuals have a role to play as producers of meaning and in determining their own actions.

Rivera is not unlike other Christian, and especially Catholic writers, in his urgent need for the negation of what he portrays as repressive ideologies. However, Rivera will turn in the second half of his novel from these isolated rebellious individuals to the more important affirmation of the whole. And as if to stand the religious opposition of spirit and matter on its head, Rivera effects a relocation of the spirit toward a communal cohesiveness, a desire for change arising out of the material conditions of existence.

Rivera's depiction of changes in Chicano farm worker culture of the fifties is not an idealistic one. Although the seeds of change are apparent in both men and women, young and old, some will not escape their historical circumstances. A case in point is the representation of male-female relationships in "La noche que se apagaron las luces" ("The Night of the Blackout") and "La nochebuena" ("Christmas Eve"). These tales that deal with two generations of women are placed side by side to be compared by the reader. For doña María of "La nochebuena," who aspires to change by liberating herself from her confinement to the home, her moment of courage will end in failure. However, the young Juanita of the companion tale will stand up against the foolish phallocentric attitudes of her boyfriend, Ramón. Juanita's future will, perhaps, be different from doña María's. We should recall that Juanita's family wants her to finish her education before she marries.

Other examples of change include the fragment (No. 11) in which a whole community of parishioners rise up against the priest who had exploited farm workers by charging them for his blessings. With the money saved the priest had visited his native Spain and returned with picture postcards to encourage more financial support for his church. This priest could not understand why his new pews and postcards were disfigured by his angry parishioners. The tale that follows, "El retrato" ("The Portrait"), concerns a father who does not accept exploitation and eventually, after searching in San Antonio, finds the wrongdoer.

These exemplary tales that readers have been reconstructing into a legible whole reach a utopian conclusion in the final tale, "Cuando lleguemos," in which different voices echo the desire to break out of the cycle of migrant work and in which the narrator, in the ending frame, completes his search for identity through the characters of his tales. The locus of hope for the older generation, the celestial paradise, is displaced by a desire for a yet unrealized transformation of the present (see also Jameson 1981, 281–99, and J. D. Saldívar 1985, 100–114). This concluding utopian vision of the future is due as much to the expression of collective hope as to the decentering of individualism. Admittedly, Rivera's literary context is the individualistic one of print capital; he writes for the individual reader. And certainly the triumphant moment of struggle that gives the title to his narrative is a private one which leads the protagonist to feel happy and detached from everything, from "todo." This thematization of individualism, however, is structurally counterbalanced by the tales and fragments with their many nameless characters and the ending frame.

Rivera's novel, therefore, offers Chicano readers an empowering collective vision in which the narrator (ultimately the writer) tries to harmonize individualistic tendencies with society as a whole. Rivera's desire for community is all the more evident when we read him against other early Chicano narratives in which the male subject is represented or characterized through generational conflicts or sexual rivalries. The absence of a proper name, a patronymic, for the central narrator and protagonist indicates Rivera's perspective on egocentrism, Chicano machismo, and the Hispanic version of the Oedipal triangle of father, mother, and son. Rivera does not dwell on these elements of individualistic writings as do other writers like Villarreal in *Pocho*, Oscar Zeta Acosta in *Autobiography of a Brown Buffalo* (1972), and Rudolfo A. Anaya in *Bless Me, Ultima* (1972). And while Rivera's protagonist is an exemplary figure guiding the reader through a process of learning or maturation, he is not a preordained hero in any romantic way as are Antonio Márez y Luna of *Bless Me, Ultima* or Don Fausto Tejada of *The Road to Tamazunchale* (1975), nor must he prove himself as a Don Juan as must the central characters of Villarreal's and Acosta's narratives. The kind of unity between the narrator-character as singular subject and his community that Rivera was striving for is realized by the impersonal epic moment of the ending frame when the novel form yields up its individualistic conceptualization. The narrator momentarily disappears, not to withdraw from his culture, but to take a stance like the prenovelistic oral poet; he surrenders his consciousness and allows the collective voices of his people to speak through him. This last frame, therefore, is emblematic of the entire plot.

IV

Given the historical and social conditioning of Chicano culture, the possibility of a Chicano readership in the late sixties and early seventies was itself a revolutionary idea. Early Chicano writers were thus able to seize upon utopian currents already present in the Chicano movement and give expression to them. And while Chicano readers will be able to identify with the world depicted in *Tierra*, many other readers may find Rivera's world remote and alien. This is so because Rivera is mediating between a First World aesthetic and what should be judged a Third World experience. In this sense, unlike José Antonio Villarreal's *Pocho*, Rivera's novel-as-tales shares much with other emerging national literatures of the sixties. In these litcratures of emancipation native writers were able to combine an older literary realism and modernist strategies with traditional storytelling or oral consciousness to address problems of a peasant, rural, or agricultural world as it was being transformed by new economic and superstructural realities. Thus Rivera looks back to his childhood and adolescence, from the thirties through the fifties, in south Texas when this region was being transformed into the Winter Garden Area as earlier Mexicano ranching communities were being replaced first by cotton farming and then by large-scale citrus orchards (Menefee [1941] 1974, A. Paredes 1958, 106). A similar phenomenon occurred in the San Joaquin and Imperial valleys of California where the increasing population of Mexican migrant families supplied the seasonal labor force. From the point of view of the nineties this reinvention of a prior historical moment and the consequent emergence from a colonial mentality can now be reconceived as a Chicano version of a Third World postmodernism evident, for example, in Latin American and African literature. I am constructing this master narrative for Chicano literature because one is already implicit in the work of Rivera and because this a necessary task to understand the emergence of a Chicano consciousness from economic and ideological structures that were set in place with the conquest and colonization of the Americas. And the salient features of this new consciousncss were the rejection of the metaphysical and the acceptance of the social, the decentering of the autonomous subject and the reconciliation of individual desire with a wider social movement.

Rosaura Sánchez

Ideological Discourses in Arturo Islas's
The Rain God

Literature is a cultural and semiotic practice. As such it provides through signifying practices an ideological representation of culture, what, to rephrase Lotman and Uspenskii (1985, 30), we could call an ideological system of "collective memory and collective consciousness." If, as Lotman and Uspenskii allege, culture evidences "clear-cut divisions into stages that replace one another dynamically" (31), each period making a decisive break with what preceded it, even while repeating or regenerating certain aspects of the culture of the past, then an analysis of the discursive practices in Chicano literature should disclose not only the group's ideological memory but its "lived" experiences of the continuities and discontinuities in its history as well.

The literature of the population of Mexican origin in the United States since 1848 is increasingly being brought to light through continued research into newspapers, journals, and unpublished documents. These new findings enable us to retrace and formulate ideological models textualized in the narratives of two centuries of discourse. With these earlier texts as benchmarks, we will increasingly be able to note not only the ruptures in the discourse but also the links and differences between what was produced in the late nineteenth century and what has been produced in the twentieth century. In the most recent stage of literary production, which is the one most studied and best known, several novels have appeared dealing with experiences of occupational and geographical mobility and changing power relations within the family as experienced by a child growing into adulthood. These issues are also central to feminist literature, in particular the works of Chicano female poets, texts which offer additional examples of ideological transformations which are taking place alongside shifts in power relations arising from the questioning of male-dominant cultural practices. But there are other examples of shifts in the collective memory to be explored as yet. A study of both earlier and recent narratives will allow us to track down evolving ideological discourse and cultural practices within the multifaceted Chicano community.

These cultural breaks are a result of internal and external contradictions. Externally the contradictions are multiple and varied. Internally, cultures, as Lenin pointed out, are characterized by both progressive and reactionary elements (1968, 80); these ideological contradictions invariably give rise to conflicts, struggles, and shifts, especially when cultural practices are perceived to be forms of exploitation and domination or when they are no longer deemed to be viable given the presence of alternative practices. Such is the case in *Pocho* (Villarreal 1959); here the main character, Richard Rubio, rejects his family's patriarchal prescriptions for male sons and joins the navy, not for any patriotic reason, but simply to get away from his family, to escape and thus avoid a restrictive situation that suffocates him with expectations of domestic and filial obligations and forces his transformation into what to him is a nonentity, that is, into a steel mill worker, a family man. Much like his father, who in his youth had set his political and personal allegiance to Pancho Villa above the needs of the family to the point of neglect, the protagonist Richard too felt that his personal goals should take priority. Trapped and confined by those collective bonds which kept him from developing his individuality and from attending the university in order to become a writer, he embraced the anonymity of a military order which, though confining, would free him of family obligations and, if he wasn't killed, allow him to work toward his goals. Obviously these middle-class aspirations, while unheard of in his lower-income community, fitted in perfectly well with a growing capitalist economy.

Thus Richard does not indict society for his predicament but rather accedes to the dominant ideologies and accepts their definitions of reality. In consenting to his own subordination and making sense of his options, the protagonist attempts to mask and displace what is at odds with the dominant ideologies, but even his passing acknowledgment of social subordination and blatant discrimination against Mexicanos reveals the contradictions and problematic areas. In accepting the myth of individualism, the Chicano of the early forties in effect accepted the ideological representations, discourse, and power configurations of entrepreneurial capitalism. Later stages of multinational capitalism with its corporate structure and centralization of capital in core firms would emerge as the dominant form of big business in the United States with World War I (Edwards 1979, 69) and become fully consolidated after the twenties as the economy expanded then and again after 1940 (Edwards 1979, 81). With this shift of control in the firm would come an undermining of previously necessary myths, among them notions of the individualist subject. The novel *Pocho* appears then at the end of an era, while the novel *The Rain God: A Desert Tale* by Arturo Islas, published in 1984, begins in a sense where *Pocho* leaves off, that is, in the decade of the forties. It moves, however, not so much within a historical time-space as within a subjective timeless frame in which historical references are blurred and earlier social practices are recalled and mapped out in order to be finally expunged from the character's memory, as we shall see.

I read Islas's novel as a literary text made up of a multiplicity of discourses which dialogue with past and present signifying practices in society while at the same time providing a textualization of extradiscursive cultural and social practices. Within this discursive approach all discourse will be viewed as ideological and experience will be seen to be the product of these ideological practices. The novel—and like it all texts—is not analyzable in terms of the author's intentions, but as a product of those social and cultural practices and ideological discourses which interact to determine the experiences of the individual who actually writes the work. This network of interacting practices and discourses constitutes the signifying practices which make up the text.

In this analysis, then, ideological practices are said to be discursive and representative of "lived experience," what Althusser calls "the 'representation' of the imaginary relationship of individuals to their real conditions of existence" (1971, 162). Here Althusser retains the notion of ideology as illusion, as false consciousness and distortion, not of men's real conditions of existence, but of their relations to those conditions. This imaginary relation of individuals to the real relations in which they live is necessarily complex since an individual is involved in a plurality of relations, assumes a number of positions in society, and interacts with numerous practices of various social institutions, such as family, schools, government, the legal system, media, etc. In fact it is ideology, or more specifically, bourgeois ideology, that, like language, is said to constitute or interpellate concrete individuals as subjects (Althusser 1971, 171). The entire notion of the individual subject, as noted earlier, once generally accepted as a given, is today questioned and viewed as a myth, as an imaginary representation, which in fact never really existed but was created by bourgeois ideologies (Jameson 1983, 115). Current trends assume a decentered subject, a multiple subject, notions which alongside those of the individual autonomous subject are evident in Islas's novel, albeit in a rather fragmented fashion.

It is the Althusserian analysis of ideology as imaginary or unconscious which led to Jameson's notion of the "political unconscious" (1981). Unfortunately this notion of the unconscious gives the analysis of ideology a definitely Lacanian bent which is misleading. Today we can no longer accept idealist notions of deep structures distinct from surface structures, nor can we posit ideology at some hidden or repressed underlying level, for it is manifest at a conscious surface level. Marx's example of the fetishism of commodities (Marx 1967, 71) best clarifies the problem arising with hermeneutic notions of levels. The labor time congealed in a commodity may be ignored or negated to the point that value is attributed to the commodity itself as if it were inherently present, but the value determined by the labor is never absent or hidden at some deeper structural level. The value added by labor (Marx 1973, 354) is present at the surface level, in the very production of the artifact, waiting only to be deconstructed. In a similar manner ideology is present in the very discourse, in the very signs used for communication (Vološinov 1973, 22), and even in the textual surface gaps, lapses, silences, and absences (Althusser 1977). Ideology, moreover, cannot be reduced to a functionalist practice which merely ensures the maintenance of the mode of production which gives rise to it, for it is always contradictory and it always harbors countertendencies. For this reason theorists like Callinicos (1985) and Hall (1977), citing Gramsci, prefer to speak of "ideologies" or a "field of ideology" which bears " 'traces' of previous ideological systems and sedimentations." Disjuncture thus may arise within ideological hegemony, made up of an alliance of dominant class fractions, to produce counter practices. The mode of operation of these dominant groups is a complex matter, for, as explained by Hall: "they not only possess the power to coerce but actively organize so as to command and win the consent of the subordinated classes to their continuing sway" (1977, 332). Subordinate classes in effect accede to representing their experiences in terms of discursive frameworks set up by the dominant classes; if on the other hand, they refuse to identify with the established definitions of reality and produce counterdiscourses, they face numerous strategies of co-optation, as discussed by Hebdige (1979) in his work on subcultural styles. As a result, the discourse of opposition can be easily appropriated and incorporated into dominant ideological practices through their reduction to a commodity-form or through a redefinition which trivializes, naturalizes, or domesticates what originally may have seemed subversive (Hebdige 1979, 94–97).

This essay then will focus on the representation in *The Rain God* of the social practices of three generations of the Angel family as well as on the ideological discourses used by the characters to represent, interpret, and make sense of their experiences. The older generations will be seen to conform to dominant ideological practices and identify with them while the younger generations counter specific but limited aspects of parental practices; their counterdiscourses, however, will be seen to be tied to the same formulations and power systems, so that the rejected practice is either simply reversed or replaced by different but analogous power relations. But that is the nature of counterdiscourse; it does not formulate a distinctive alternative but merely opposes what it, ironically, affirms.

The novel addresses three important social practices: the patriarchy and all it connotes in terms of family practices and gender roles; ethnic and class prejudices; and, to a lesser extent, religious beliefs. Countering these practices are strategies which contain or restrict problematic events and relations within a limiting framework (Hall 1977, 341) wherein individual differences are opposed to family norms and traditions. Among the principal "strategies of containment," to use Jameson's phrase (1981), are resentment, which in time turns into disdain, and deviance or departures from accepted norms, as evidenced in suicide, drug addiction, and homosexuality. Here the affirmation of difference arises not at a collective level but strictly at an individualist one.

These cultural practices are textualized in six separate segments which make up the novel, with each segment projecting a particular image of the family. The totality of the novel produces a fragmented and discontinuous extended-family portrait which includes three generations of the Angel family plus the sister-in-law of one family member. Each segment of the novel focuses on one of the households represented in the overall picture and details the crisis of that particular family unit. The fragmented structure is spiral-like with each segment advancing and retreating in time to cover a period extending from the decade of the thirties to the present, with two brief references to an earlier period, the Mexican Revolution of 1910 and the year of immigration, 1916. Each segment narrates an episode which contains dialogue between various members of the family, as well as intratextual references to events reiterated from different perspectives in third-person narration; although the segments internally assume a certain chronological framework, there are numerous flashbacks (analepsis) and flashforwards (prolepsis) within the episodes.

The first segment, "Judgment Day," serves as an introduction to the entire family and juxtaposes the main character's early childhood with his near-death experience in surgery at the age of thirty. It also provides the most vivid image in the novel, that of the main character's colostomy, which forces him to wear an appliance to which a plastic bag, regularly changed, is attached. Twelve years after leaving the desert of his youth, Miguel Chico, a university professor in San Francisco, recalled his family, especially its sinners, as he lay on his deathbed, half-conscious and longing for the desert of his childhood, the place where his aunt Nina feared being buried. His earliest childhood memories were of love, death, religion, and bigotry, evoked along with other subsequent events, not with nostalgia but with resentment; his life-threatening experience would in a sense free him and allow him to deal with his memories, to face up to them, to feel no longer compelled to hide the family's secrets. It is this experience which serves to explain the desert tale, as Miguel Chico is the presumed narrator, although all mentions of the character are in third person as well. The final segment, "The Rain God," ends with the death of the matriarch, Mama Chona, a scene recalled in the first segment, many years after the fact.

At her deathbed Mama Chona entrusts the family to Miguel Chico, a burden that he rejects yet still bears. Many years later the grandson would still be looking for a way to stop being haunted by his dead. The novel itself ultimately is the answer; it assumes the form of a collective confession, an act of exorcism, a ritual within which the writer is both confessor and collective sinner. The narrative is thus a cathartic experience, a way of consuming the past, a way of forgetting (Jameson 1984, xii), as well as of doing penance. The character proposes to tell all the family secrets and in that way to be free of them:

> He needed very much to make peace with his dead, to prepare a feast for them so that they would stop haunting him. He would feed them words and make his candied skulls out of paper. He looked once again, at that old photograph of himself and Mama Chona. The white daisies in her hat no longer frightened him; now that she was gone, the child in the picture held only a ghost by the hand and was free to tell the family secrets. (160)

Once narrated, discourse becomes estranged, *ajeno;* in this way the narrator means to be free of this burdensome collective memory, this textual "other" which is a multitextual "inner speech" (Vygotsky 1978), in effect the discourse of the living and dead. The novel deals then with a need to exteriorize the private sphere, the family circle from which the character is estranged. In an effort to collect his images of the past, Miguel Chico resolves, like the quoted fifteenth-century king of Texcoco, Netzahual-coyotl, to recall his dead through written discourse: "Nothing recalls them but the written page" (162).

As noted before, resentment is the major ideological strategy in the novel, but it is not the resentment of subordinated classes against the upper classes but rather that of sons and daughters who reject the authoritarian position of the father and the deleterious effect of the family on its members, a discourse that runs entirely counter to the words of Mama Chona who assured her grandchildren that within the family no harm would come to them.

The principal resentment is thus against the patriarchy as constituted in traditional Western society, with its gender roles, power relations, and values. The patriarchal code is particularly explicit in terms of male behavior. A son must not be weak, delicate, or effeminate, but rather strong, independent, aggressive, competitive, and ambitious. Wives, on the other hand, are deemed to be subordinate creatures, whose principal duties are to reproduce and nurture children and attend to the various needs of the husband. The father figure, proudly masculine and dominant, is established as the authority to be unquestionably obeyed. In the novel Miguel Grande, the husband of Juanita and father of Miguel Chico and two other sons, is a policeman, an authoritarian father and husband, and a womanizer. His pernicious influence is countered throughout the novel in various ways. First of all, the son, his namesake and first born, Miguel Chico, grows up to be an academic, a bookworm who cares little about bodybuilding and who as a child preferred the company of his mother, grandmother, and the maid, a domestic worker from across the border who enjoyed dressing the child in a skirt and teaching him to dance. When the child is stricken with polio, he is not taken to the doctor immediately because his father, who does not wish to pamper a sickly son, forbids his mother to take him until it is too late and he is, as a result, left with a lifelong limp. Many years later the son's education and economic independence, his professional career as a professor, and his bachelor status would allow him to escape the stranglehold of his father's patriarchal standards but not to subvert the power relations altogether. In fact the son develops such a strong resentment against his father and considers him to be so despicable that he finds that he will never be able to trust another man again (97). Resentment eventually turns to disdain and ultimately to arrogance, when the son becomes his father's confessor and feels a triumph in the knowledge that his father will never be able to come between him and his mother. For a brief moment, then, the roles are reversed, but significantly they are not undone. Resentment is thus a form of adherence and consent in the end.

Resentment against the patriarchal family structure is tied to the very textualization of the patriarchy in the novel. Years after his grandmother's death and after visiting his drug-addicted cousin in a halfway house, Miguel Chico would dream of being raped by the monster that killed his grandmother. If we recall that her monstrous abortion was actually a fallen uterus, it becomes evident that the monster symbolizes the family, the patriarchy; it is a monstrous synthesis of exploiter and exploited, loved and unloved, judge and advocate, and the only way to destroy it is to destroy oneself. The plunge that in the dream the character takes off the bridge with the monster represents his decision to commit suicide with his violator, that is, to end the silence and begin writing the story of his family and thus of himself.

Miguel Chico's rejection of the patriarchal norm has to be viewed in terms of other social practices. In effect, patriarchal discourse is often tied to capitalist ideology in the text and it is not always of male origin. In one case, for example, it is reproduced by a woman, Miguel's aunt and god-mother, Nina, whose stubbornness and authoritarian ways and middle-class patriarchal expectations for her son, Tony, lead to a confrontation between mother and son. Tony's sisters are barely mentioned in the novel; it is the son who represents the family's aspirations and for whom the purchase of a new home is made, as an investment, the future sale of which will provide the funds for his college education. The son, on the other hand, resents having to change to a high school in a new neighborhood and scorns his mother's constant interest in making a profit. To protest the move he threatens to stop studying; moreover he sees no reason to make plans for college when the Vietnam War draft awaits him. After his threats fail to have any effect and he is locked up in his room to force him to do his work, the son determines to counter his family's and, more pointedly his mother's, authoritarianism in a most violent way: he commits suicide. Another central character in *The Rain God* is the uncle Felix, a contradictory figure, rain dancer, free spirit, and bisexual who seemingly subverts but in fact conforms to patriarchal practices as he governs his home in a typically authoritarian way. The text is ambivalent about Felix, presenting him as a kind and gentle man, who is not bigoted like the rest of the Angel family, while at the same time revealing his seduction of young men and narrating aspects of his life which point to his exploitation of the Mexican workers whom he hires as factory foreman and fondles under the pretext of a necessary medical examination. His death at the hands of a reluctant Anglo victim is portrayed as a case of civil rights discrimination against Mexicans when it is covered up by the military personnel at the base where the young man was stationed; it is also said that the dismissal of the case is accepted by Miguel Grande, then concerned with his candidacy for police chief. Felix's homosexual preferences, however, cannot be seen to negate patriarchal structures, for not only is he an authoritarian husband with a wife and four children at home, but in his relations with men he also assumes the position of power and takes advantage of his subordinates. Resentment of the offspring toward the authority figure also comes into play here as Felix too faces the resentment and loss of his son, JoEl, whom he adores but who in time also begins to seek "his own space" by retreating to the printed world of his books and his poetry. Once again individualism and the desire to affirm individual differences counter traditional family roles and create father-son conflicts, even though bonds are not entirely severed. In fact JoEl too, like Miguel, will carry the burden of his dead throughout his life; his plunge, however, will be into the oblivion of a drug-induced idiocy.

The women in the novel, on the other hand, are true to patriarchal prescription; they are passive, spineless, gentle creatures, except for Nina, Juanita's sister, who is said to be like her authoritarian, half-French father, whom she hated. The main character's mother, Juanita, on the other hand, is described as a "selfless angel," who loves her husband dearly and even her best friend, Lola, who would then betray her by becoming her husband's lover. If Lola represents the conniving yet glamorous seductress, the ideal woman is undoubtedly the mother figure as represented by Juanita and Angie, Felix's wife, but this male idealization of women is challenged if only somewhat by Juanita's son who considers his mother masochistic and is repudiated entirely by Angie's son JoEl, who scorns his mother for putting up with Felix's injustices: "Wordlessly, he let Angie know that she deserved the pain she endured and that she was no better than a worm for letting Felix take advantage of her goodness" (125).

The novel thus captures a generational conflict as it both reconstructs patriarchal images of women as angels or whores and deconstructs them by uncovering the wives' oppression and their subjection to cultural norms. The text, however, deals only with the subordination of women within the home, as it focuses exclusively on the private sphere and neglects the public domain. The chronotope (Bakhtin 1981) of the home as an idyllic refuge for the patriarchal family is thus thoroughly negated and seen instead to be a space wherein tension, oppression, and domination take place. The home is truly the cave where the monster resides.

The novel begins and ends with a portrait of Mama Chona, the grandmother, the transmitter of patriarchal and capitalist practices and discourses. A woman who had suffered the loss of three children by the time she immigrated to the United States, Mama Chona lived in constant expectation of suffering and death. A judgmental, pretentious, and proud woman, she ensured the transmission of her class ideology and bigotry, practices which would characterize all but two of her children, Felix and Mena, the daughter who also would suffer the consequences of patriarchal practices when her illegitimate child was born and she was forced by the family to give him up. In protest Mena would cross the border to live with her man and to look for her son. Six years later Mena would find the boy begging in the streets of Juárez and with the help of Felix have him brought back to the United States where his grandmother would raise him, as if attempting to undo her own deed.

The hypocrisy and snobbery of the Angel clan are part of a network of contradictions in the family. The two matriarchs, Mama Chona and Tia Cuca, for example, are in effect poor women with aristocratic airs who consider menial labor beneath them. An earlier situation which had allowed for hired domestic workers in the home had left its ideological traces in the grandmother's discourse long after she had ceased to be able to afford a maid. Her refusal to do her domestic chores because she associated this work with members of the lower working class or undocumented workers, whom she identified as "Indians," revealed the racist ideology of an ethnic classification system in which class relations were displaced and a chain linking illiteracy with paganism and servility with dark skin was created. Thus Mama Chona assumed an air of superiority, a class condescension with those she considered her inferiors, "the illiterate riffraff from across the river" (15). Miguel Chico, who resented this snobbery, understood it as a remnant of colonial discourse in women who were obviously of Indian heritage themselves. The grandmother's imaginary representation of her relations to her own conditions of existence served in fact to hide her actual poverty and mask her Indian features to none but herself. The ideological nature of this perspective was clear to Juanita, who likewise saw through this pretentiousness and noted the little means of the Angel family (14–15). On the other hand this ideology was not unconscious; it assumed concrete manifestation at every turn. Because fair skin was a mark of worth for the Angel family, Felix, for example, had to marry Angie without his mother's blessing since his wife was considered a "lower-class Mexican," and an "Indian" for being dark-complected. Felix's sister best summarizes the inherited discourse:

> She said she did not understand how Angie had even gotten through school. Obviously she belonged to that loathsome group of Indians who were herded through the system, taught to add at least since they refused to learn any language properly, and then let loose among decent people who must put up with their ignorance. Jesus Maria knew that her family was better than such illiterates and she would prove it by going on to college. (128)

After Mama Chona's children grow up, they attain a lower-middle-class or middle-class status; this can be inferred from the sparse mention made of their means of support, since the public sphere constitutes a notable gap in the narrative. In their conversations, and in the entire novel for that matter, their relation to the dominant class in society is never analyzed or questioned; in fact they are strong proponents of the dominant ideology, consenting, as Hall explains in his analysis of culture (1977), to their own subordination. Miguel Grande, as one of the first policemen of Mexican origin in this border Texas town in the desert, was convinced that the "North American dream had worked for him. Only his family reminded him of his roots, and except for his mother he avoided them as much as possible" (78). Although apparently alienated from his own ethnic group and from his own family, Miguel Grande's best friends are Mexican as well, and he is said to have worked to integrate the police force until more than half were Mexican (76). Strong defenders of the power structure in this country, Miguel Angel and his buddy, El Compa, were convinced that the United States was the best country in the world; they considered themselves Americans and were totally unaware not only of international affairs, as the narrator point out in reference to the Spanish Civil War (57), but also of their own historical circumstances. It is Felix's daughter Lena, the one who ran around with lower-class Mexicanos, who is glad to find out that Miguel Grande "had not been selected chief, thinking it might force him to understand what life was really like for 'low class' Mexicans in the land that guaranteed justice under the law for all" (88). The loss of this promotion was to be a shock for Miguel Grande, and he is said to have lost faith in "what he had believed in all his life about this country" (91).

While ethnic solidarity and discrimination are not primary issues in the novel, they, along with deviance, are presented as explicit constituents of difference. Class structure, on the other hand, although less visible, is an implicit presupposition for only it can explain the Angel resentment toward the lower classes and their consent to the dominant ideologies.

The third cultural practice inherited from Mama Chona is the other side of bigotry: Catholic guilt and a desire for punishment. Although the institution itself—the church—is not represented, its ideology raises its ugly head as its practices are visited even on to the third generation, so that the Angel grandchildren feel burdened by the sins of their fathers. JoEl seeks relief in drug addiction but it proves to be no escape; we last see him in a halfway house for addicts, a riddle-spouting lunatic. Nina, on the other hand, though Catholic, searches out additional occult practices which eventually allow her to overcome her fear of death. On the other hand, Jesus Maria, who had married against her mother's wishes, is a shrieking replica of her mother; she attends mass daily and follows her mother's religious norms faithfully, but her hypocritical harangues make her intolerable even to Mama Chona. The third generation of the Angel family continues to evidence vestiges of this practice as well. Miguel Chico, for example, grows up to assume an air of self-righteousness and superiority, thinking himself educated and beyond the plague of guilt and beyond the maid Maria's distortions of religion, but he too is obsessed with the sins of his fathers and his own. Later, and wiser, like a Foucauldian genealogist, he resigns himself, if not to being totally free of his family's influences and distortions, at least to the illusion of going beyond these practices through his knowledge of them, for "he believed in the power of knowledge" (28). To escape from the power of secrecy, deformation, and mystification, Miguel Chico invokes the privileges and power of knowledge. The narration of the family secrets itself thus becomes a strategy of struggle.

This genealogical analysis focuses, then, on various cultural practices but without discussing their relation to an entire network of social practices which are economic and political in nature, preferring to limit itself strictly to power relations within the family. Consequently the Angel family seems to have lived in a vacuum, untouched by World War II, the Korean War, the McCarthyist period, the Vietnam War, the civil rights movement, labor struggles, political struggles, overt racial discrimination, and other forms of class struggles in the United States. It is only by searching through numerous traces of other texts to be found in the novel that we encounter texts of poverty that go beyond Tia Cuca's eccentric life-style and allude to an entire population of "low-class" Mexicans in Lena's high school with whom she associates, to the family's consternation. After this rapid mention, however, the text is bracketed and never taken up again. In a similar way we discover that Felix's work as foreman puts him in a position as *coyote,* recruiting Mexican laborers for the plant. However, it is the men's physical beauty which attracts Felix; their plight beyond this sexual abuse is also bracketed. In a similar fashion we learn that the murder of Mexicans is a routine, casually treated matter in the city while being offered the exceptional case of Felix's murder, which attracts a good deal of attention since the victim is the brother of a candidate for police chief. The family is thus enclosed in a cocoon, a world all its own. Only brief asides, like that of the Catholic president being assassinated, situate the episodes in time. But what is edited out, though absent, is clearly leading to social changes that pit the younger generation against the power positions of the older generations and against the entire family structure, despite provoking pangs of guilt for so doing. The three kinds of social and ideological struggles suggested in the text against the patriarchy, against ethnic, sexual, and class prejudice, and against the teachings of the Church are cast in a subjective objectivity in defense of the status and primacy of the individual; these serve in this regard as counterdiscourses which although critical of family relations of power do not question the larger economic and political structures of power within which they arise.

These struggles take place in the desert, a place of both life and death, the place to which the Rain God sends rainstorms as a respite from the hot dry winds that blow the desert sands. This seemingly lifeless area wherein men toil and die is also a chronotype, a discourse strategy which serves to mirror the lives of the characters and provides the text a unifying thread that ties various deplorable acts together: suicide, murder, poverty, infirmity, and death. The smell of a rainstorm in the desert is said to be the Rain God's covenant with mere mortals, assuring them of the one sure thing in life: death. The desert and its rainstorms thus capture the novel's deconstructive and reconstructive strategies as the text allows a reconstruction of cultural practices and ideologies, collective memories which are subsequently deconstructed to reveal their contradictions. The novel's metaphysical strain serves only as a secondary motif and strategy, itself deconstructed by the novel's cynical discourse. The novel does in fact embrace another ahistorical, theological proposition: Miguel Chico's vision of the writer as god, as transcendental signified of the text, as the purveyor of meaning of a text, as individual subject. But even this ideological discourse allows for its own deconstruction within the text, since the main character and presumed subject of the narration is a fragmented subject; in fact he sees himself as a "grafted" subject, whose symbolic "colostomy" and "severe pruning" allow his discourse to be grafted with a multiplicity of discourses, contradictory in nature and voicing both dominant and counterdiscourses. Although it is again a need to affirm difference and individualism, as in the case of Richard Rubio, that will lead Miguel Chico to leave the desert, it is now a multiplicity of voices which question the experience of subjectivity and individualism and, in a sense, lead him back to the collective.

Angie Chabram

Conceptualizing Chicano Critical Discourse

A los críticos de
la literatura chicana.

But I am saying that we should look not
for the components of a product but for
the conditions of a practice.
—*Raymond Williams,* Problems in Materialism and Culture

Charting the Terrain

This essay examines some of the recent developments that have surfaced in Chicano critical discourse—that body of writing which emerged in response to the artistic practices generated by the Chicano movement in select cultural institutions. Rather than providing a metacommentary on individual critical works in the fashion of its predecessors, this essay sets out to identify general trends within contemporary Chicano criticism and to examine some of the problems that have arisen in its conceptualization as an emergent critical discourse.

This deviation from the norm is conscious; it is intended to draw attention to the fact that Chicano criticism, as it exists today, is a dynamic, ever-changing field, which requires much careful scrutiny and a wide-ranging integrated approach, capable of responding to its multifaceted existence within various forms and spheres of critical activity.

Chicano Critical Situations

Since its inception in the sixties, Chicano literary criticism has undergone profound transformations which are readily evident in its cver-

I would like to express my gratitude to those Chicano critics whose voices are recorded in this essay.

increasing sophistication and its now substantial volume. Nonetheless, relative to its significant maturation in recent years, its scholarship has lagged notably behind. To date there are no extensive histories, encyclopedias, or monograph-length theoretical accounts dedicated to its appraisal. Of those Chicano metacritical works which have appeared over the last eleven years, Joseph Sommers's "From the Critical Premise to the Product: Critical Modes and Their Application to a Chicano Literary Text" (1977) is undoubtedly the most comprehensive study that has appeared on the topic.

With this essay, which stands as a benchmark in the development of Chicano critical thought, Joseph Sommers succeeded in bringing Chicano criticism to the forefront as an important domain of scholarly investigation. He not only shed light on many of the basic critical assumptions which underlie its early critical modalities (the historical-dialectical, the culturalist, and the formalist), but he inspired a string of writers to take cognizance of the developments in Chicano criticism, thus setting the stage for the expansion of the Chicano critical essay into yet other forms of metacritical activity.

In the period since the appearance of Joseph Sommers's ground-breaking essay, record numbers of critical monographs on Chicano literature, several issues of literary journals dedicated solely to the diffusion of critical essays, and a significant body of unpublished dissertations on Chicano literature have surfaced.

This proliferation of critical texts has been accompanied by a steady growth of international attention to Chicano literature and criticism in countries such as France, Germany, Spain, and Mexico. Several prominent foreign-based publishing outlets have also begun to carry the works of Chicano critics. Among the most notable examples in recent years are Mexico's Siglo Veintiuno, *Texto Crítico, Plural,* and Fondo de Cultura Económica. Conversely, with greater frequency than ever, European and Latin American critics are circulating their Chicano critical essays published abroad within various national literary institutions.

Significant trends in publication can also be discerned within the United States, where a good number of critical monographs have been published by prestigious university presses and regular mainstream publication outlets. Chicano critical essays have also made sporadic appearances in such mainstream journals as *Modern Language Notes, Diacritics, Ideologies & Literature, The Denver Quarterly, Hispania, Latin American Literary Review,* and *Latin American Theatre Review,* although the bulk of these essays is still concentrated in ethnic or Chicano journals. Outside this sphere Chicano critical works have begun to surface in feminist journals such as *Third Woman, Feminist Studies,* and *Signs,* primarily as a result of the growing number of Chicana critics (Sylvia Lizárraga, Marta Sánchez, Rosaura Sánchez, Norma Alarcón, María Herrera-Sobek, Yolanda Julia Broyles, and Yvonne Yarbro-Bejarano) who are examining women's writings and, in the process, *re*writing Chicano criticism.

It would not be an exaggeration to suggest that we are rapidly moving into an "Age of Chicano Criticism." Not only has this production fared considerably well in relation to the total volume of literature produced within the same time period, but recent trends defy previous years when literary anthologies prevailed over critical monographs by substantial margins.

Signs of this critical passage can also be detected in the progressive movement toward more professional forms of critical discourse and in the proliferation of modern literary theories and perspectives (especially Marxist, formalist, mythic, feminist, poststructuralist, semiotic, and phenomenological) throughout recent Chicano critical endeavors. The growing number of works dedicated to Chicano critical reflection and evaluation is also symptomatic. As Terry Eagleton has suggested elsewhere: "The moment when a material or intellectual practice begins to 'think itself,' to take itself as an object of intellectual enquiry, is clearly of dominant significance in the development of that practice; it will certainly never be the same again" (1976, 17).

The significance of these developments can only be fully appreciated when considering that they have taken place within a critical discourse, whose existence (in the present form) only dates back a few decades and which, for all practical purposes, has experienced the theoretical revolution in literary studies from the very periphery of the dominant critical culture and its supportive institutions. If this were not enough, passage to "critical self-consciousness" has meant movement away from nationalistic paradigms and the creation of new forms of metacritical inquiry for "thinking" this intellectual watershed.

Any discussion of the transformations that have swept Chicano criticism which does not mention the plight of the critic is incomplete, for it is the critic who initially generates the critical text and places it in the literary circuit, thus contributing to its multiple affiliations with other textual practices, critics, and institutional sectors. The critic does not, however, escape the influences of the specific context in which s/he operates; as Edward Said explains: "critics are not merely the alchemical translators of texts into circumstantial reality or worldliness; for they too are subject to and producers of circumstances, which are felt regardless of whatever objectivity the critic's method proposes" (1983, 35).

One area where these mutually confirming forces come together is in the altered professional circumstance of the critic. In contrast to the early years, which saw an onslaught of "popular" (uncertified) critics who worked in nonspecialized informal sectors, the majority of critics of Chicano literature are now members of national literary academies—generally at the assistant and associate professor level. Increasingly their critical production is oriented toward the completion of professional obligations when this is possible.[1] This formation has undoubtedly contributed to the growing professionalization of Chicano critical discourse and to the proliferation of book-length monographs.

Another development which is rarely mentioned, but nonetheless significant for understanding the types of alterations experienced by Chicano criticism in recent years, is the ongoing tendency of critics of Chicano literature to cluster into individual "circles" or "schools" of criticism. Thus, it is now possible to speak candidly, though modestly, about the existence of a Yale circle of Chicano critics, an Austin circle, a Santa Barbara circle, and last, but not least, a La Jolla circle of Chicano critics. While these institutional affiliations do not signify that the circles of Chicano critical thought necessarily replicate the predominant theoretical perspectives associated with specific educational settings, they do illustrate the literary-institutional forces which are affecting the conceptual development of this emerging critical practice.

The Chicano presence at Yale offers an interesting case in this regard. Several prominent critics of Chicano literature, including Juan Bruce-Novoa, Ramón Saldívar, José David Saldívar, and Héctor Calderón, met at Yale and all have had important affiliations there, either in the capacity of professors, graduate students, or undergraduates. In a series of interviews which I conducted with each of these critics, they acknowledged that this professional affiliation with the "Yale Critics" and "Yale Deconstructionist Movement" did have a significant impact on their critical work—though the nature of this impact varied tremendously with each individual critic.

Ramón Saldívar, for instance, in recalling the culture shock which he experienced upon moving from Edinburg, Texas, to New Haven, Connecticut, cites "Paul de Man as the single most important intellectual influence" on him during the course of his study at Yale. Saldívar's professional biography exemplifies the manners in which diverse critical traditions and professional experiences have converged to produce new theoretical directions in Chicano criticism. As a graduate student at Yale he produces a dissertation on narrative theory, which later culminates in the publication of *Figural Language in the Novel* (1984), under the direction of J. Hillis Miller and Paul de Man, while at the same time teaching courses on Chicano literature and culture. Upon arriving at the University of Texas at Austin as a professor, his interest in narrative theory is directed toward Chicano literature, and he writes the much cited: "A Dialectic of Difference: Towards a Theory of the Chicano Novel" (1979). Saldívar charts the process that led him to adapt certain aspects of poststructuralist theory to the Chicano literary experience:

> I had already evolved from my original work in literary theory on Jacques Derrida and the whole structuralist and post-structural debate to the notion of "difference." It struck me that in the case of the Mexican American you had precisely a concrete historical example of what Derrida was talking about in abstract, philosophical terms. It seemed like a fitting parallel, especially to what he was saying in his essay "Difference." Juan Bruce-Novoa was making a similar kind of argument, though not from Derrida's point of view . . . he was moving in another direction and exploring some of the possibilities of thinking theoretically and abstractly and in a non Anglo-American critical tradition, about Chicano literature. So his notion of Mexican American existing in the space between Mexican and American was something which I sympathized with very much. (Chabram, interview with R. Saldívar, January 1987)

A very different trajectory can be followed in the case of Juan Bruce-Novoa, author of *Chicano Authors* (1980) and *Chicano Poetry* (1982) and scores of critical essays, who joins the Spanish faculty at Yale in 1974 (after completing a dissertation on Juan García Ponce at the University of Colorado) and soon thereafter launches his highly polemical "The Space of Chicano Literature" (1975). Here Bruce-Novoa downplays the influence of poststructuralism on his intellectual formation, reformulating as well, the phenomenological orientation that distinguishes his view of Chicano literature from Ramón Saldívar's:

> When I came to Yale, I had a strong theoretical background, but it wasn't the type prevalent in the English Department. . . . Most of my readings were oriented through Mexican essays from the generation of Juan García Ponce. . . . They . . . took me to Bataille and Blanchot. . . . Derrida was not one of my principal readings . . . but through García Ponce, I read the people who influenced Derrida. . . . I always rejected the binary oppositions of French linguistic theory. . . . I saw that binaries are anti-Chicano; as soon as we adopt binaries we're in trouble. In the first essay . . . I talk about the Chicano as an inter-space; that is, neither one of the poles. . . . It's really the synthesis. . . . Ramón Saldívar says there's no synthesis, but synthesis does not mean end. . . . it's a

constant dialectic that can never be achieved until death. . . . I really do
believe in this other space . . . where it [the literary object] has its own
subject. (Chabram, interview with Bruce-Novoa, August 1987)

Yet another perspective on the Yale experience is recorded by Héctor
Calderón, professor and former graduate of Spanish literature, who studies
with Fredric Jameson at the School of Criticism and Theory (1978) and
completes a dissertation (1981) on language and consciousness in the novel
under the direction of Emir Rodríguez Monegal "in an attempt to bring
historical depth to poststructuralism." Subsequently, Calderón publishes
Conciencia y lenguaje en el "Quijote" y en "El obsceno pájaro de la noche"
(1987) along with various critical essays that examine Chicano narrative
genres from the perspective of "the ideology of literary form" (see Calderón
1986). In this excerpt he chronicles his initial impressions of Yale:

> You have to understand what it was like when I came to Yale . . . The
> tremendous excitement. . . . It was the period from '75 to '77 . . . [and]
> everything was in the formative stages, a very exciting time to be in
> literature. So then maybe my third or fourth week at Yale, I walked into
> an auditorium to hear Derrida speak, and I remember having people
> point out Geoffrey Hartman and Paul de Man, J. Hillis Miller. And the
> atmosphere was sort of: "Here is the word." The final answer was about
> to be given, and these critics were gathered to hear it. . . .
>
> Another thing that bothered me about Yale, offended me even, was
> this notion that history does not exist. You know . . . That you can't
> write history anymore. That even the subject doesn't exist. Again, that
> seemed to exclude a whole group of people who were very much in-
> volved with history. . . . The Chicano Movement itself was not only
> making history at that moment, but it was a process in history, and
> there did not seem to be a space for thinking about that within a frame-
> work that says: "there's no subject, there's no history". (Chabram,
> interview with Calderón, May 1987)

José David Saldívar, himself a former student at Yale, professor of
literature at the University of California at Santa Cruz, editor of the much-
acclaimed *The Rolando Hinojosa Reader* (1985) and author of critical essays that locate the emergence of a Chicano-Chicana subject in narrative
(see J. D. Saldívar 1986) coincides, elaborating:

> It seems a bit ironic that just when all of these [mainstream] critics are
> talking about the end of the subject . . . that we should have Chicanos,
> peoples of color, and feminists, finally beginning to see themselves as
> subjects, as capable of action instead of just being acted upon. . . . It may

not be a coincidence that mainstream critics are talking about the end of the subject just when those people who have been cut off from power become aware of their potential role—as subjects—within the historical moment. (Chabram, interview with J. D. Saldívar, May 1987)

These excerpts are of interest not only because they allow us to speculate on the impact which intellectual formation exerts on a critic's work, but also because they furnish an example of the way in which the *Chicano* critical tradition and the Chicano movement itself mediated the professional experiences and literary perspectives of these critics at Yale. This type of mediation, aside from producing a substantially different set of cultural problematics from those initially registered by Arac, Godzich, and Martin in their account of *The Yale Critics* (1983), also explains the types of adaptations which are produced in contemporary literary theory by Chicano critical discourse.

It would, however, be erroneous to universalize the professional affiliations described above to other circles or even to assume that Chicano critical activity is limited to the institutional settings mentioned in this essay—the range of possibilities is as varied as are the individual critical histories which, together, make up the Chicano critical experience. What is undisputable, however, is the decisive role which Chicano writers and critics have played in fomenting Chicano critical expression in their capacity as mentors. Though space does not permit acknowledgment of all the deserving, the most visible include: Américo Paredes, Rosaura Sánchez, Gustavo Segade, Arturo Madrid, Sergio Elizondo, Jorge Huerta, Arturo Islas, Sylvia Lizárraga, Philip D. Ortego, Juan Bruce-Novoa, Juan Rodríguez, Nicolás Kanellos, Tomás Ybarra-Frausto, Rolando Hinojosa, Alejandro Morales, and Tomás Rivera. Hispanists such as Luis Leal, Joseph Sommers, Carlos Blanco-Aguinaga, and Justo Alarcón have also done their part in training future critics of Chicano literature.

The most influential circles of Chicano criticism have also made contributions worthy of note: the Santa Barbara circle has contributed to the development of a tradition of historical scholarship which has unearthed many early Chicano literary texts; the San Diego circle to a budding Marxist tradition which dialogues with the works of Eagleton, Jameson, and Sánchez Vázquez; the Yale circle to the consolidation of various poststructuralist and phenomenological trends; and the Austin circle to the writing of literary histories which draw from folklore and cultural studies methodology.

An idea of the diverse elements which have converged to produce influential Chicano critical perspectives or networks can be gotten upon examining the Texas circle, which surfaces largely as a result of the appearance of seminal literary histories inspired by Américo Paredes's *"With His Pistol in His Hand"* (1958), a text which itself prefigures the Chicano critical tradition in its contemporary renditions. The now classic "The Evolution of Chicano Literature" (1978), for example, was written by Raymund Paredes, who not only studied with Américo Paredes at the University of Texas at Austin, but coauthored one of the earlier anthologies of Chicano writers with his mentor (R. Paredes and A. Paredes 1972). After producing a dissertation on the Mexican image in American literature, which sought to "rewrite Cecil Robinson's *With the Ears of Strangers* (1963) from a Chicano point of view," Raymund Paredes writes several essays that identify the origin of anti-Mexican sentiment in the United States and examine the folk base of Chicano literature. In this passage he discusses the significance of Américo Paredes's work for contemporary literary scholarship:

> Yes. There is definitely a group of students trained at the University of Texas at Austin, heavily influenced by Américo Paredes' work. It is important that Paredes is both a literary scholar and an anthropologist; many people tend to forget his training as a literary critic. But up until about fifteen years ago, when he began attracting graduate students whose emphasis was in Chicano Studies, he taught conventional American literature courses. . . . You know, they talk about Paredes, and the obvious influence he's had on a generation of critics. . . . But you can see why the response has been so overwhelmingly positive. If you go back and reread his criticism, it continuously holds up. . . . He makes it clear how important it is to establish the cultural landscape in which Chicano writers are composing their works. (Chabram, interview with R. Paredes, June 1987)

This type of "generational" distribution among critics of Chicano literature, with a range of two and often three tiers, is a relatively new phenomenon. So, too, is the appearance of the literary critic, reared and saturated in the field of Chicano literary studies. While doing fieldwork for an unpublished monograph entitled "Conversations with Chicano Critics," I was taken aback by the overwhelming number of prominent critical figures who had never had formal instruction in this area of study. More often than not, they had actually gained access to the discipline through individual study and the teaching of Chicano literature and culture courses in prominent literary institutions. The experience of one of my respondents is not atypical. When asked if he had ever taken a course in Chicano literature, he answered, "No, there were no courses; I taught the first course myself. . . . I wasn't exactly assigned, more like recruited."

The institutional challenges which these critics encountered—and continue to encounter—within national literary institutions are exemplified in the case of a pioneer Chicano critic, Juan Rodríguez, who narrates his stormy entrance:

> I went there as a Chicano professor, and I was very conscious of being a Chicano professor. . . . I became involved with the students. . . . [T]he first week I was there, my picture appeared in the paper. . . . The Chicano students and I went to ask for funds and it got violent. . . . I was called into the Chair's office and I was told: "If your picture appears in the paper again, you won't have a job with this university." (Chabram, interview with Rodríguez, May 1987)

Not only were these critics faced with negotiating the place of Chicano literature within established literary circles less than sympathetic with their objectives, but, they were also faced with the arduous task of laying the foundation for studying a literary tradition in the absence of readily available reference works. As Juan Rodríguez, compiler of *Crónicas diabólicas de "Jorge Ulica"* (1982), responded when asked about the critical figures who had influenced him:

> There were no critics of Chicano literature, as far as I knew, . . . so I was working on the basis of my own perception of the world. . . . But there were two things I was trying to do. . . . One was to make sense of what was before me in terms of Chicano literature, to put it into some type of context. And the other thing was to make it legitimate. . . . So I was conscious of defending Chicano literature. (Interview, May 1987)

The experiences of these as well as many other critics of Chicano literature—their valuable service activity, formidable intellectual strides, unyielding persistence in the face of minimal professional retribution—form an important chapter in Chicano critical history. Their contributions also deserve a place—if not within—at least alongside of, monographs of the nature of *The Yale Critics, Twentieth-Century Literary Criticism, American Critics at Work, Contemporary Literary Critics*, and *American Literary Criticism*, as evidence of the "other" literary revolution, which has yet to universally populate libraries, bookstores, and graduate seminars.

Together with the previously mentioned developments, these experiences offer valuable insights into the processes and forces which are currently shaping the contours of an emergent critical practice as it passes into a qualitatively new phase of its existence, simultaneously charting terrain which is familiar and unfamiliar to general critical sectors. Much groundwork will have to be laid to do justice to the breadth and depth of this critical passage.

Present lacunae in the field point to the need for additional metacritical studies that could explore the historical trajectory of Chicano criticism—its early origins, critical influences, and associations—and the need for an update of Joseph Sommers's classificatory schema to reflect the new approaches to Chicano literature that have surfaced since the publication of his seminal work. Recent developments should also be reviewed in light of new conceptual frameworks that assess and evaluate the altered nature of Chicano critical discourse, its linkages with other emergent discourses, its appropriation of contemporary literary theory, and its relationship to greater critical traditions.

This is one of the most challenging and exciting of present metacritical endeavors, for it entails bringing together traditions that have been linked by contradictory relations of rupture and continuity, as well as operating within a mode of intellectual inquiry whose perimeters have yet to be defined in a manner that could respond effectively to such a formidable historical challenge. Charting this new critical terrain will require much reflection and evaluation, not only of future possibilities of broadening the scope of existing metacritical studies, but of past metacritical studies—their priorities, limitations, and lacunae—for it is "in history" (to quote Fredric Jameson) that criticism is practiced.

What follows is my own reflection on the state of metacritical studies pertaining to Chicano criticism; though tentative, it identifies some of the problems which have surfaced in the conceptualization of Chicano critical discourse, while proposing areas of critical research that could permit a redefinition of its current perimeters. More attention to the particular concerns it raises is essential if this critical discourse is to shed its marginal status within contemporary critical problematics. It is in this spirit that critical trends are examined, beginning with those which concern Chicano critical studies.

Chicano Metacritical Studies: Expanding the Perimeters

In many respects Chicano critical studies have thrived in recent years. In addition to their notable proliferation, they have increasingly grown into specialized domains of critical inquiry. The upshot of this is the appearance of several Chicano critical essays which evaluate critical approaches to Chicano literature, offer commentaries on the works of individual critics, or reflect on the problems involved in classifying Chicano literature or criticism (see Salazar Parr 1977, 1982; Alarcón 1979; Epple 1983; Lizárraga 1982; Bruce-Novoa 1982–1983; Flores 1981). Nonetheless, these studies have only succeeded in offering a partial description of the significant developments which have transpired in Chicano criticism, ignoring as well, the complex processes which have generated these developments. For the most part the literature on Chicano criticism has tended toward comprehensive inventories of literary perspectives, which, while illuminating basic critical assumptions, have fallen short in accounting for the noteworthy historical trajectory of Chicano criticism and its participation in multiple sectors of literary production.

Studies of this nature also generally fail to articulate their assumptions regarding Chicano critical discourse, or even to consider the ways in which general critical works, which ponder on the nature and function of criticism itself, might be incorporated into a theoretical rendition of Chicano criticism. In this particular respect Chicano critical studies have fallen well behind much of the vanguard of Chicano literary criticism itself, a domain which is increasingly conscious of the theoretical presuppositions that inform its reading of any number of texts and its dialogue with any number of traditions.

This gap between these two domains of literary scholarship must be eradicated if the potential of Chicano critical theory is to be fully realized and if the breadth of its fields of material and symbolic production are to be properly accounted for. But the negative repercussions of this hermetical tendency in Chicano critical studies assume even more widespread proportions when considering that the function of studies of this nature is that of discerning questions of vital significance for the entire discipline.

Further development and refinement of the scope of Chicano metacritical studies are of particular importance at this point in history, especially in light of the fact Chicano criticism is undergoing, on a reduced yet accelerated scale, many of the earthshaking developments experienced within the Anglo-American and European literary contexts from the early seventies onward. The appearance of new critical perspectives, forms of analysis, and terms of critical discourse in Chicano literary criticism are symptomatic of other, more sweeping critical transformations such as the radical reformulation of the accepted notions of Chicano literary genres, the nature and lineages of the Chicano literary tradition, and the boundaries of Chicano critical discourse itself (see R. Sánchez 1985a, 1985b; Calderón 1983, 1986; Saldívar 1979; Herrera-Sobek 1985; Broyles 1986; M. E. Sánchez 1985).

Documenting the extent of this transformation is essential if we are to gain an understanding of the significant roads traveled by Chicano criticism within the past decade or so. It is also essential that this transformation be contextualized in terms of a new critical movement, which has altered not only the types of theoretical frameworks deployed in the analysis of Chicano literature, but also current notions of Chicano criticism and its function in society.

No longer can this function be considered in isolation from the problematics of general critical discourse as was true in the early years. The heightened development of Chicano criticism, together with our growing awareness of its linkages with other critical sectors, requires that this function be dialectically articulated from within the very critical traditions and institutional contexts that are mediating its symbolic readings or interpretations of reality under the impact of determinate social and historical conditions.

Likewise, examination of the types of literary perspectives which inhabit Chicano critical discourse should ideally include attention to the manner in which Chicano critical theory travels from one institutional environment to another; to the manner in which this movement gives way to a dynamic process of appropriation and adaptation, where critical theories are constituted and reconstituted—often completely transformed—by virtue of their accommodation to the exigencies of new and distinct textual and cultural milieus.

This is not to suggest, as Henry Louis Gates, Jr., does, that the circulation of ideas necessarily involves a unidirectional movement from the mainstream to the alternative sector, where "non-Western," "noncanonical" critics appropriate the most sophisticated theories in order to *re*appropriate and "legitimize" their own literary discourses (1986, 14). Evidently, alternative sectors are not static repositories of critical problematics; they, too, generate them and, I might add, not "outside" the Western conventions of literary receptivity. As Héctor Calderón in my interview remarked when asked to comment on the problems involved in classifying Chicano narrative genres:

> It is a very difficult issue, and it's a problem of applying the notion of genre to Chicano Literature, which is, after all, a very specific literature. It's not "Western" literature in the conventional sense, yet it has grown both from within the tradition of Western literature, and in response to the pressures from the periphery of Western culture. If you think in terms of where we're educated, the universities we attend, the institutional framework which transmits a European, in some cases a very British tradition, and then you examine the cultural bonds with Mexican or Latin American tradition—this dual formation, First World and Third World, is going to come through. . . . A Chicano writer has a certain social formation that may run counter to the Western tradition at the same time that he or she has an ideological formation that is Western. It's there, we can't deny either aspect. (Interview, May 1987)

Not all the distinctive features of emergent critical discourses can be traced to ethnic content, intellectual formation, and specific ideological frameworks or cultural experiences. Irregular conditions of literary (and therefore, critical) production have also negatively affected the way in which these discourses relate to other critical discourses and movements, often functioning to limit the scope of their influence and capability of promoting emergent literatures within the extant primary and secondary literary institutions, such as literary academies, societies, book clubs, and producers. It is the disparate nature of these conditions of production that has largely nurtured the illusion that alternative emergent discourses exist "outside" general critical practice.

These conditions of production are well illustrated in the case of Chicano literary criticism. Not only is this criticism practiced within multiple channels of literary production, but these channels coexist within varying relations of homology, conflict, and disjuncture, and they potentially differ insofar as their intended objectives, perceptions of Chicano literature, and reading publics are concerned.

The most prevalent channels of Chicano literary (and critical) production are alternative ones. These include both specialized channels for the diffusion of literary works (namely, Chicano literary journals, conferences or associations, or book distributors that deal strictly with literature) and nonspecialized channels such as Chicano studies programs, reference libraries, and interdisciplinary journals such as *Aztlán*. Chicano literary criticism also participates in specialized established literary channels (when incorporated into regular literature departments, mainstream publication outlets, bookstores, and libraries) as well as in nonspecialized channels for the diffusion of general cultural activity.

These channels (the established and the alternative) do not, however, exist with complete independence of one another. Nowhere is the overlap more vividly illustrated than in the not-so-common professor of Chicano literature, who teaches in Spanish or English departments and Chicano studies programs, who publishes critical essays in both mainstream and alternative literary journals, and whose critical work is then listed in bibliographic indexes such as the *Modern Language Association Bibliography* and the *Chicano Periodical Index*. Also of significance in this regard is the frequency with which the alternative channels serve as catalysts for the reception of Chicano literary texts in college libraries, language departments, and bookstores.

These patterns suggest that the channels of production and consumption of Chicano literature and criticism are both interactive as well as relatively autonomous from one another. Together they form a complex, asymmetrical totality of structures which do not duplicate one another's functions and which are not uniformly incorporated into the various national cultural institutions in the patterns described here. While differing in the manner and extent to which they promote Chicano literary activity, they remain bound to the predominant structures of literary production by contradictory and unequal relations of subordination and marginalization. Viewed from this perspective, all Chicano critical activity (including that which inhabits the established sector) can be seen as participating in an "alternative" production insofar as this production seeks to promote a body of writings that continues to exist on the periphery of the greater literary world.

To be sure these conditions of production have left their imprint on Chicano critical discourse: they have contributed to the uneven and fragmentary nature of its articulation; they have retarded its organization in the manner typical of other more established critical traditions; and they have functioned to distance it from the mainstream of critical activity. Future studies would do well to detail the manner in which these conditions of production have affected Chicano critical expression—both materially as well as ideologically—throughout its most salient periods of historical development.

Exploring the Horizons: General Critical Studies

Along with these elements, an assessment of the nature of the representation of Chicano criticism within the broader sphere of general critical studies is desirable if the extent and domains of its activity are to be properly charted in future metacritical endeavors. Nonetheless, here as well we encounter problems, but of a substantially different nature. While the most politically and historically engaged accounts of criticism have already tacitly acknowledged the existence of emergent critical formations, even calling for a reappraisal of their importance for recent critical history, this reception has been less than satisfactory. It is generally the case that when a passing allusion is made to the alternative critical sector, it is a means of documenting the "crisis" in the institution of criticism or of applauding the consolidation of "oppositional" literary perspectives. While such allusions lack in depth and acumen, nowhere is the lack of rigor more evident than in the pervasive tendency of mainstream critics to include emergent critical formations under homogeneous categories of "ethnic" or "countercultural" criticism with little or no regard for their concrete particularities, their unique historical trajectories, and internal dynamics.

Contemporary poststructuralist readings of modern critical history provide a recent example of this problematic tendency within recent literary scholarship. Upon identifying emergent critical formations in terms of a basic "differential" relation to general critical discourse, they generally nullify or flatten the distinctive features which set these critical traditions apart.

Some of the problems which arise when these particularities are not addressed become evident upon considering the manner in which they interact with mainstream literary institutions. Though generally marginalized, emergent formations do not experience this condition uniformly. The irregularities which are characteristic of their representation within the greater literary culture can be readily noted upon comparing the growing reception of feminist criticism to the scant reception of African-American criticism and to the almost nil reception of Chicano criticism, which has suffered from the exclusionary practices of both the Anglo-American as well as the Spanish-speaking literary worlds.

Another domain where the lack of consensus can be witnessed is at the level of ideology. Until only very recently it was believed that emergent critical formations, by virtue of their critique of the marginalization of the artistic practices of specific racial, gender, and cultural groups, had delivered a uniform response to mainstream practices and literary assumptions. Nonetheless, studies have begun to unearth their heterogeneous—and oftentimes contradictory—responses.

The culturalist movement, which almost virtually dominated the early phase of Chicano criticism, serves as a case in point. Although this movement successfully combated the stereotypical representations of Chicanos within the greater literary culture, it frequently drew from idealist mainstream perspectives that postulated a basic separation between literature and social life. The extremes to which it was possible to arrive with the partnership between certain variants of phenomenological criticism and cultural nationalism made it possible to castigate the mainstream for its omission of Chicano cultural products, while at the same time offering philosophical configurations (nonhyphenated spatial metaphors, ethereal or racial essences) of Chicano culture which posited its virtual absence as a form of material production.

Insufficient attention has been paid to examining the manner in which the "counter-discourse" appropriated and modified existing literary perspectives in the early phase of its existence, although this topic promises to yield much in the way of broadening our understanding of its conceptual development. What is clear thus far is that early Chicano critical works—like their African-American counterparts—generally avoided inserting themselves into mainstream critical traditions, though they were adamant about demarcating the boundaries of the Chicano literary tradition. In fact many of the debates which were being waged within the greater literary culture appeared in an often concealed, often inconspicuous fashion in Chicano critical discourse, almost overshadowed by the desire to use critical practice as a domain for cultural affirmation. Almost, but not quite. In his preface to *Literary Theory* Eagleton has suggested that "[h]ostility to theory usually means an opposition to other people's theories and an oblivion to one's own" (1983, viii). While a measure of both of these elements contributed to the markedly antitheoretical flavor of much of early Chicano literary criticism, this attitude cannot be properly understood without accounting for the particular objectives that marked its inception.

Along with the general movements of the sixties which challenged the social, cultural, and political practices of the dominant social formation by proposing other modes of social development, the eruption of the Chicano movement gave birth to a criticism wedded to alternative literary values and committed to bringing about significant transformations in the existent structures, values, and boundaries of literary production and consumption. If the dominant literary culture had responded with censure or neglect to Chicano literature, classifying it as nonexistent, scant, or unworthy of incorporation because of its unconventional format, then this emergent criticism would exalt Chicano literature's merits, outline its significant historical and geographical lineages, and reiterate the innovation transmitted through popular flavor. If dominant notions of critical receptivity—transmitted throughout mainstream literary institutions—had functioned as real material constraints for the diffusion of Chicano literature and criticism, then it was necessary to create new critical perspectives, new alternative literary institutions, and new reading publics. If the legacy of literary marginality had condemned this corpus to relative obscurity and/or isolation, then it was necessary to rethink the relations of literary production and to substitute the peripheral position of Chicano literary forms on the literary map for a central one.

While this reorganization, reevaluation, and reaffirmation of Chicano literary and critical perspectives signified a break with the idea of a "singular" national literary tradition free of rupture, conflict, and contradiction, it did not refashion alternative values in a literary, ideological vacuum. It took from existing conventions, approaches, and traditions, nourishing them with the conventions embedded in alternative as well as established literary institutions of cultural production. In the final instance the articulation of this discourse involved a unique conjuncture between the general ideological formations of the larger social order, the particular ideological formations of the group (particularly of those associated with the Chicano movement), and their foregrounding in aesthetic categories derived from various literary sectors.

From this particular conjuncture a wide array of Chicano literary perspectives—mythic, culturalist, existentialist, formalist, historical, and phenomenological—flourished under a metacommentary whose referent was generally cast as the "Chicano experience," though this experience was not always well served by such definition. This practice was especially common among the culturalist variants; even in their most sophisticated renditions of immanent and formalist criticism, they would succeed in organizing their principles and couching their terms around a discourse of culture whose loyalty was directed toward the "authenticity" of the Chicano, but rarely toward the literary theories and traditions which they also spoke and disseminated.

This privileging of the ideological formations associated with the group, combined with the objective fact that Chicano criticism developed with a certain degree of autonomy from mainstream literary institutions, did produce interesting innovations in the critical format, innovations which continue to appear in more sophisticated renditions. Unlike most conventional academic literary criticism which had already passed through years of professionalization, altogether subordinating popular forms of criticism to more scholarly endeavors (such as the critical essay, the monograph, and the literary article), Chicano literary criticism—aside from including these forms—drew widely from the literary manifesto, newsletter, chapbooks, and journalistic criticism, generally flaunting this usage in the most academic of professional settings. Such a practice was intentional; as Juan Rodríguez describes when speaking about his literary newsletter, *La carta abierta:*

> On the other hand, I wanted that informal tone. As a matter of fact I'd played with the idea of calling it "Chismes." Because I believed at the time and believe to this day that if we start doing everything just like the academy does it—it means essentially sterilizing our communication. And when that happens, we've lost the battle. . . . You don't have to use 19th century Spanish to say something that's legitimately critical. This I think is especially true when you're dealing with a literature that grows so immediately out of a popular background. . . . You can even use Chicano slang, and there can still be a critical judgement. (Interview, May 1987)

These objectives did affect the type of expression utilized in the early period. Chicano critical discourse incorporated any number of (popular or standard) variants of Spanish or English, frequently code-switching from one language to another or else mimicking the popular lingo of university students and community activists. It also encoded as its audience a greater "Chicano community" through the use of the collective voice in literary analysis, generally as a means of fostering the political and social concerns associated with the Chicano movement. These trends offer a marked contrast to the contemporary period where critical endeavors are tending toward more conventional forms of expression and appealing to a general literary audience not explicitly differentiated on the basis of ethnicity, culture, or class. The long-range effects of this growing professionalization require much scrutiny, particularly if the collective spirit of the early years is to be safeguarded alongside the growing theoretical impulse in Chicano critical endeavors.

Reconceptualizing Chicano Critical Discourse: Global Perspectives

This brief overview of some of the features of early Chicano critical discourse highlights some of the interesting dynamics which emergent critical formations have brought to general critical practice. Though rarely credited for doing so, they have enriched critical history by virtue of their popular thrust, decentering of the dominant literary tradition, and broad interdisciplinary perspectives. While these elements may have initially placed them at odds with the "organic" sensibility of previous decades, new and exciting possibilities now exist for examining them within a larger theoretical context, particularly now with the growing intersection between literary theory and cultural studies and the rising dissatisfaction with the institution of literary criticism.

Nevertheless, any "serious" attempt to do so would have to begin by examining the chain of events which have for so long muted the voice of this budding critical discourse within the greater literary culture. It is not by accident that the "Chicano Renaissance" of the sixties was inaugurated with literary journals, publishing houses, and anthologies which carried the headings *Chicano Voices, Grito de Aztlán,* and *El Grito.* As the editors of *El Espejo* made clear in the opening pages of their anthology, the idea was to authorize the work to "speak for itself" and "for the people" that it represented. The discursive character intentionally assigned to this cultural production was a means of gaining control over a collective destiny through the reappropriation of language. Bakhtin describes the significance of such a process in *The Dialogic Imagination:*

> [L]anguage, for the individual consciousness, lies on the borderline between oneself and the other. The word in language is half someone else's. It becomes "one's own" only when the speaker populates it with his intention, his own accent, when he appropriates the word, adapting

it to his own semantic and expressive intention. Prior to this moment of appropriation, the word does not exist in a neutral and impersonal language (it is not, after all, out of a dictionary that a speaker gets his words!), but rather it exists in other people's mouths, in other people's contexts, serving other people's intentions: it is from there that one must take the word, and make it one's own. (Bakhtin 1981, 293–94)

"Taking the word" in the sixties translated into writing Chicano literary histories and critical essays that counteracted the pejorative images and values associated with the cultural production of the Mexican population in the United States. "Taking the word" in the eighties and nineties translates into rewriting not only histories of Chicano literature and criticism, but also the histories of the greater tradition, from the perspective of these and other formerly excluded or partially incorporated sectors. As Raymund Paredes remarked when asked about his preference for Edward Said's *Orientalism*.

Another thing I like about Said's book is the way he recognizes that you cannot talk about minority cultures without a considerable amount of reference to the majority culture; . . . you have to take the majority culture into account. This is a process already familiar to us from studies of American slavery, whether in the United States or Latin America. The slave has to know the master better than the master knows the slave. It seems to me that Chicano writers have always understood American culture very well. They have responded to it with a sensitivity that a lot of Chicano critics haven't noticed. (Interview, June 1987)

Populating critical histories with the intention of the newly discovered sensibilities and expressive modes of national minorities, women, and working-class sectors involves more than just refurbishing linkages obfuscated under the weight of deliberate cultural suppression and/or benign neglect. It also involves exploring how one's word has populated the discourse of others and discovering to what ends it has done so. Viewed from this standpoint, the problematic reception of alternative emergent formations—their omission and qualification as "anthropological" (not "critical") ventures, designated to illuminate "foreign" (not "national") literary cultures—provides ample ground for examining the formal, institutional, and textual strategies and the ideological perspectives that have gone into shaping the greater critical tradition. In this light recent trends in general critical studies would appear to confirm Edward Said's observation that the significant alterations which have swept literary institutions since the decline of New Criticism haven't substantially curbed "the prevailing ideology of even advanced literary criticism," which continues to be "pronouncedly ethnocentric" and "indifferent to everything but the political-social status quo" (1977, 54).

Notwithstanding these ideological choices, and notwithstanding the fact that criticism has been inordinately slow in recognizing and documenting the links between the critical "boom" (the proliferation of European theory in the United States) and the eruption of alternative emergent critical formations, parallels can and should be drawn between them. Both of these movements were symptomatic of the decentering of the Anglo-American literary tradition, insofar as this tradition drew from a moral and spiritual ideal of the English classics; both signified a departure from the orthodoxy and parochialism of New Criticism; and both unwillingly elicited nationalistic responses from mainstream elements, which identified these movements as "foreign" and warned against their adverse effects upon the then consecrated language of criticism.

What distinguished these movements—aside from their most immediate critical influences, perspectives, readership, and geographical affiliations—was the nature of their reception within prominent literary institutions. The transplantation of European critical theory shook the center of the professional critical world, affecting every level of its language, and creating a new set of "star critics" whose work would formulate the new literary canon, ultimately reconstituting what has been termed a "New new criticism."

Although the eruption of national alternative critical formations such as Chicano critical discourse also produced noteworthy critical figures and literary perspectives, their influence has remained largely peripheral to greater critical developments—no doubt as a result of history of cultural suppression and the lack of a solid material infrastructure of artistic production associated with these writings. However, the fact remains that, along with other critical formations of the period, Chicano critical discourse took part in the social thrust, cosmopolitanism, proliferation of new critical journals, renovation of critical discourse, comparative studies, critique of liberal humanism, and speculative spirit—elements which Elizabeth Bruss (1982) links to an "Age of Theory" dating back to the late sixties.

Only a broad-based theoretical perspective, which accommodates the multifarious expressions of critical discourse in its diverse cultural and textual milieus, can do justice to the complex dynamics which have historically engaged emergent critical discourses with larger movements such as the one described above. Only a perception of Chicano critical enterprise as an extensive, dynamic field of symbolic and material practices, which unites diverse intellectual and cultural spheres into historically variable forces and relations of literary production, can begin to unravel the complexities of its existence as a partially incorporated emergent critical formation.

Already the most provocative theoretical works have begun to outline the merits of such "global" or "systemic" visions of criticism, suggesting that these perspectives could, in fact, signal the way toward the return of criticism to its rightful and original public mandate, where it served as purveyor and commentator of a larger social dynamic. Not so long ago, Edward Said, in *The World, the Text, and the Critic*, crystallized this notion upon identifying a fifth form of "secular" criticism which he envisaged would function as a new "critical consciousness" and a "bold interventionary movement," engaging in the political questions of power and authority which involve men and women in contemporary society (1983, 5).

Taking the Word

Chicano criticism, with its particular manner of configuring varied cultural and linguistic traditions, its participation in an expansive constellation of "alternative" and "established" literary institutions, and its dual critical dialogue, provides a viable starting point for laying one of the foundations of such a global cultural vision. Certainly, the popular origins of this criticism, together with its vital links with an informal public sphere and its engagement with such questions as class oppression, sexism, and political domination, confirm its involvement with a "worldly circumstance," as surely as does its recent incorporation of any number of readings or interpretations of social reality communicated through modern literary theory.

With reference to the latter I might add that the indissoluble bonds which link Chicano critical discourse to a greater critical dynamic are not to be limited to the contemporary period, which has seen a narrowing of the intellectual horizons that inform these divergent critical spheres. Since its emergence, the fate of Chicano criticism—its initial consolidation as a counterdiscourse, its erratic development, and its limited incorporation into prominent literary institutions—has been sealed to the modes and patterns of development of the greater literary world. It could, in fact, be argued that the tardy appearance and progressive marginalization of Chicano critical discourse played a central role in the constitution of the dominant literary canon and modes of production as we know them today. This becomes clear when considering that criticism plays an important role in defining social perceptions of what constitutes literature insofar as it selects, processes, and rewrites literary texts, reconstituting the writings of a people into an object as well as a subject of academic inquiry. Without the benefit of a supportive institutionalized body of criticism to promote them in the early years of their existence, it is not surprising that alternative traditions (like Chicano literature) were systematically excluded from this type of literary definition.

As we rapidly move into what proves to be a rich and productive phase in the development of Chicano critical discourse, we will be faced with the substantial challenge of defining the perimeters and objectives of this discourse in ways that would no doubt seem inconceivable to that early generation of Chicano critics, who boldly inaugurated it with their admirable struggles within the institution of literary criticism. Our success in responding to this challenge will depend largely upon our ability to circumvent those strategies of containment that would sever Chicano critical discourse from its multiple determinants and expressions and upon our ability to reconceptualize it within the various domains of its influence, directing it toward the values, practices, and social realities that engendered it. Though formidable, this slanting of criticism toward questions of pedagogy, education, and social and cultural practice promises much in the way of contributing to a second theoretical revolution, where criticism ceases to be a self-contained field or the privileged discourse of an enlightened and culturally dominant few.

Notes

1. In describing critics of Chicano literature, Charles Tatum effects an unfortunate division between "young relatively inexperienced academics who are searching for their own critical approach" and "critics well established in their fields" who are applying their own well-defined approaches. Suffice it to say that youth does not exclude the possibility of expertise in a field or the possibility of possessing a well-defined critical method. Perhaps most serious is Tatum's negligence of the fact that one of the most pressing concerns among critics in recent years has been to find adequate theoretical approaches for the study of Chicano literature (see Tatum 1982, 193).

Barbara Harlow

Sites of Struggle: Immigration, Deportation, Prison, and Exile

I

In her 1977 essay, "The Chicana Labor Force," Rosaura Sánchez presents an analysis of the recent history of Mexican-American working women and examines the consequences of such an analysis for rethinking the interference of issues of race and class in the construction of a women's movement in the United States. The place of Chicana laborers in the field and within the family, followed by their subsequent displacement in the process of urbanization, provokes a further critique of traditional family and kinship structures and the differentials of ethnicity which can be enlisted both in the service of and in resistance to capitalism and patriarchy. Sánchez concludes her analysis of the Chicana labor force, however, by addressing herself to Chicanas in the academy: "It is imperative that those few Chicano women attaining professional status or higher education recognize the low economic status of the majority of Chicano women and identify with their struggle rather than with feminist middle class aspirations, for most of us Chicano women have working class roots" (1977, 14).

The emphasis on class differences within the Chicana constituency, and the attendant need to organize around the issues of working class women, is established in Sánchez's essay on the grounds of "identity," the "working class roots" of "most Chicano women." Chicana feminism in its development over the last decade and through the internal debates it has waged over identity and categories of gender, sexual orientation, race, and class thus becomes exemplary in important ways for the history of the United States women's movement more generally. Not only has it become necessary, that is, to "identify with" other struggles—on an individual or personal level or even on the basis of "roots"—but furthermore to participate actively in identifying those struggles according to political and historical exigencies. The very question of identity is at stake, a question which Chicana writing poses in ultimately urgent ways—for non-Chicanas as well as for Chicanas, for cannery and field workers no less than for academics. Too limited a definition of identity politics only leads, as Jenny Bourne has pointed out, to a "discourse of equal oppressions" (1987, 11). How then is it possible to "identify with" the struggle so that the struggle is itself identified in such a way as to enable collective participation, political participation of the kind that Cornel West has enjoined, in the Afro-American context, as "strategies (as opposed to personal moral duties) of struggle against racism" (1988, 19).

"Immigration, deportation, prison, and exile," each differently, but nonetheless complicitously, indicate what might be called "extradiscursive formations," institutions and mechanisms initiated by state bureaucracies to control the borders of dissent within their territorial domain. As such, they also serve to manipulate a "discourse of boundaries" from within the sites of hegemonic power. The supervision of national borders is part of this "discourse of boundaries," described by Rosaura Sánchez in her 1987 essay, "Ethnicity, Ideology and Academia," the legislation of entry, rights of passage, and expulsion. Nationalism itself legitimizes its position of ideological ascendancy as a cover for more coercive stratagems of power, from the United States Immigration and Naturalization Services (INS) to the university's literary critics who superintend the distinctions of genre and national literatures and discipline their practice. These external borders are again internalized inside the national confines through the state prison itself.

If prisons, deportations, immigration control, and enforced exile indicate a nexus of bureaucratic power and its deployment in the service of the state, functioning as "structural constraints [which] impose limits upon historically constituted agents," they also provide at the same time "conjunctural opportunities [which] can be enacted by these agents" (West 1988, 24). The borders they define and on which they are premised determine sites of struggle and potential social transformation. Prison, deportation, immigration, and exile have in recent decades become central to the contemporary historical experience of much of the world's population. Rampant statistics and the documentation by individuals and organizations which have become almost legend attest to the decisive interference in daily life practiced by systematic state oppression against its various peoples. In Argentina, for example, at least 11,000 people "disappeared" between 1976 and 1983 under the dictatorship of the generals and the army. Approximately 30 percent of the Palestinian population living in Israel or under Israeli occupation in the West Bank and Gaza has passed through the

Israeli prison system.[1] In South Africa some 10,000 individuals, many of them children, were detained since the state of emergency was declared from 1986 until 1991. And there are an estimated 13 million refugees in the world today. According to the Independent Commission on International Humanitarian Issues (1986), 700 people per day have been forced to leave their country over the last thirty years (9). In El Salvador as in Cambodia and elsewhere, the situation of internal exile and displacement characterizes the existence of a large proportion of the country's inhabitants.

Although what is currently known as the "Third World" functions as the primary focus for these figures and data, this same geopolitical category—Third World—can also serve rhetorically to distantiate the self-appointed First World from the political phenomena isolated for attention by such statistics and to obscure further the degree in which they transgress and challenge the protective barriers of national borders. Similar figures are produced as well from within certain neighborhoods, barrios, and ghettos in the United States. The social pattern of systematic oppression and displacement which they reveal exemplifies the daily lives of First World ethnic minorities no less than those of Third World populations. In 1960, for example, 1 out of every 26 African-American men between the ages of twenty-five and thirty-four was in prison on an average day, as compared with 1 out of 163 white men in the same age group (Wright 1973, 31–32). Two and a half decades later, according to a report from the California state attorney general's office, among a group of 240,000 California men, "65.6 percent of the blacks were arrested at least once, compared to 33.9 percent of the whites. Latinos were included with the whites because law enforcement agencies often list them that way" (*Los Angeles Times*, 1 March 1987).

In two stories by Chicana writers, each based on the narrative and political manipulation of a discourse of boundaries, the apotropaic distance granted by the very term "Third World" is strategically collapsed and the political complicity in this data of the dominant ideology is exposed. "The Ditch," written by Rosaura Sánchez and published in 1979, is the story of an INS raid on migrant workers picking in the cotton fields. Alerted to the approach of the officials, the pickers run. The short narrative which tells the tale of their flight toward the ditch and safety contextualizes the personal fate of the illegal aliens from south of the border within the larger historical narrative of United States predations in Vietnam: "He ran fast, head down, stepping on whatever was in his path, be it cocklebur or thorny plants. He saw himself running through the field as others before him had run through rice paddies in Vietnam, as he himself had run when he crossed over the wire fence on the border" (1979, 182). The "illegal aliens'" historical consciousness acknowledges the political duplicity of hegemonic language of nationalism: "It was an often repeated scene. They had only recently set up the radars on the border: it was hardware left over from the Vietnam War" (182). That same consciousness further reveals the agenda of destruction concealed in the duplicity: "Immigration officials were planning to clear the thicket with a little Napalm, left over as well from Vietnam" (183).

Whereas "The Ditch" is premised on the historical continuity between First and Third Worlds concealed in and by United States policy and the complicity of its "domestic" and foreign agendas, thus collapsing the dichotomies from within the system itself, "The Cariboo Cafe" makes the border between the United States and its Central American "neighbors" a site of contestation. In Helena María Viramontes's story from *The Moths and Other Stories* (1985), borders become bonds among peoples, rather than the articulation of national difference and the basis for exclusion enforced by the collaboration of the United States and Salvadoran regimes. Borders, that is, function as a site of confrontation between popular and official interpretations of the historical narrative. "The Cariboo Cafe" is set in an unnamed United States city which numbers Salvadoran refugees amongst its populations. Much as these refugees transgress national boundaries, victims of political persecution who by their very international mobility challenge the ideology of national borders and its agenda of depoliticization in the interest of hegemony, so too the story refuses to respect the boundaries and conventions of literary critical time and space and their disciplining of plot genre. No markers indicate the narrative's breaks and shifts from the United States to El Salvador and history remains to be reconstructed. Implicit in Viramontes's storied narrative, as Sonia Saldívar-Hull points out in her essay in this volume, is a documentary critique not only of the U.S. INS and the Salvadoran semiofficial paramilitary death squads, but of their active collaboration as well. The story of the Salvadoran woman refugee, expelled from her country when her son is abducted, and the Chicano children, locked out of their home when they lose the key, thus enjoins an historical awareness and a political reading on the part of its audience no less than from its characters. It proposes too another historical narrative. Restructuring the traditional family order, "The Cariboo Cafe" assigns to women the task of a reformulation across borders of gender and race and insists on their place in the construction of identity and political struggle.

Stories such as "The Ditch" or "The Cariboo Cafe," like Sánchez's critical essays "The Chicana Labor Force" and "Ethnicity, Ideology and Academia," or the international reports of nongovernmental human rights agencies, collectively challenge on the discursive level, irrespective of genre distinctions, the arbitrary deployment of boundaries, both as practiced by the United States government and as professed from within the academy. Area studies programs and departments of national literatures discover their extracurricular analogues in the state bureaucracy which closes its internal borders as readily as it allows for a calculated permeability of its external boundaries. On 29 October 1986, for example, the U.S. Bureau of Prisons opened at the cost of some several millions of dollars a maximum security prison for women in Lexington, Kentucky. Designed to house sixteen inmates, the facility until recently contained only two detainees, Alejandrina Torres, a Puerto Rican nationalist, and Susan Rosenberg, a "self-proclaimed revolutionary" from New York City, both confined under extremely brutal conditions deemed by Amnesty International as constituting "cruel and unusual punishment" (*Nation*, 27 June 1987).[2] Less than a year later, in July 1987, death squads from El Salvador extended their sphere of activity into the United States, to the streets of Los Angeles when three Central American women were abducted, tortured, and then returned to the street badly beaten, as a "message" to them and their supporters (*NACLA*, 21, 3, 1987). The ultimate intended effect of such a "message" and the dominant discourse of boundaries and border defenses which it bespeaks is to disenfranchise the political for the sake of the national patriotic.

The writings of "Third World women" participant in the political arena challenge that message and the discourse of boundaries which underwrites the construction of domestic prisons and the practices of foreign death squads. The politics of place are problematized in these writings and their analysis in turn allows for an immanent reading of the "conjunctural opportunities" contained in these spaces.

In the following sections I will briefly examine a not altogether random selection of texts from across the geopolitical divide of First and Third Worlds, texts which elicit the collective cultural habits of survival and resistance as these have developed among social groups growing up under conditions of political oppression and dispossession. Implicit in this examination will be the further question of how the United States academy, as a political institution, can respond to the conditions which have generated this oppression, respond, however, without falling into what Armand Mattelart has aptly criticized as "ethnocentric cosmopolitanism" (1986, 7).

II

Sahar Khalifeh is a Palestinian woman novelist from the Occupied West Bank (currently completing her doctoral work in American Studies at the

University of Iowa).³ Her second novel, *Wild Thorns* (1985), published in Arabic in 1976, engages the problem of intersecting and competing borders, both territorial and ideological, which interrupt the contemporary situation of Palestinians living under Israeli occupation in Gaza and the West Bank since the June war of 1967 when these territories were captured by Israel from Egypt and Jordan. A "green line," recognized internationally but effaced, for example, on maps distributed by Israel's tourism industry, separates the state of Israel from the territories which it has occupied militarily for over twenty years. These Occupied Territories, the setting for *Wild Thorns*, delineate a liminal geopolitical space, created by historical circumstances and contested by multiple parties with divergent political agendas. The most significant opposition remains that between the state of Israel and the Palestinian people, but equally dramatic, and critical to Khalifeh's novel, are the divisions amongst the Palestinians themselves. Such divisions are created by borders, between those living in exile, or *manfā*, and those living under occupation (*taht al-ihtilāl*), or again under occupation, between those who live in Israel proper and those living in occupied Gaza and the West Bank. But the divisions are produced by economic differentials as well, as indicated in the novel in a conversation among passengers in a service taxi: what is the difference, after all, they argue, between working "inside" or "outside," in the Arab Gulf states or in Israel, since wealthy Palestinians and Arabs are no less guilty than Israeli employers of class exploitation. Within this contested space which functions as the setting of the novel, a Palestinian *feda'i*, a commando from the resistance organization in Jordan, has been sent to sabotage the system of economic co-optation between Israel and the Palestinian work force by blowing up the buses which transport Palestinian day laborers from the Occupied Territories to the factories and construction sites on the other side of the Green Line.

If *Wild Thorns* is premised on a history of territorial occupations and settler colonialism, the force of the novel's plot is to disrupt the Western historical narrative organized according to a model of linear stages of progressive development and the cultural synchronicity which such a model entails. By locating prisons and factories as primary sites of confrontation, *Wild Thorns* challenges not only the Zionist program of Israel but the romantic idealism of Palestinian cultural symbolism and its focus on land and peasant. The feudal estate lies untended in the novel, its patriarch surviving only with the aid of a kidney dialysis machine and ignorant of the fact that his eldest son travels daily across the "border" as a worker in Israeli factories. In the prison, meanwhile, young Basil, arrested for hurling epithets at Israeli soldiers on patrol, attains symbolic manhood and Zuhdi learns the significance of solidarity and collective endeavor. The Israeli factories, by contrast, are scenes of violence and strife provoked by ethnic and racial contentions fostered by the state's discriminatory labor policy which divides Israeli and Palestinian workers amongst themselves. Adil, however, the landowner's proletarianized son, who seeks indemnification for his coworker and compatriot who has lost his hand in a work accident, emerges as a proto-trade union organizer.

The country/city dichotomy, based like the rhetorical division between First and Third Worlds on an unreflected idealism and exploitative nostalgia as models of development and underdevelopment, is collapsed in *Wild Thorns*, thus requiring another explanation of historical exigencies, one which would involve what Cornel West has called an "explanatory commitment" invested in an "emancipatory vision of the future" (1988, 25). In the end Usama (the commando) and Zuhdi (from the workers' buses) are killed in the attempt to explode the process of the proletarianization of the Palestinian peasantry. Buses then, which traverse the space between rural and urban, like prisons and factories, situate new forms of struggle and immanent historical change through organized resistance. In Luz Garzón's story, "Going for a Ride" (1979), the INS buses "repatriate" illegal Mexican aliens. But in *One Day of Life* (1983), by the Salvadoran writer Manlio Argueta, the buses which carry peasants to demonstrate in the capital city are attacked by government forces and their passengers assassinated. *Cuzcatlán* (1987), a sequel to *One Day of Life*, opens in turn with Beatriz, nicknamed Ticha, a partisan in the Salvadoran resistance, reflecting to herself as she rides the microbus to San Salvador, "if the [North American] advisers knew our history, would they still treat us the same? I don't know. Besides, our history is sad and boring. Maybe they're not interested in hearing about it. We're interested, though, because it gives us strength. It teaches us to survive. We've learned how to survive. That's why I use an alias" (1987, 5).

The current debate over the "proletarianization of the peasantry," which informs Sahar Khalifeh's novel *Wild Thorns* and which critically determined Rosaura Sánchez's analysis of "the Chicana labor force," is a debate which focuses on class issues and eschews finally a strict nationalist position, whether on the part of dominant institutions or as an ideology of resistance. It raises too the question of the "task of the intellectual" and the class position of an intellectual partisan within the opposition. The problem, however, becomes again more complicated when the class relationship of the woman is at stake and more urgent still when her role within the resistance movements which have emerged out of traditionally patriarchal social orders is examined. How, that is, beyond "identity," does the university-educated Chicana "identify" with "the struggle of the Chicana labor force"? Or how does the Western academic, more generally, participate in Third World forms of resistance? In *Wild Thorns* the role of Palestinian women in the opposition remains unspoken, tacit: a female fellow passenger, her arm in a plaster cast, in the service taxi which takes Usama into the Occupied Territories to carry out his mission is shortly afterward observed in Nablus with her arm finally exposed to view and no evidence as to its erstwhile sheath. The other women, more prominent in the novel, remain to varying degrees confined by tradition: Um Usama, the *feda'i*'s mother, consigns her fate to Allah, and Niwar, a university student, refuses to defy openly her infirm father's wishes. Her engagement to an imprisoned comrade from the resistance is in the end revealed by her younger brother.

III

The decades from the fifties to the seventies have been described as the era of national liberation, an era which culminated in the national independence of most formerly colonized territories. This epoch has given way now to variant forms of neocolonialism or neoimperialism, of cultural, economic, and political dependency, which have replaced the classic versions of territorial imperialism from the nineteenth and early twentieth centuries. Two ongoing national liberation struggles continue, however, still unresolved, as if "left over" from the decades of "high" national liberation: Palestine and South Africa. Are these resistance movements, therefore, avatars, atavistic anachronisms, remnants of a past abandoned by historical developments? Or has their own development in response to changing historical conditions so proceeded as to enable perhaps a renewed "emancipatory vision of the future," one which ultimately intersects with the immanent agendas of liberation within the Chicana/o context, for example, as well as with the programs of other "Third World" population groups located under First World territorial dominion? These movements provide new critical possibilities for a rethinking of traditional nationalism and its attendant discourse of boundaries, as well as strategic means for intervening in the broader debate over the conflicted relationship between the First and the Third Worlds. Together with nationalism, this dichotomous, even separatist, relationship demands now a historical reformulation.

According to George Katsiaficas, for example, "Because the extreme economic, political and social problems of the Third World demand radical solutions, it is in the underdeveloped countries that revolutionary movements today are most viable. As in 1968, social movements in the industrialized societies will continue to be motivated by international dynamics, but the differing material conditions of existence which define the core and the periphery of the world system make the organizational models of Third World movements highly problematic for social movements in the capitalist metropoles" (1987, 207). Among these conditions Katsiaficas cites "different immediate aims: decentralization of increasingly powerful centers versus national consolidation of power in the face of international imperialism" and "different primary contradictions: technological and economic overdevelopment and political/cultural overdevelopment versus economic underdevelopment and intense class struggles/cultural awakening" (207). While acknowledging the urgent significance of organized resistance in the Third World, as well as the historical specificity of these different movements, Katsiaficas's analysis reasserts once again the binarism of First World/Third World relationships and with it the primacy of place conventionally assigned to the First World. The borders remain still unassailed, and the political potential of the question, "What does the First World have to learn from the Third World?", remains unanswered. The "border problems" which traverse Chicana and other Third World women's writings begin to suggest the important strategic possibilities inherent in such a question for a reconsideration of nationalism and a critique of various forms of fundamentalism.

Black Gold is a study of Mozambican migrant workers in the mines of South Africa, published in 1983 under the name of Ruth First, a white South African woman active in the ANC and the South African Communist party in the sixties. A journalist and a historian of Africa as well, Ruth First was arrested during the Rivonia raids on the ANC in 1963 in South Africa and sentenced under the Ninety Day Detention Law. Her prison memoir, 117 Days, takes its title from this law which allowed for automatic renewal at the discretion of the authorities of the detention period. Eventually, following various banning orders and restrictions on her work, and later a period in England where she coauthored a biography of Olive Schreiner with Ann Scott, First went into exile in Mozambique. Her activities as a researcher at Eduardo Mondlane University in Maputo came to an end when she was assassinated by a parcel bomb in 1982. At Mondlane University she had been part of a large research collective studying migrant labor patterns in the countries of southern Africa and their effects on historical transformations in the indigenous social structures. The volume entitled Black Gold was part of that collaborative research effort and combines historical background and sociological analysis of the "proletarianization of the peasantry," interviews with miners and their families, and work songs composed and sung by male migrants in the mines as well as by those men, women, and children who remained behind.

Black Gold was published posthumously in the year following Ruth

First's death, posthumously, that is, only if one considers the function of "author" according to the most limited definition of the word, as referring to the personal identity of the authorial individual. The contribution of *Black Gold*, however, to a reconstruction of political strategy and the ideology of literary critical practice is manifold and includes an implicit critique of authorship and the "task of the intellectual" in the resistance struggle. The reformulation of genre, together with its textual analysis of class and race in the migrant labor movement, which confute "nationalism" as an enabling paradigm, are reiterated on a sociopolitical level over the issue of authorial identity. The very circumstances of "exile" which condition First's participation in the research require a particular construction of nationalism and departure from it. Unlike her compatriot Nadine Gordimer for whom exile from South Africa is construed, in her novel *Burger's Daughter*, as escape to Europe or as an existential flight in the case of Maureen Smales's headlong plunge at the end of *July's People*, Ruth First would seem to have reworked exile imposed by the South African state as continued participation in the popular history of African resistance. Ruth First's biographical narrative intersects with the labor history of the migrant worker, and *Black Gold* can be read critically as an active, indeed committed, conflation of the two modes, otherwise separated by disciplinary strictures and a cult of individual authorship. If *Black Gold* is read as the autobiography of the partisan intellectual subject in which a personal itinerary is assimilated into a larger historical narrative of resistance and struggle, then First's own exile becomes crucial as part of the means to the narration of the history of the migrant workers. Her political task as an intellectual is subsumed by the cooperative research project in which the laborers themselves acquire authorial voices and historical agency. The issues of authorial identity and the work of the intellectual are reconstituted across national borders. Ruth First's identification with the resistance movement thus allows as well for an identification of the resistance movement within an expanded emancipatory agenda.

The same interplay and continuity of authorial identity and sociopolitical critique are rearticulated again, albeit differently too as informed from within the First World territorial context in and against which she writes, by the Chicana writer Gloria Anzaldúa in her self-critical autobiography *Borderlands/La Frontera* (1987). Whereas *Black Gold* displaces the author's persona and relocates it within the problematic of migrant labor in southern Africa, *Borderlands/La Frontera* foregrounds the issue of the personal identity of the subject and complicates it by an analysis of the mythic and historic elements which have contributed to its constitution: the legacies of Aztec civilization and Spanish culture, a *mestizo* heritage and the recent past of legal and illegal Mexican-American immigration across the United States borders, and women's traditions of compliance with the opposition to the machismo-sanctioned practices of their men. That already complex identity is fragmented further in the bilingual, even trilingual, multigeneric textual composition which disarticulates Anzaldúa's expression—at once intimate and scholarly. The academically footnoted autobiographical narrative of the first half of the book, with its combined sense of fabled past and political present, gives way in the second part to a more lyrical disquisition on the contradictions of class and race as these are implicated in questions of gender and sexual identity.

The collection of poems is in Spanish and English, some (but not all, thus enjoining not only a historical consciousness but a linguistic responsibility from the reader) in both their Spanish and English versions, while still others combine both languages in challenging even a coherent linguistic identity. The poems are further sequenced critically to move along a personal trajectory, from childhood's sense of fullness and loss to the painful rewards of women's homosexual love. That personal axis is embedded in the historical itinerary of development and the passage from field to city which charts the narrative of a "proletarianization of the peasantry." Central to this fragmented developmental process are two poems which speak to the emergent historical consciousness of their narrators and the ways in which that historicity both interrupts a prelapsarian sense of self and posits the conditions for its historical reconstruction under political pressures. Each of these poems further elicits the issue, already posed in "The Chicana Labor Force" and elaborated by Ruth First, of the "identification" of the educated Chicana with "the struggle of the majority of Chicano women."

> I left and have been gone a long time
> I keep leaving and when I am home
> they remember no one but me had ever left.
> I listen to the *grillos* more intently
> Than I do their *regaño.*
> I have more languages than they,
> am aware of every root of my *pueblo;*
> they, my people, are not
> They are the living, sleeping roots.
> (1987, 113)

Again, in a critical change of person, the narrator observes, of herself:

> If she hadn't read all those books
> She'd be singing up and down the rows
> like all the rest.
> (1987, 117)

Is it that books and their writing intervene/interrupt/inhibit the identification of the woman intellectual with the resistance, the class struggle, the struggle against racism, the independence movement? "The insider-outsider dilemma," according to Patricia Zavella who did anthropological fieldwork among Chicana cannery workers in California's Santa Clara Valley, "is still salient for minority researchers doing fieldwork in minority communities" (1987, 20–21).

IV

The fields upon fields of rows up and down which Gloria Anzaldúa, privileged now by her learning, no longer moves, have become proletarianized as factory assembly lines for the cannery workers, in whose midst Patricia Zavella carried out her academic study, and for the women too of northern Mexico who are employed in the *maquiladoras* on the southern side of the United States-Mexican border; the story of the latter is told by María Patricia Fernández-Kelly in *For We Are Sold, I and My People* (1983). In Judy Lucero's prison poem, "Jail-Life Walk (1980)," these rows are in turn made part of the "politics of punishment." The poem, signed like all of her writing by the poet-detainee's prison identification number, uses ellipses and the letter "U" to transform the sense of self in a struggle against the coercive machinery of the prison apparatus:

> Walk til you . . . See the sign
> Look at the sign . . . Walk in line
>
> [. . .]
> The only thing free
> is your mind
> Free to count
> As U walk in line.
> #21918

The reconstruction of identity practiced in Lucero's poetry from prison is located in topography and the neighborhood in Sandra Cisneros's volume, at once novel and collection of prose poems, *The House on Mango Street* (1988). The disassembled narrative is premised on the alienation between the young girl's emergent sense of a socially conditioned self and the new neighborhood where the Mango Street house has failed to actualize the child's aspirations of status and comfort raised by the promise of "moving," a promise which is critical to the inherently political ideology of the "American dream." That ideology is subjected in Cisneros's book to a radical critique when the flawed discrepancies are realized in the anecdotes and stories which follow, stories which recount the short histories of the neighborhood's inhabitants embedded in the longer history of Hispanic immigration, relocation and political displacement in the United States. In *The House on Mango Street*, alienation becomes a border problem: the isolated women who sit daily, routinely, at their window sills are as much of a piece with the neighborhood as "Geraldo No Last Name," the illegal immigrant who refuses to identify himself against the threats of the INS.

The internal borders which disrupt the Mango Street neighborhood and redefine its characters are reproduced by the cordon principle of immigrant and ethnic neighborhoods in the major cities of the United States where urban planners provide the blueprints for the dominant discourse of boundaries. According to the labor historian Mike Davis, such designs, from skyscrapers and Hyatt Regency hotels to the freeways, are indicative of the "decisive role of urban counter-insurgency in defining the essential terms of the contemporary built environment" (1985, 113). These hegemonic urban plans, in containing the ghettos and the barrios and their "Third World populations," serve also to sabotage their internal coherence and historical continuity. Helena María Viramontes's story "Neighbors" (1985) narrates the deterioration of community in the life history of one Aura Rodríguez:

> Aura Rodríguez always stayed within her perimeters, both personal and otherwise, and expected the same of her neighbors. . . . People of her age died off only to leave their grandchildren with little knowledge of the struggle [. . .] Like those who barricaded themselves against an incomprehensible generation, Aura had resigned herself to live with the caution and silence of an apparition [. . .] without hurting anyone, including herself. (1985, 102)

The revisionary rebuilding of such neighborhoods is part of the larger task of a counter-hegemonic ideological production. The "structural constraints" force as well "conjunctural opportunities," as when the neighborhoods of the past are reconstructed in the prisoners' movement, in the Chicano movement and in Raúl Salinas's 1969 prison poem from Leavenworth penitentiary, "Un Trip through the Mind Jail."

LA LOMA
Neighborhood of my youth
demolished, erased forever from
the universe.
You live on, captive, in the lonely
cellblocks of my mind.
(1980, 55)

The relationship of the prison system to its inmates, and the connection between the inmates and the sociopolitical world outside is exemplary of the need to politicize the "discourse of boundaries." Erik Olin Wright studied the United States prison system from within through ministry work with prisoners in the early seventies, particularly with reference to the ethnic populations and "political prisoners" it incarcerated. According to Wright, "in certain situations, the relationship of crime to political decisions is very direct [. . . but even] broadly speaking, the pattern of crime in America is a product of the basic political choice to maintain the existing structure of wealth and power in this society" (1973, 4). The calculated distinction between criminal offenses and political activities is one that is manipulated by the dominant ideology precisely in order to maintain its control over the borders of dissent. As Lorri Martínez writes in her collection of prison poetry, *Where Eagles Fall*,

> Remember—technically.
> I'm doing time
> because I used to be
> a drug addict.
> (1982, n.p.)

That punctuated technicality is decisive to the hegemonic discourse of depoliticization and its legislation of the "extradiscursive formations" of coercion of its disposal. It is a technicality which the prison counterculture exposes as illusory and ideologically overdetermined. As Judy Lucero writes in "I Speak in an Illusion," "the bonds are real" (1980, 396).

Even the critique of the prison system, however, is subjected to the consent of that same prison system and its apparent insistence on a language of authority and objective responsibility requiring a complicit compromise from the would-be researcher and attempting a usurpation of his/her own project. Thus, R. Theodore Davidson, who investigated social formations and networks amongst Chicano prisoners in San Quentin, introduces his study with an explanation of his own situation within that system: "Prison administrators realized the delicate nature of the information I would probably encounter if I were to accomplish my task, so it was agreed that I would not have to reveal any confidential information to the staff. The only exception would have been if I had learned that someone was going to be physically harmed or that the prisoners were going to destroy the prison in some manner" (1974, 1). This "only exception," however, is twofold, and the requirements of the prison administration and the unitary language serve only to conceal a concern for the stability of the prison system itself ("destroy the prison in some manner") under an ostensibly humanitarian sensitivity for the safety and well-being of the anonymous prisoners ("someone was going to be physically harmed").

In the introduction to the collection of essays entitled *Women and Political Conflict*, Rosemary Ridd describes what she calls a "counterweight to this privileged insider[/outsider] view" (1987, 10). This counterweight is the "particular responsibility the writer has to the community she studies and to her informants who may risk much danger in sharing information with her. Sensitivity to this danger then calls for some commitment to the community on the part of the writer and, in many cases, makes it unfeasible and inappropriate for her to become involved with people on more than one side in an issue." (10) The insider/outsider contradiction is not an academic question, nor a scholarly dilemma over scientific objectivity or neutrality. "Identification with" is not a "personal moral duty," but a political choice. What these writers, Chicana, Palestinian, and South African, writing from "inside the struggle," discover through their writings is that borders and the discourse of boundaries that patrols them are designed as part of hegemony's self-interest in maintaining its border controls intact. It is these border controls, which govern national boundaries and university disciplines alike, that must be dismantled. An "identification with" the struggle requires other strategies in the identification of the struggle, strategies suggested by these writers. As Rosaura Sánchez puts it, in her essay "Ethnicity, Ideology and Academia," "all that is inside is not center" (1987, 82).

Notes

1. This number has increased significantly since the beginning of the intifada in December 1987.

2. The Lexington facility was closed in August 1988 in response to national and international pressure.

3. Having completed her degree, Sahar Khalifeh has returned to the West Bank.

Part IV

Aesthetics

of the

Border

José David Saldívar

Chicano Border Narratives as Cultural Critique

"Culture" is always relational, . . . between subjects in relations of power. . . . Culture is contested, temporal, and emergent.—James Clifford, Writing Culture *(1986)*

In this essay I want to examine the cultural conversation in and around Chicano border narratives, paying particular attention to the political and ideological rhetoric of the text and the way its arguments relate both to the larger institutional quarrels of the forties, fifties, and sixties in south Texas and to academic discussions of the American canon in the eighties. My study locates Chicano border narratives within the debates over white supremacy[1] in Texas and the Southwest, when these texts were first published.

At the outset let me emphasize that literature's relationship to ideology, institutional practices, and cultural critique is quite complex. But as Steven Mailloux suggests in a recent study of Mark Twain's *Huckleberry Finn*, a text "can be a topic in the cultural conversation, or it can be a participant who is motivated by and has effects on the conversation. As a participant, a literary text can take up the ideological rhetoric of its historical moment—the rhetoric of political speeches, newspaper editorials, book reviews, scholarly treatises, and so forth—and place it on a fictional stage. Readers thus become spectators at a rhetorical performance" (1985, 108). With Mailloux's ideas of the cultural conversation and the rhetoric of the text as performed ideology in mind, we can turn to some of the staged arguments in contemporary Chicano border narratives. Specifically, I argue that there has been in south Texas between 1958 and 1987 a unique Chicano intellectual and artistic response to the white supremacist scholarship of the thirties and forties by Walter Prescott Webb and his followers. Increasingly in the years after 1958, the "official" white supremacist tradition of Walter Prescott Webb in Texas was progressively demystified and negated by Américo Paredes, Tomás Rivera, and Rolando Hinojosa, among others.

Ideological Rhetoric in Texas

[Mexicans are] vaguely considered as degenerate and degraded Spaniards; it is at least, equally correct to think of them as improved and Christianized Indians. In their tastes and social instincts, they approximate the African. The difference between them and the Negro is smaller, and is less felt, I believe, than that between the northern and southern European races.—Frederick Law Olmsted, Journey Through Texas: Or a Saddle-Trip on the Southwestern Frontier, *1857*

I thought I could shoot Mexicans as well as I could shoot Indians, or deer, or turkey; and so I rode away to war.—Creed Taylor, reminiscing about his role in the struggle between Texas and Mexico

Then the Rangers rode onto the field of San Jacinto where the Mexicans lay dead in piles. Smithwick said the buzzards and coyotes gathered to the feast, eating the horses but refusing the Mexicans because of their peppery skins.— Walter Prescott Webb, The Texas Rangers *(1935)*

Ask the Apache the why of his going.
Ask the Comanche, he's not knowing;
Question the Mexican thief and marauder
Why his respect for the great Texas border;
Question them all, these beaten-back strangers.
White-lipped they'll tremble and whisper, 'The Rangers!'—Albert Edmund Trombly, "Texas Rangers"

Then said Gregorio Cortez. With his pistol in his hand. Ah, so many mounted Rangers / Just to take one Mexican.—"El Corrido de Gregorio Cortez"

[There were many] 'rocky times' in Texas between Texicans and Mexicans.— J. Frank Dobie, A Vaquero of the Brush Country *(1929)*

Américo Paredes's *"With His Pistol in His Hand": A Border Ballad and Its Hero* appeared in 1958 in the midst of a long, heated political quarrel over what U. S. historian Walter Prescott Webb, among others, had to say about Mexicans in the United States. By the end of the nineteenth century the ideological rhetoric of white supremacy dominated southern and southwestern politics and eventually became institutionalized in state discourses, laws, and narratives regulating relations by whites and nonwhites, especially African-Americans and Chicanos. As we know, Walter Prescott Webb was one of the leading spokespersons of the institutionalized racism of this period. As one of his close friends, Necah Furman, said, Walter Prescott Webb "subconsciously . . . had the Alamo-Texas Ranger chauvinistic myth deeply engraved" (1983, 35). Throughout Webb's book, *The Texas Rangers: A Century of Frontier Defense* (1935), for example, he characterized Mexicans in the following manner: "Without disparagement, there is a cruel streak in the Mexican nature, or so the history would lead to believe. This cruelty may be a heritage from the Spanish of the Inquisition; it may, and doubtless should, be attributed partly to the Indian blood" (1935, 14).

Although Walter Prescott Webb had proposed the integration of African-Americans into the Texas State Historical Association, he, like other native white supremacists in Texas, had a profound prejudice against Mexicans on both sides of the border. Sentences like the one I quoted above in *The Texas Rangers* illustrate Webb's regional stereotyping of Mexicans. To understand the cultural conversation in Texas more fully, then, it is important to examine Webb's institutional study of the Texas Rangers.

When, in 1918, Walter Prescott Webb joined the history department's faculty at the University of Texas at Austin, he began doing scholarly research on the institution of the Rangers, which culminated in his master's thesis on the Texas Rangers. Years later, in 1935, he published his institutional history of the Rangers with an East Coast press (Houghton Mifflin) in Cambridge, Massachusetts. Almost overnight Webb's study of the Texas Rangers became, in the words of Necah Furman, "acknowledged as the definitive study on this frontier law enforcement agency" (1983, 33).

With a southern white supremacist orientation, Webb traced the changing functions of the Texas Rangers, from the "heroic" roles they played in frontier and border communities in the 1830s to their institutional reorganization in 1935, when a Texas-Mexican state representative, J. T. Canales, from Brownsville, led an investigation of the Texas Rangers' abuse of power as "peace officers" (see Webb 1935, 513–16).

Although Webb's "objective" and "disinterested" institutional history of the Texas Rangers was filled, in the author's own words, "with deadening facts," *The Texas Rangers* soon became a popular academic best seller. Webb's description of the Rangers as "very quiet, deliberate gentle person[s]" (ix) became so popular in fact that Paramount Pictures purchased the film rights for $11,000, a fee that undoubtedly made Professor Webb's depression days at the University of Texas at Austin easier to bear. Paramount Pictures, it must be emphasized, made a Western out of Webb's study, even using Webb's original title. *The Texas Rangers*, the movie, ninety-five minutes in length, was directed by King Vidor who also had directed such classics as *Billy the Kid*. Fred MacMurray, Jack Oakie, Lloyd Nolan, and Elena Martinez were the featured stars. Not surprisingly, this movie was made in association with the state's centennial celebration. A mediocre sequel, *The Texas Rangers Ride Again*, was issued in 1940 with John Howard and Ellen Drew. The 1936 original was remade as *Streets of Laredo* in 1949, with William Holden, MacDonald Carey, and William Bendix in starring roles. Unfortunately, the racial strife that existed between Mexicans and the Texas Rangers was characteristically absent in both Webb's and Hollywood's dashing and daring portrayal of the Texas Rangers. To understand the underside of Texas Ranger history in more detail, I believe we need to examine the cultural work of Américo Paredes, Tomás Rivera, and Rolando Hinojosa as socially symbolic responses to Walter Prescott Webb.

Into this institutional and rhetorical context came the oppositional voice of Américo Paredes, a Texas-Mexican, from south Texas, the son of a revolutionary father who "rode a raid or two with Catarino Garza" (1958, 136). By the thirties Paredes was a superb singer of *corridos*, or ballads, and an accomplished composer and guitarist. He had even performed with Chelo Silva, the well-known Texas-Mexican vocalist. During World War II Paredes became a political editor for the U. S. Army's *Stars and Stripes*, its institutional daily. After the war he returned to Texas, and he entered the University of Texas at Austin—coincidentally, Walter Prescott Webb's home turf. According to José Limón, one of Paredes's brilliant students, "By taking course overloads and summer school, [Paredes] compressed two years of college work into one and took his B. A. in 1951 with highest honors. . . . Then, for Américo Paredes anyway, it was quite simply a matter of five years for a master's degree and a Ph.D. in English" (1980, 4). In 1957 Paredes joined the English Department at the University of Texas at Austin, and by the end of that year the University of Texas Press accepted his doctoral dissertation for publication. It would have been controversial enough if Paredes's *"With His Pistol in His Hand"* had been written by an Anglo-American northerner, but a book taking on Walter Prescott Webb and the Texas Rangers, written in the Southwest by a Chicano, with its polemical argument, its deconstruction of established authority and hierarchies, was almost unthinkable.

Paredes begins his narrative of Gregorio Cortez, a border vaquero of the early 1900s who resisted legal "Texas" justice, fought the Texas Rangers, and became a folk hero for the Texas-Mexican community, by giving the reader a lengthy chapter on the border culture and aesthetics of south Texas. In the words of Teresa McKenna, Paredes here "gives an encompassing view of an area which geographically, as well as politically and culturally, stands as figure and metaphor for the transition between nations and the complex of connections which continue to exist for all Mexicans whether border residents or not" (McKenna, forthcoming). Moreover, for our purposes,

Paredes begins in this chapter to give us, in thick detail, a critique of southern white supremacist ideology: he claims that "the English speaking Texan . . . disappoints us in a folkloric sense. He produces no balladry. His contribution to the literature of the border conflict is a set of attitudes and beliefs about the Mexican which form a legend of their own and are the complement to the *corrido*, the Border-Mexican ballad of border conflict" (15).

Paredes then goes on to analyze the "set of attitudes and beliefs about the Mexican which form a legend"—in other words, the ideology of Texan white supremacy which perpetuates the power of the ruling races by defining Mexicans as "cruel," "cowardly," "inferior," "passive," "mongrel," and "treacherous" (16). This ideological definition of the Mexican allows Texas Anglos thus to justify their abridgment of the Chicano's liberties. According to Paredes, however, this invidious, crude, and humiliating view of the Mexican is found not in folk tales of the people of Texas, but in nonfolk origins: "It is in print—in newspapers, magazines, and books" (16).

Into the highly charged and polarized argument about Mexicans, thus came Paredes's more explicit debate with Walter Prescott Webb. By choosing to analyze "El corrido de Gregorio Cortez," a border ballad of resistance, Paredes critiqued Webb's romanticized and ideological reading of the Texas Rangers. For to investigate the *corrido*'s rhetoric, according to Paredes, is to unfold its complicated critique of white supremacy as ideological performance. And by staging rhetorical exchanges and debates with Webb—in his story of Gregorio Cortez—Paredes maneuvered his audience to cooperate with him in his narrative performance. As we retrace the progression of some of Paredes's strategies, we will follow the reader of *"With His Pistol in His Hand"* through a series of reading events that encourages him or her to take a stance on the rhetorical attitudes invoked and ultimately on a society's ideological politics.

Paredes's debate with Webb begins in the following manner: "In more recent years," he writes, "it has often been the writer of history textbooks and the author of scholarly works who have lent their prestige to the legend [about Mexicans]" (17). He then counters Webb's proposition about Mexicans in *The Texas Rangers* ("there is a cruel streak in the Mexican nature") by noting, in an ironic mode, that: "One wonders what [Webb's] opinion might have been when he was in a less scholarly mood and not looking at the Mexican from the objective point of view of the historian" (17). The irony, of course, is that what Paredes here denies playfully about Webb's "objective point of view" as historian, Webb affirmed in action and deeds.

Not surprisingly, then, the ideological drama of Paredes's *"With His Pistol in His Hand"* relies for much of its persuasive success on the author's irreverent sense of humor and irony. This tropic irony is perhaps the most visible part of Paredes's more general attack on social authority in Texas, an attack that Paredes carries out through a relentless questioning of rhetorical authorities that serve ideologically dubious ends. As he says about the voluminous books written about the Texas Rangers, Paredes's cultural critique is often humorous: "If all the books written about the Rangers were put on top of the other, the resulting pile would be almost as tall as some of the tales they contain" (23).

The historical and biographical information contained in the first part of *"With His Pistol in His Hand"* is meant as a tonic for those readers, like Paredes, for whom the objective historian's, Webb's, and also Hollywood's portrayal of the Texas Rangers had for so long been anything but "objective," neutral, or scholarly impartial. "The shoot-first and ask questions later method of the Rangers," Paredes writes, "has been romanticized into something dashing and daring, in technicolor, on a wide screen, and with Gary Cooper in the title role" (28).

After weaving several elements into his critique of Texan white supremacist ideology into his narrative—the history of Nuevo Santander, the aesthetics of the border, the *corrido,* and its folkways—Paredes then turns to the rhetorical analysis of "El corrido de Gregorio Cortez." Part II of *"With His Pistol in His Hand"* concentrates on the many versions of the *corrido* of border conflict and on a close reading of the *corrido* proper. In the course of his dialectical reading of form and content, of the *corrido,* Paredes established the following crucial points about the border ballad's ideological form and content: (1) the *corrido* is a multifaceted discourse, with reflexive, narrative, and rhetorical-propositional elements; (2) *corridos* as social texts tend to be historical and personal; and (3) *corridos* make assertions which derive from the collective outlook and experience of the Mexican ballad community on the border.[2] Finally, of course, as a trained composer, guitarist, and singer, himself, Paredes saw the *corrido* as what it patently was: a unit of musical sound—a performance-oriented genre sung mostly by men, but also, occasionally, by women.

But it must be emphasized: Paredes was no mere formalist. He interpreted the *corrido* as a literary form of resistance to the encroachment of Anglo-Americans. As a socially symbolic act, Paredes argued that the *corrido* usually recounted the exploits of a hero who surpasses all odds to prevail against those in power with dignity, grace, and courage. Specifically, in the example of "El corrido de Gregorio Cortez," Paredes analyzed how the hero, Cortez, who was falsely accused of horse stealing and murdering Sheriffs Morris and Glover, outran and outsmarted a wild, whirling posse of Texas Rangers over half the state of Texas. Briefly stated, Paredes, in overturning the passive view of the Chicano, recounted how common Mexicans defended their border communities and families through confrontations with the Anglo-American ruling class and their state oppressors—the Texas Rangers. As the *corrido* asserts of Gregorio Cortez (which I often heard as a young boy in Brownsville, Texas), Cortez was exemplary of those who defended his or her rights, "con la pistola en la mano"—"with his pistol in his hand." Paredes's *"With His Pistol in His Hand": A Border Ballad and Its Hero* thus was the first sophisticated Chicano narrative to begin to overturn established authority in Texas and the Southwest. Paredes showed how the *corrido* itself broke down white supremacist hierarchies: the "gentle," brave men of Texas, the Rangers, were, in fact, cowardly and foolish ("All the rangers of the county / Were flying, they rode so hard" . . . "But trying to catch Cortez / Was like following a star") (Paredes 1976, 64–67); a "macho" Major Sheriff screams out to Cortez "as if he was going to cry." The inferior slave, Cortez turns out to be superior to his Anglo masters: "Then said Gregorio Cortez, With his pistol in his hand, / Ah, so many mounted Rangers / Just to take one Mexican." This overturning of hierarchies functions in the *corrido*, Paredes argued, to dismantle the opposition upon which much of the white supremacy of Webb, among others, was based.

It is not surprising, then, that Chicano literary historians and cultural critics often mention the momentous impact Américo Paredes's *"With His Pistol in His Hand"* had on Chicano literature. Renato Rosaldo, for example, writes, "Ahead of its time, [*"With His Pistol in His Hand"*] embodied a sophisticated conception of culture where conflict, domination, and resistance, rather than coherence and consensus, were the central subjects of analysis" (1986, 6). Similarly, Ramón Saldívar, in his essay, "The Form of Texas-Mexican Fiction," asserts: "With impeccable scholarship and imaginative subtlety, Dr. Paredes' study of the *corridos*, the border ballads, concerning Gregorio Cortez may be said to have invented the very possibility of a narrative community, a complete and legitimate Texas-Mexican *persona*, whose life of struggle and discord was worthy of being told" (1983, 139).

Finally, the south Texas writers, Tomás Rivera and Rolando Hinojosa, have acknowledged, in different places, the influence that Paredes's narrative of resistance had on their own emergent literary production (see Bruce-Novoa 1980, 49–65, 139–61). In the remainder of this essay I will examine briefly how Rivera's and Hinojosa's rhetorical performances in their narratives were just as subversive of racist, white supremacist ideology as Paredes's more explicit attacks.

Tomás Rivera's Quinto Sol prize-winning novel, *"Y no se lo tragó la tierra"*—misread in its early years—is one of the Southwest's richest dialectical novels. It is the story of the subjective and collective experiences of Texas-Mexican migrant farm workers. Rivera's novel delves deeply into the life of a young anonymous migrant worker by analyzing his growth and maturity within the cyclical frame of reference of a year. *Tierra,* however, not only studies the protagonist's rites of passage, but also, shows how his solitary, chaotic life fits together within a collective class pattern of solidarity among other migrant farm workers. This class pattern, in turn, has its own utopian patterns, because Rivera's performed ideology of the text is not a picture of an American social and economic world in an uncritical perspective, but a reality apprehended in terms of a larger American cultural and political conversation during the forties and fifties in south Texas. The aesthetic quality of the work, moreover, is achieved by means of a dialectical folkloric and postmodernist conversation with the contemporary Latin American new narrative—specifically, the narrative strategies rendered by Mexican novelist and short story writer Juan Rulfo in his *El llano en llamas (The Burning Plain).*

Among existing dialectically mediated fields of semiotic forces, the most significant in Rivera's *Tierra* are a negation of a fixed, coherent, narrative sequence and the structural breakdown of a conventional cause and effect sequence. Rivera's new narrative, like Rulfo's text, offers a disordered and fragmented story line, but succeeds in creating a view of the Chicano migrant world from the protagonist's consciousness.

Rivera's world is an extremely condensed rural world, and a profoundly accurate rendering of the migrant farm worker's stark social and economic conditions. The atmosphere of *Tierra* is full of shocks, tragedies, and political and social regressions. Unfulfilled passions and desires, fear and chaos, stand out as tangible phenomena in Rivera's work of art.

The migrant farm workers who live and die on the agricultural fields of south Texas and on the long, lonely roads of Midwestern America are treated by Rivera as nameless individuals whose lives are full of suffering, misery, and anguish. Collectively, however, these migrant farm workers, like their honorable and dignified ancestors celebrated in the *corridos* of the Southwest borderlands, struggle against injustice, hardship, and physical as well as psychological abuse. Beyond our anonymous protagonist's inner world of fragmentation often lurks an unspeakable world of violence and suffering: murder, child abuse, labor exploitation, guilt, and grief. Nevertheless, the protagonist, like his fellow migrant farm workers, lives on and struggles. Indeed, as I have argued elsewhere (1985), a covert utopian impulse, though it scarcely appears explicitly in the novel as a whole, plays implicitly an important role in Rivera's novel, for those farm workers who must work and produce *surplus value* for others at the center of American culture necessarily grasp their own solidarity—initially in the unarticulated form of rage, helplessness, victimization, and oppression by a common enemy—before the dominant or ruling class has any incentive to do so. Tomás Rivera's contribution to the cultural conversation in American culture, I suggest, is about this dawning sense of solidarity of migrant farm workers with other members of their race and class. Class consciousness, as such, in Rivera's *Tierra* is, therefore, utopian, insofar as it expresses the unity of a collectivity; yet it must be stressed that this rhetorical proposition in the text is an allegorical one.[3]

Because I have spent so much time on the local cultural conversations and conflicts dramatized in the narratives by Paredes and Rivera, I leave myself little space for commenting on the broader cultural conversations between Chicano border narratives and the Latin American "new narrative." Let me note that with Rolando Hinojosa's *Klail City Death Trip Series* (1973, 1976, 1977a, 1977b, 1981, 1982, 1985, 1986), Chicano border narratives begin to speak an "international" language. From his wonderful Faulknerian blending of history and myth in *Estampas Del Valle* (1973) to his postmodernist detective novel, *Partners in Crime* (1985), Hinojosa's *Klail City Death Trip Series* is itself a *mestizaje,* a cross-breeding of North American and Latin American literary and cultural traditions. As I explained in my introduction to *The Rolando Hinojosa Reader* (J. D. Saldívar, ed., 1985, 44–63), the *Klail City Death Trip Series* is both integrated and disintegrated. Each novel in the series about Belken County, Texas, Hinojosa's mythical county, participates in composing an integrative work while, at the same time, it works out its own individual detachment from it.

In the fifteenth- and sixteenth-century Hispanic chronicle-writing tradition of Fernán Pérez de Guzmán and Hernando del Pulgar, in the Caribbean Third World American tradition of José Martí's "Nuestra América," in the Texas-Mexican tradition of Paredes's *"With His Pistol in His Hand,"* and in the disintegrating Americas of William Faulkner and Gabriel García Márquez, Hinojosa's *Klail City Death Trip Series,* through its own doctrine of the political unconscious, counters historical amnesia by restoring to the materiality of its signifiers that buried reality of south Texas history. Structurally, it can be argued that Hinojosa's new narrative, like William Faulkner's *Absalom, Absalom!* (1936) and García Márquez's *Cien años de soledad* (1967), is a multidimensional, historical novel: it is first an ascent, insofar as the Texas-Mexican community struggles, lives, and survives in a white supremacist, segregated society, and second it is a descent from its Nuevo Santander past, insofar as the old and new guard Texas-Mexican borders grow more alienated and marginalized by an overpowering and reifying North American culture and economy. This profound reification is discernible in many sections of *Klail City Death Trip Series* but is especially dramatized in Hinojosa's *Claros varones de Belken* (1986), in a section of the chronicle entitled "Con el pie en el estribo" ("Going West"), where the eighty-year-old Esteban Echevarría, one of the principal "native informants" of the novel, confides the following to Rafa Buenrostro, one of the novel's principal narrators-historians:

> ¡Qué me echen al canal grande! ¡Ya! Ahorita mismo. ¡Je! Y que pensar que en mis tiempos se sabía más que ahora con sus radios y teléfonos y sus vistas. Sí. . . . Tiempos malos fueron aquellos tambíen con sus rinches, la ley aprovechada, los terratenientes, las sequías y el engruesamiento de la vida misma . . . pero . . . al fin y al cabo era mi tiempo, mi gente, mi Valle querido . . . antes de que hubiera tal cosa como el condado de Belken y Klail City y todo de lo demás . . . había gente, Rafa, gente. . . . Labores y rancherías, y ese Río Grande que era para beber y no pa' detener los de un lado contra el otro . . . no . . . eso vino después con la bolillada y sus ingenieros y el papelaje todo en inglés. (207)

> Let them throw me in the big canal! Now! Right now. Heh! And to think that in my day we knew more things than they do today with their radios and their telephones and the movies. Sure. Bad times with the Texas Rangers; *upholding the law!* Ha! And the big landholders who brought the Rangers in. And the droughts, the pure hell of life. . . . But those were my times, my people, my Valley. Yeah. Before there was such a thing as a Belken County or a Klail City and the rest of it, there were people, Rafa, people. Fields and small towns and that Río Grande, which was for drinking, not for keeping those on one side away from the others on the other side. No, that came later: with the Anglos and their civil engineers and all those papers in English. (206)

Echevarría's task here and throughout the *Klail City Death Trip Series* is to restructure the problem of ideology, of the unconscious, of desire, and cultural production around the process of oral narrative. Put differently, Echevarría spells out for us in this passage the reification process in south Texas. Essentially, reification, for Echevarría, stands for the labor process, the division of labor, modernization, and for social and psychic fragmentation. A whole new dimension of conceptual abstraction, what Echevarría refers to in his border vernacular as "el papelaje todo en inglés" is characteristic of reification and the notarial arts on the border.

Briefly stated, Hinojosa's *Klail City Death Trip Series* is a sensitive and skillful literary social history of the Río Grande valley. As I see it, his new narratives, the nine novels about Klail City, Texas, and its environs in Belken County, are situated in a society whose traditional organization is being transformed locally by global changes in the world market (see Wallerstein, 1974). Only by situating Hinojosa's *Klail City Death Trip Series* in relation to the historical conflicts that erupted in the Texas-Mexican border region can we begin to grasp the social meanings of his avant-garde, formal innovations.

Hinojosa's two hundred year history, the *Klail City Death Trip Series*, I believe, provides the reader with two distinct worlds in his novel: one, a Mexican ranch society, and the other, a white supremacist, Anglo farm society. His new narrative thus dramatizes the triumph of farming over ranching in south Texas and with that triumph the emergence of a striking segregation of the races. What is essential in my reading of race, writing, and difference in south Texas, then, is the view that the white supremacist farm society did not implant itself peacefully. Rather, as Paredes taught us in *"With His Pistol in His Hand"* and as Hinojosa dramatizes throughout his *Klail City Death Trip Series*, it was a violent intervention. In its most dramatic form, Hinojosa's Chicano border novel shows us how the conflict between the old ranch society and new farm society expressed itself in the armed rebellion of Texas-Mexicans and their thorough suppression by the Texas Rangers.[4] This suppression is thematized boldly at the end of Hinojosa's novel, *Rites and Witnesses*. I will quote Abel Manzano's oral reconstruction of events, in detail, because his oral discourse functions in the text to counter, in a direct manner, Walter Prescott Webb's representation of these events in *The Texas Rangers*:

> [Near] El Carmen Ranch . . . the Texas Rangers shot the three Naranjo brothers in 1915. In cold blood. At night. And in the back. I was the same age as Jesus Christ then, and I found them where they were left: on the Buenrostro property, the Buenrostros were blameless, and they had nothing to do with that. They were left there until I cut them down. With this. Look.
>
> It was the Rangers who took them from the deputies, and it was the Rangers who executed them. I have heard *now* and for the last twenty years, that Choche Markham had nothing to do with the shooting; . . .
>
> I am saying it *now, right now* that Choche Markham was one of the seven Texas Rangers who took the Galveston Ranch hands from the Relámpago jail; they were going to Ruffing, but they never got there; listen to this [*corrido*]:
>
> En el camino a esa ciudad mentada
> En un domingo por la noche con nubarrón

Estos rinches texanos de la chingada
Mataron a más mexicanos del Galvestón.
. . .
Yes. I covered the bodies with the tarp from my roll and took them to
Santa Rita Mission—near El Carmen, by the bend of the River, and they
were buried there. (1982, 109–10).

As a direct refutation of Walter Prescott Webb's representation of events in
The Texas Rangers, Hinojosa's socially symbolic text, like Paredes's *"With
His Pistol in His Hand,"* engages the reader in an alternative reconstruction
of Texas border history. Moreover, Hinojosa, through Abel Manzano, articulates a cultural poetics that is not only prefigured visually, but also as an
interplay of voices, songs (Abel Manzano sings a *corrido*), and positioned utterances, what Houston A. Baker, Jr., calls Caliban's "vernacular rhythms"
(1986, 387). What characterizes Hinojosa's border aesthetics, then, is what
Baker refers to as New World discourse, "A world of oppression, a *sound* of
conflict between invader and the indigenous" (387).

Hinojosa's *Klail City Death Trip Series* functions simultaneously as
historical record, as genealogy, and as a rousing cultural critique of Texas
Ranger mythography in general, and of south Texas history in particular.
Like other historical novels, *Klail City Death Trip Series* is the creation of
its own public, its own audience in the creation of self-consciously "historical subjects."

Conclusion

*¡Ay! Este recuerdo pasado / se ha sangrado el corazón . . . / sólo un mesquite ha
quedado.—Famous décima cantada on the Texas Mexican Border*

Gente del Valle; gente trabajada, mal comida y bien cojida. [sic]—*Rolando
Hinojosa,* Claros varones de Belken

In this essay I have traced a rather small group of south Texas writers
and intellectuals between 1958 and 1987—a progress in Chicano self-
consciousness. The term "progress" is, of course, an optimistic reading of
Chicano self-consciousness, for the metaphor suggests a positive connota-
tion. Stretching my organic metaphor to include such tropes as "growth,"
"rebirth," and "emergence," I believe that the narratives by Paredes, Rivera,
and Hinojosa may be seen as replacing the old, shrill, and racist narratives
about border history and culture by Walter Prescott Webb and his followers.
An invidious, white supremacist rhetoric of performance thus gives way to
the possibility of a revitalized Chicano present and future.

But let me be clear about this intellectual and artistic flourishing of
resistance literature, to use Barbara Harlow's term (Harlow 1987), in south

Texas. First, I believe that the emergence of Chicano oppositional thinking in south Texas is more than "just" a literary movement. It is certainly that, but it also represents an outpouring of art, as in the silk screens and paintings by Amado Peña at El Taller Gallery in Austin, Texas; an outpouring in history, Arnoldo De León (1983), Emilio Zamora (1983), and David Montejano (1987); musicology and folklore, Manuel Peña (1985); ethnography and cultural studies, José Cuéllar (1971) and José E. Limón (1978, 1980, 1986a, 1986b); and feminist critique, Pat Mora (1986), Evangelina Vigil (1985), and Gloria Anzaldúa (1987). The work of these aforementioned Chicana and Chicano artists and intellectuals, to be sure, are as central to the flourishing of a south Texas Chicano resistance literature as the cultural works of Paredes, Rivera, and Hinojosa.

In the end the unresolved legacy of Gregorio Cortez, dramatized explicitly in Paredes's Chicano narrative and implicitly in Rivera's and Hinojosa's texts, is still part of our world, more than eighty-five years after the death of this border hero. Under other names the struggle unleashed by Cortez against the Texas Rangers for equality in social relations still continues in our postmodernist age.

Finally, I do not think it would be too farfetched to say that Chicano border narratives, like Faulkner's modernist novels about Mississippi and the (post)modernist Latin American new narrative (I'm here referring to García Márquez's *Cien años de soledad*, Carlos Fuentes's *Terra Nostra*, Alejo Carpentier's *El siglo de las luces*, Mario Vargas Llosa's *La guerra del fin del mundo*, and Isabel Allende's *La casa de los espíritus*) all appear to be obsessed with New World history and myth. What is characteristic of all these New World narratives is the following: (1) in these new narratives we are given history and the mediating elements through which history is narrated; (2) there is usually in these texts the existence of an inner historian who reads the cultural conversation, records the oral text, interprets it, and writes the history; and (3) there is usually an unfinished history that the inner historian is trying to complete.[5] If I were to make a totalizing proposition about the new narrative in general, and Chicano border narratives in particular, it would echo Perry Anderson's thesis in his Marxist book, *In the Tracks of Historical Materialism* (1983): "Theory [in these narratives] now is history, with a seriousness and severity it never was in the past; as history is equally theory, in all its exigency, in a way it typically evaded before" (1983, 26).

Notes

1. In George M. Fredrickson's *White Supremacy: A Comparative Study in American & South African History* (1981), the author tells us that "the phrase 'white supremacy'

applies with particular force to the historical experience of two nations—South Africa and the United States. As generally understood, white supremacy refers to the attitudes, ideologies, and policies associated with the rise of blatant forms of white or European dominance over 'nonwhite' population" (13).

2. For an incisive metacommentary on the *corrido*, see John Holmes McDowell's "The Corrido of Greater Mexico as Discourse, Music, and Event" in *"And Other Neighborly Names": Social Process and Cultural Image in Texas Folklore*, ed. Richard Bauman and Roger D. Abraham (Austin, 1981): 44–75.

3. See Fredric Jameson's *The Political Unconscious: Narrative as a Socially Symbolic Act* (Ithaca, 1981), especially his chapter, "The Dialectic of Utopia and Ideology." Here Jameson argues that "all class consciousness . . . all ideology in the strongest sense, including the most exclusive forms of ruling-class consciousness is in its very nature Utopian" (289). Such collectivities are allegorical insofar as they are "figures for the ultimate concrete collective life" (289).

4. For a full account of the history of this suppression, see David Montejano's *Anglos and Mexicans in the Making of Texas, 1836–1986* (1987).

5. My reading of New World history and myth is indebted to Roberto González Echevarría's penetrating essay, *"Cien años de soledad:* The Novel as Myth and Archive," *Modern Language Notes* 99, no. 2 (March 1984): 65–80.

Teresa McKenna

On Chicano Poetry and the Political Age: *Corridos* as Social Drama

The performance transforms itself. . . . Traditional framings may have to be reframed—new bottles made for new wine.—Victor Turner

On January 29, 1973, the following was published in the community-based newspaper *El Grito del Norte* from Española, New Mexico:

A year ago at midnight, on top of a desolate mesa just outside Albuquerque, Antonio Córdova and Rito Canales were gunned down by a group of six New Mexico police. Nine or ten bullets were pumped into Antonio while six bullets were fired into Rito's body, mostly his back. Although police claimed they had caught the two 29 year old Chicanos trying to steal dynamite, few of our people were convinced by the police explanation of events and almost none believed that such terrible force was really needed to stop them. People knew that both Antonio and Rito worked with Las Gorras Negras, a Chicano community organization and had recently been collecting information on state prison conditions (Rito was an ex-pinto) and police brutality. Antonio had also worked with *El Grito* as a reporter and photographer until shortly before he died. The killings of Jan. 29 have never been forgotten, although no state or federal agency took any action for justice. Attorney General David Norvell white-washed the police in his so-called report. The U.S. Civil Rights Commission promised action but. . . .

On Jan. 24, 1973, María Córdova—mother of Antonio—filed a suit for $300,000 damages in Albuquerque District Court against the six police. (Editorial 1973, 4)

This article and the action by María Córdova follow intensive presentation of the events of January 29, 1972, in the newspaper over a period of approximately two years. Not only were there feature-length articles and biographies of the victims, but also excerpts from the Norvell Report and testimonies about the men's value to the community in a segment entitled, "Unheard Voices of the Families." In addition, letters were published by well-known Raza leaders from throughout the nation in a section, "Raza Speaks Out on the Murders." Interspersed through these segments were numerous *corridos* and poems about the January 29 alleged murders, which were signed by members of the slain men's families (María Córdova, the mother, and Carlos Córdova, the brother) as well as interested friends and political supporters, including one poem by José Antonio Soler del Valle, from Puerto Rico.

In conjunction with the reportage and editorial commentary, the poems constitute an important aspect of the entire rhetorical presentation of the event over a period of a year prior to, and almost a year following, the filing of the suit by María Córdova. This configuration of reportage, *corrido*, and poem suggests important questions regarding the development of Chicano poetry during the years 1965–1975, a time which roughly corresponds to the public stage of what has been called the Chicano movement and poses issues of interest in understanding the evolution of poetry in what might be called the post-movement era. Chronological divisions of social activity, such as these, will become a central aspect of this discussion when the parameters of the social drama are discussed. We will leave expansion of these issues for later.

In his seminal essay, "The Folk Base of Chicano Literature," published in 1964 and reprinted in 1979, Américo Paredes delineates an ideological framework under which implicitly most critics of Chicano literature have since operated. In it he posits the notion of two Mexicos, "Méjico de adentro" and "Méjico de afuera," where the former refers to all that is encompassed within the territorial boundaries of the Republic of Mexico and the latter to all those Mexicans and all the "mejicanidad" which remains outside. By noting the two categories, he not only attests to differences between the two groups, but to linkages as well. His perspective gives us an understanding of the Mexican-American as an entity in himself who is linked to, and yet opposed to, both Mexican and Anglo-American cultures. Of greatest concern to us here, however, is this later assertion: "The Mexican saw himself and all that he stood for as continually challenging a foreign people who treated him, for the most part, with disdain. Being Mexican meant remaining inviolable in the face of overwhelming attack on one's personality. Under these circumstances, for a Mexican to accept North American values was to desert under fire" (A. Paredes 1979, 10). Although Paredes's comments refer to a particular era (the period immediately preceding and following the Mexican-American War), his ideas are germane to the Mexican experience which followed. Paredes implicitly argues the existence of the "other," the foreign power, the enemy who threatens the continuity and survival of a people in their cultural and psychological integrity. In the time about which Paredes writes, the "other" was the Anglo-American and in particular his institutional representative, the Rinche (Texas Ranger); later on the "other" became the Anglo-American dominant authority, either the police or the amorphous "they" of the hegemony under which contemporary Mexicans felt themselves to be living.

According to Paredes, it is in folklore that the Mexican finds and retains his identity. He clearly posits this idea in his essay, "Folklore, lo Mexicano and Proverbs," initially published in 1970 and reprinted in 1982, when he states:

> In other words, folklore is of particular importance to minority groups such as the Mexican Americans because their basic sense of identity is expressed in a language with an "unofficial" status, different from the one used by the official culture. We can say then, that while in Mexico the Mexican may well seek lo mexicano in art, literature and philosophy, or history—as well as folklore—the Mexican American would do well to seek his identity in his folklore. (1982, 1)

For Paredes the *corrido*, because of its nature as a folk-determined genre, was uniquely suited to present the interethnic conflict of the period. And as we can see from *El Grito del Norte*, the *corrido* continued to be similarly used. The difference between the classic *corrido* dealing with border conflict and the contemporary *corrido* (as represented by the Canales/Córdova one we will be discussing in this essay) are technical, structural, and, as we shall see, functional as well. By examining the divergence between the two, we also see similarities and in so doing more closely approximate and understand what Paredes ideologically posited as the "folk base" of Chicano literature. That Chicano literature proceeds out of a "folk base" has been a common assumption of most Chicano critics. That it evolves out of an oral tradition is a widely held corollary to this belief. The implications of these notions for the conceptualization of Chicano literary criticism are my concern in this essay. Since "folk base" does not necessarily carry the verbal connotations of "orality," it would be beneficial to examine these fundamental critical assumptions more closely through an investigation of folk song, or the *corrido*, which has become, as I have argued elsewhere, the emblematic form of Chicano literary activity.[1]

In the 1964 essay, "Some Aspects of Folk Poetry," Paredes isolates three important elements of folk song: (1) a binary structure producing balance and contrast, (2) conventional language and use of formula, and (3) performance. For our purposes here we need not discuss the first two points since they have been addressed at length by others, particularly by Manuel Peña in his "Folksong and Social Change: Two Corridos as Interpretive Sources" (1982, 1985). Rather, we will focus on the third aspect, performance, since most Chicano critics have interpreted Paredes's notion of the "folk base" of Chicano literature to refer to its origins in oral forms.

Paredes tells us that there are three factors which must be taken into consideration when discussing performance: (1) the influence of chant or song on both rhythm and diction, (2) the context in which a folk poem is performed, and (3) the performer himself as an actor, a personality (1964). In analyzing the *corridos* produced in reaction to the Canales/Córdova situation, the latter two points are most useful. Paredes clearly is correct in his assessment that "when folk poetry is written down . . . the repetitions, the refrains, the strong parallelistic devices that hold it together may become too monotonous to an ear that is guided by the eye" (1964, 217). We proceed, then, with the given that the *corridos* we are concerned with here lack the felicity of song and strike us with their questionable diction. These *corridos* do present, however, an innovation in the notion of context and performance. While Paredes focuses on the contextual relationship of the *corrido* to the politico-historical milieu, as well as to the event of its performance, his emphasis lay on the individual folk performer. I would argue that in these *corridos* a more encompassing type of "performance" is evident—one which emphasizes the notion of the actor and which more closely approaches Victor Turner's notion of the social drama.

In *Dramas, Fields and Metaphors: Symbolic Action in Human Society* (1981) Turner presents the major tenets of this theory concerning the processual nature of human activity and defines in more detail these "structures of experience" which he considers to be fundamental units in the study of human action. He explains that he focuses on a "species of 'element of the historical field' or 'event' . . . which is cross-culturally isolable and which exhibits, if it is allowed to come to full term, a characteristic processual structure that holds firm whether one is considering a macro- or micro-historical event of this type"; he proceeds to argue that this unit, the social drama, is "the social ground of many types of narrative" (1981, 139, 141). Furthermore, in "Social Dramas and Stories About Them," he explains: "I tend to regard the social drama in its full formal development, its full phase structure as a process of converting particular values and ends, distributed over a range of actors, into a system (which is always temporary and provisional) of shared and consensual meaning" (1981, 152).

The elements, "event," "narrativity," and "shared consensual meaning" are fundamental to the social drama. Moreover, reflexivity attends all these elements since social dramas constitute "ways in which a group tries to scrutinize, portray, understand and then act upon itself" (1981, 152). These activities, Turner argues, are processual; that is, they contain a structure which roughly conforms to four phases: breach, crisis, redress, and either reintegration or recognition of schism. And these phases "occur within groups of persons who share values and interests and who have a real or alleged common history" (Turner 1981, 145).

A cursory look at Mexican history shows that it lends itself easily to the social drama interpretation. Turner acknowledges this fact in his prolonged study of Hidalgo and his role in the events of the struggle for Mexican independence. Recently, José Limón argues the benefits of the social drama as the interpretive vehicle for looking at Chicano political events by focusing on two periods of, what he calls, "greater Mexican history" 1890–1930 and 1966–1972, which he explores in his *Mexican Ballads, Chicano Epic: History, Social Dramas and Poetic Persuasions* (1986a). He bases this periodization on Turner's requisites of a politically keyed conflict situation which are based on certain dramatistic elements. Of primary importance to Limón's formulation is Turner's third phase of the social drama, redressive action. He quotes the following by Turner: "It is in the redressive phase that both pragmatic techniques and symbolic action reach their fullest expression. For the society, group, community, association, or whatever may be the social unit, is here at its most 'self-conscious' and may attain the clarity of someone fighting in a corner for his life" (Turner 1974, 41). The key elements in this passage for Limón are "pragmatic techniques and symbolic action," which he perceives to be essential to understanding the two periods of Mexican/Chicano social drama which he isolates below:

> The first social drama I have in mind is the dualistic international "disharmonic" social process that, on the Mexican side of the border, reaches its utmost clarity in the extended event we call the Mexican Revolution of 1910, and, on this side of the border, although with less clarity, consists of an extended radical questioning of Anglo-American political authority, particularly in Texas. . . . The second social drama emerges between 1966 and 1972 and also consists in part of a radical Mexican American political critique of Anglo American authority although encompassing an extended Southwestern regional zone. (1986a, 2)

In this schema of the Mexican/Chicano social drama, Limón goes on to argue, the *corrido* becomes a significant form of symbolic redressive action. Limón's assertion is well-grounded in the generative nature of the social drama which Turner clarifies in the following: "The social drama, then, I regard as the experiential matrix from which the many genres of cultural performance, beginning with redressive ritual and juridical procedures and eventually including oral and literary narrative have been generated" (Turner 1981, 154). Taking his cue from Turner, Limón understands the *corrido* to be not only a form of redressive symbolic action, but also a form in transformation, that is, one which bridges the periodization he develops of the Mexican/Chicano social drama and which becomes a key element in the residual effects of the drama which are still being played today.[2]

It is not necessary to recount all of Limón's useful argument here, except to reaffirm his analysis of the *corrido* as a symbolic form which changes and is transformed by the particular events which compose his two periods of social drama. Turner lays the groundwork for this notion of the transformation of symbolic forms when he writes: "I would point out at the linguistic level of 'parole,' each phase has its own speech forms and styles, its own rhetoric, its own kinds of nonverbal languages and cultural performances may be viewed as 'dialectical dancing partners' . . . of the perennial social drama to which they give meaning appropriate to the specificities of time, place and culture" (1981, 155). We can infer from Turner's analysis that this proliferation of expressive forms takes place in time, demonstrates a temporal structure, and, as such, is subject to change. The textuality of the social drama, then, can only be understood keeping these temporal dimensions in mind. Frank Lentricchia understands this textuality when he reconsiders Raymond Williams's thoughts on the issue of hegemony. His analysis is instructive for our discussion. Lentricchia reminds us that hegemony too "is a process that 'has continually to be renewed, recreated, defended, and modified' because it is continually being 'resisted, limited and altered, challenged by pressures all its own.' That is to say that hegemony is 'never either total or exclusive' and that it is best understood agonistically" (1983, 15). His comments are germane considering that Mexican history has been characterized by hegemonic conflict. Paredes has formulated this history in terms of the antagonistic "other," Turner has characterized it as social drama, and Limón postulates it as social drama attended with symbolic action in the services of transformation.

If we use Limón's schema, Gregorio Cortez is a figure who is associated with the first period of the Mexican/Chicano social drama and who reflects his community in his resistance, an attitude which is crucibled in his celebrated flight from a posse over the state of Texas. But most importantly he is the subject of one of the most well-known *corridos* of the time. Less than one-hundred years later, Antonio Córdova and Rito Canales also resisted what they perceived to be their unjust domination by the Anglo-

American and were allegedly murdered for their efforts. They too became the subject of *corridos*, but the circumstances of the production and presentation of this symbolic form differ significantly from that which chronicled Cortez's exploits. Whereas "El Corrido de Gregorio Cortez" was performed by numerous folk performers over the Southwest region, in small groups or large, the mode of communication was primarily oral. For the chroniclers of the Canales/Córdova situation the poem operates in concert with significantly different actants; the report, the biography, the epistle take the place of the figures surrounding the campfire. The process of transformation of symbolic forms which Limón discusses is evident here. Yet, the political/cultural nature of the activities which produced both of these symbolic forms connects them together. They emerge from different historical moments in the social drama, but their essential political nature remains, if by political we take to mean action associated with struggle. Turner confirms the political element in the social drama when he observes that social dramas are in large measure political. He means that they arise out of crisis and function to redress a social breach. Moreover, he points out that "There is an interdependent, perhaps dialectical, relationship between social dramas and genres of cultural performance" (1981, 149). In both cases (Cortez and Canales/Córdova) the *corrido* is a genre of cultural performance which acts dialectically within the larger social drama. The link, then, between the *corrido* and the social drama does not lie in orality per se, but in narrativity itself, in the politically laden event upon which the narrative is based, and most importantly on the social group from which it springs, whose constant crises revolve around the dysfunction or breach produced by the Anglo-American "other." These elements are the paradigmatic dimensions of the saga of Mexican/Chicano resistance to domination; it is the root metaphor from which others are born. Turner's observation, then, that the story feeds "back into the social process, providing it with a rhetoric, a mode of emplotment, and a meaning," seems to hold true (1981, 149). Moreover, these genres of cultural performance which attend the drama/story also appear to function as "our native way of manifesting ourselves, to ourselves and of declaring where power and meaning lie and how they are distributed" (1981, 154).

We must underscore, again, that cultural performances are time-bound: they provide meaning by positing a past and a history—a fact which draws attention to these forms as reactions to, recorders of, and producers of social change. Turner tells us that, "the performance transforms itself. True, as I said, the rules may frame the performance, but the flow of action and interaction within that frame may conduce to hitherto unprecedented insights and even generate new symbols and meanings, which may be incorporated into subsequent performances. Traditional framings may have to be reframed—new bottles made for new wine" (1981, 146). I suggest that the *corrido* is reframed in the context of a type of social drama performance which is defined within the rhetorical boundaries of, in the case under discussion here, the newspaper. Other reframings are possible and occur as *corridos* are generated, for example, in the Delano strike picket lines or in inclusion in memorial documents for dead leaders.[3] Yet always two essential elements remain that confirm the political functionality: (1) the overt and implied "other" and (2) the emphasis on event or on narrativity to transform that event into larger social action.

Let us begin our discussion of the rhetorical presentation of the Canales/Córdova slayings in *El Grito del Norte* by first considering the following *corrido* by María Córdova which was published in the newspaper on May 19, 1972:

Una poema por la madre de Antonio[4]

Voy a escribir unas linias
de lo que hace poco pasó
Mataron a Antonio y Rito
en Albuquerque Nuevo Méjico

Mil novecientos setenta y dos
El veinte y nueve de enero
Mataron a Antonio y Rito
pero hicieron sus planes primero

Callaron en Manos de hombres
de duro corazón
los Mataron en Black Mesa
sin ninguna compasión

Seis tiros le dieron a Rito
a Antonio le dieron diez
ellos querian estar seguros
que no se levantaron otra vez

Los sacaron a Black Mesa
los mataron a traición
para que ellos pudieron
aparecer en el programa de la televisión

Toda la gente sabe
que los mataron en sangre fria
el crimen que les levantaron
no lo han podido probar todavía

El dia veinte y ocho de enero
hicieron todos sus planes
para cometer este crimen
y quedar ellos libres de sus afanes

Estos eran dos hombres
que no temían morir
pusieron sus vidas en peligro
porque no querian ver a su pueblo sufrir

Dos hombres que los mataron
eran seis hombres inhumanos
pero la sangre que se derramieron
será requirida de sus manos

Había doscientos personas
que demandaron la Verdad
pero ellos estaban dentro de cuatro poderes
cubiertos con la capa de la autoridad

Antonio no necesitaba dinamita
para defender sus derechos
tenía pluma, papel y su cámara
para proverles sus hechos

Ellos no saben que un día
que al juicio tendran que pasar
y alli delante de un juez justo
no se podran escapar

Vimos el retrato de Anita
con su pequeño niñito
Y nos parte el Corazón
porque su padre no pudo ver a su hijito

No soy poeta ni soy nada
solo soy una madre de un hijo querido
y hoy mismo me encuentro
con mi corazón herido

Ya con este me despido
teniendo mucho mas que decir
y esperando que la Raza Nuestra
En lo futuro se sepa unir.

Note that the author of the poem has observed some of the conventions of the *corrido* form.[5] We are privy to the retelling of the event with attention

to date and place: "Mil novecientos setenta y dos / El veinte y nueve de
enero / Mataron a Antonio y Rito / pero hicieron sus planes primero"
(Nineteen hundred and seventy two / the 29th of January / They killed
Antonio and Rito / But they made their plans beforehand). From here we are
led through the details of the story—where and how they were killed:
"Callaron en Manos de hombres / de duro corazón / los Mataron en Black
Mesa / sin ninguna compasión" (They fell into the hands of men / with hard
hearts / who killed them at Black Mesa / Without any compassion). And:
"Seis tiros le dieron a Rito / a Antonio le dieron diez / ellos querian estar
seguros / que no se levantaron otra vez" (They shot Rito six times / they
shot Antonio ten / They wanted to make sure / that they would not ever get
up again). The action moves from the actual murder to a recounting of the
investigation by authorities into the crime. Then, the speaker makes another contextual shift: "Estos eran dos hombres / que no temían morir /
pusieron sus vidas en peligro / porque no querian ver a su pueblo sufrir"
(These were two men / who did not fear death / They put their lives in
danger / because they didn't want to see their people suffer). The speaker
solidifies the communal identification of the victims with: "Antonio no
necesitaba dinamita / para defender sus derechos / tenia pluma, papel y su
cámara / para proverles sus hechos" (Antonio did not need dynamite / to
defend his rights / He had paper, pen and his camera / to prove his deeds).
The allusion is obviously to the repeated formula phrase from the border
corrido about Gregorio Cortez, who "defendió su derecho con la pistola en
la mano" (defended his rights with his pistol in his hand). The acts of
resistance of one cultural hero are superimposed on that of the intellectual
warrior who uses pens and not pistols in his fight. The play against the oral
corrido subtext is foregrounded here. Moreover, as in the classic *corrido*
form, María Córdova ends her *corrido* with the formulaic despedida or
farewell: "Yo no soy poeta ni soy nada" (I am not a poet / I am not anything),
and "Ya con este me despido / teniendo mucho mas que decir / y esperando
que la Raza Nuestra / En el futuro se sepa unir" (With this I say farewell /
having so much more to say / and hoping that our beloved people / will in
the future know how to unite).

   The shift to showing the position of the victim within the Chicano
community serves several purposes. The speaker can then proceed to the
underlying message of the poem, because it is not Antonio who has the
power to effect change, but his fellow community who must unite, become
powerful, and produce change. The event—the murder of the two men—
serves a larger meaning and purpose, that is, the unification of the community against the "other." Most importantly, the murders and the form in
which they are explained to the community (i.e., the *corrido*) compose part

of a historical and cultural drama which has been taking place since the encroachment of the Anglo-American into the Southwest. The deaths of these Chicano movement leaders are linked to a process of conflict and resistance, a text of which they form a part.

This text is significantly different, albeit, from the ballads of the border. The rhetorical function of the *corrido* as it had been sung in small communal settings in the ranchos or at familial celebrations, gives way to a much wider rhetorical situation like the one we are investigating here. The nature of the teller and the listener has changed radically. The single folk performer and the interaction in performance between himself/herself and the audience has been widened considerably. Now we have the reactions to the "drama" expressed through printed letters, poems, testimonies, and reportage. We see in *El Grito del Norte* a tableau effect in which each element in the presentation plays off against one another to produce a simulated "teller/listener" relationship. The direct address of the *corrido* provides the core situation, to which the rest of the elements in the tableau react, reflect, and provide consensual response. The series of newspaper tableaux (in the case of the Canales/Córdova situation the presentation of the event continues through several editions of the newspaper over several years) function to express the idea of crisis and the need for redress. As we have noted, the *corrido* itself carries within it the dynamics of event, narrativity, and a call to action based on a consensus of values, which are essential elements of the social drama, and as such it plays a crucial role in the architecture of the rhetorical presentation.

We see here a process of transformation of forms which Turner explains when he writes "one genre might supplant or replace another as the historically or situationally dominant form of social metacommentary. New communicative techniques and media may make possible wholly unprecedented genres of cultural performance and thus new modes of self-understanding" (1981, 155). Yet, in this newspaper presentation a conscious analogue of genres appears to be operating. José Limón comments on this type of transformative process when he analyzes Américo Paredes's "*With His Pistol in His Hand*" as a "transforming narrative response to the aesthetic influence of its scholarly subject, the border ballad" (1986b, 27). He explains that,

In this fourth chapter Paredes offers, in his own restrained prose, an equivalent of the conversations that men may have after a *corrido* performance as they evaluate the *corrido*, its hero, its circumstances and try to get at the truth. As a post narrative review, Paredes' final chapter is like this kind of polyphonic conversation and as such an integral part of his total performance as it would be for a traditional *corrido* sung to an audience. Hence, I would argue that even the seeming "review" character of Chapter IV recalls a *corrido* performance. (1986b, 27)

Similarly, I would argue that the newspaper gives us a rhetorical presentation which is an analogue to the *corrido* performance situation. The text of the Norvell Report is juxtaposed to the *El Grito del Norte* editorial, a positioning which constitutes a statement/rebuttal type of contestation. Also, the biographies of the individuals give important background information, as listeners might conversationally discuss the actors in the story from their personal experience. And the poems, authored by other family members or individuals from outside the immediate community, function as eulogies and statements of solidarity with the aggrieved parties as well as testaments about the veracity of the events. Within this presentation, which is designed to persuade the reader, the *corrido* by María Córdova is the focal point because it recalls an earlier time, one of oral performance, in which the agonistic dimensions of the Mexican/Chicano social drama resonate.

Earlier we noted that "shared and consensual meaning" was an important element of social drama. So too is it an essential aspect of the "teller/ listener" relationship, and as such it must be looked at more closely in its transformation into the rhetorical presentation in the newspaper. Renato Rosaldo's illuminating work on Ilongot narrative is instructive for our discussion here because Rosaldo details the difficulties which anthropologists, or outsiders, face when they try to listen and understand the stories being told in an Ilongot storytelling session (1986). From their etic perspective, he explains, outsiders are not privy to the emic view, that is, the internal knowledge of the wide range of history, social activity, and status demarcations which provide the necessary internal backdrop for the comprehension of all narrative texts. Consequently, the outsider receives a thread of narration which appears to have multiple gaps and to make little sense. Because of the extreme isolation of the Ilongot culture from our own, the lack of understanding on the part of the visitors becomes very apparent. Only to a limited extent can the outsider experience the shared and consensual meaning of the tribe. Similarly, *corridos* and other genres of cultural performance are produced and performed within their own sphere of shared and consensual meaning. That María Córdova's words resonate the formulaic phrase "con la pistola en la mano," as we have already observed, is a clear bid for the listener to recall the earlier *corrido* and to link the Canales/Córdova slayings to the conflict situation which gave, and continues to give, rise to forms of resistance in the Mexican/Chicano community. Those of us "in the know" will make the appropriate connections. Yet this process of engagement of consensual meaning also has a larger function. As in the Ilongot culture, it serves to elicit communitas between the teller and the listener.

Communitas is a concept which Turner describes as a key ingredient to aspects of human social activity, in fact, he remarks, "one might also postulate that the coherence of a completed social drama is itself a function of communitas" (1974, 50). "Briefly, to recapitulate the argument in *The Ritual Process*," he explains, "the bonds of communitas are anti-structural in that they are undifferentiated, equalitarian, direct, nonrational (though not irrational), I-Thou or Essential We relationships in Martin Buber's sense" (1974, 46–47).[6] In Turner's view communitas is closely associated with liminality, that creative state of betwixt and between in which old paradigms transist into new ones. Consequently, in the liminal state the claiming of a communal human identity is made possible, and moreover this process is basic to the sharing of consensus. All of these ideas proceed out of Turner's differentiation between structure and anti-structure. The first, structure, involves all that constrains people's actions and defines their differences, while the second, anti-structure, is a total and unmediated relationship between individuals, "a relationship that does not submerge one in the other but safeguards their uniqueness in the very act of their commonness" (1974, 274).[7] He means by anti-structure, not a negative corollary to structure, but rather the positive generative center of human activity. He concludes, then, that "man is both a structural and an anti-structural entity, who grows through anti-structure and conserves through structure" (1974, 298).

That growth involves a creative projection which is achieved through the development of root metaphors, conceptual archetypes, and paradigms. For our discussion here root metaphors are most important because "root metaphors have a 'thisness' or 'thereness' from which many subsequent structures may be unpacked" (Turner 1974, 50). The *corrido*, I believe, becomes transformed from a genre of cultural performance to the status of a root metaphor for the paradigmatic contestation between the Anglo-American "other" and Mexicans on this side of the border. The root metaphor is part of a larger model for activity which can be labeled a "root paradigm." If we refer back to Paredes's comments regarding the attitude which Mexicans assumed when "challenging a foreign people," we can interpret his observation to be an accurate assessment of a Mexican/Chicano root paradigm which has informed much of Mexican/Chicano cultural production. Turner remarks that root paradigms "have reference not only to the current state of social relationships existing or developing between actors, but also to cultural goals, means, ideas, outlooks, currents of thought, patterns of belief, and so on, which enter into these relationships, interpret them, incline them to alliance or divisiveness" (1974, 64).[8] The root paradigm which we have isolated here, clearly operates under these conditions and, it is important to keep in mind, functions within the realm of communitas.

The change in function and presentation from the classic *corrido* form to what has been described here in *El Grito del Norte* raises important questions regarding this root metaphor and root paradigm of which the Mexican/ Chicano social drama is a part. It appears that the framing of the cultural performance changes as the notion of the political importance of event wanes. The deaths of Antonio and Rito never reach the mythic signification level of that of Gregorio Cortez. Nor are they even considered by the wider Chicano population to be role models worthy of emulation; they have been for all intents and purposes lost to history. The political nature of the events of their deaths are secondary to the activity and response which they generated. The focus on the event appears to become subsumed by the rhetorical presentation itself. This movement away from hero and event as subject of the performance and as the model for action can be perceived in the development of much of Chicano poetry out of this tradition.

For example, José Montoya's classic poem, "El Louie," chronicles in retrospective the life of Louie Rodríguez "un vato de atolle" (1972). I do not intend to analyze the complexities of this poem here, particularly since it has been done so meticulously elsewhere by Juan Bruce-Novoa and Arturo Madrid. But it is necessary to note certain things which are important to this discussion. First, the poem is not framed in a social drama context, where redress is either desired or possible. Furthermore, no "other" is perceived by Louie as a foreign enemy which threatens his integrity. I agree with Bruce-Novoa that the only "other" which emerges for Louie is the seductive image of Bogart and Raft, characters whom he has seen in the "mono," movies, and whom he emulates in his shifting postures of illusionary selfhood. So although "El Louie" maintains the element of narrativity (we are told of Louie's life from his high riding days of "48 fleetline two-tone/buenas garras" to his service in the Korean War and finally to his ignominious death in a rented room), no longer is there a clear notion of social event nor of affirming consensual values. Yet, "El Louie" does operate against a subtext of pachuco lore. The effect, however, is ironic and not necessarily affirmative. Even so, because of this subtext, "El Louie" still is implicitly linked to an idea of community, if not communitas. Louie Rodríguez's life, moreover, bears out Paredes's view of the agonistic stance of the Mexican: "Being Mexican meant remaining inviolable in the face of overwhelming attack on one's personality" (A. Paredes 1979, 10). Despite all of his defeats, his drug addiction, and marginality, Louie remains inviolable in the only way he knows how. But his defiant stance is different from those of Cortez or even Canales and Córdova because Louie Rodríguez achieves selfhood only outside of himself, from fantasy events, the cinema, and its celluloid heroes. Louie moves deliberately outside the events of his own life to define himself. The irony of Louie Rodríguez's life is that he turns to those consumerized images of bravery fabricated by the society which impinge so destructively on his selfhood. By choosing these images, Louie entrenches himself further in the domination which is making him extinct. Consequently, Louie indirectly is accepting North American values, and his ignominious death in a rented room becomes an indirect desertion under fire, to use Paredes's words. The differences between the transformative development of the root metaphor and root paradigm through its manifestations in Cortez, Canales/Córdova, and Louie Rodríguez are suggestive. Whereas Gregorio Cortez, Antonio Córdova, and Rito Canales are shown within the events which define them and link them in a positive manner to the communal center, Louie's link to this center is mediated and ultimately ironic.

Again Américo Paredes is useful to our understanding of what has transpired in the transformation we have noted above. In discussing the differences between folk poetry and what he terms "sophisticated" poetry, he comments that "in sophisticated poetry, . . . the tendency is toward more and more subtle and individual modes of expression once poetry has ceased to be performed and has become an act of private communication between poet and reader" (1964, 225). "El Louie" is not "performance" in the folk poet's sense, nor is it a part of the type of social drama discussed above, although it is a poem which has been recorded and sung. (The musical rendering is lesser known and usually not taken into account.) Most important, "El Louie" moves toward that "subtle and individualized mode of expression" in which Louie Rodríguez becomes an indeterminate symbol of resistance to an "other" whose identity has become so blurred as to be rendered moot. Although a case can be made that the pachuco is an implicit resistance to Anglo-American domination, the integration of Anglo-American symbology into Louie's stance of selfhood complicates this interpretation. Louie Rodríguez's attitude of defiance is qualitatively different from Cortez's armed refusal of domination with a pistol or Córdova's with a pen. The defiance is turned inward against the self, not outward against an "other." Clearly, "El Louie" marks an important movement in the transformation of the root paradigm.

In some ways "El Louie" is a transitional poem in that it displays some of the dramatistic elements of the *corrido* but does not show others, such as the creative, positive invocation of communitas. We have noted that communitas refers to the recreation, always more or less provisionally, of a group which, for the time being, is strong and inviolable in the face of stress. The transformation we have been investigating above appears to support the view that some poetic efforts develop out of, and support, communitas; that is, they are integrally linked to the root paradigm of the Mexicano/Chicano social drama we have been discussing and of which the classic *corrido* is a core genre. Some, like "El Louie," bridge the gap between these and other poetic efforts which veer away from this dramatistic paradigm. As an example of the latter, consider the following poem, "The Morning They Shot Tony Lopez: Barber and Pusher Who Went Too Far, 1958," by Gary Soto:

> When they entered through the back door,
> You were too slow in raising an arm
> Or thinking of your eyes refusing the light,
> Or your new boots moored under the bed,
> Or your wallet on the bureau, open
> And choking with bills,
> Or your pockets turned inside out, hanging breathless as tongues,
> Or the vendor clearing his throat in the street,
> Or your watch passed on to another's son,
> Or the train to Los Baños,
> The earth you would slip into like a shirt
> And drift through forever.
> When they entered, and shot once,
> You twisted the face your mother gave
> With the three, short grunts that let you slide
> In the same blood you closed your eyes to.
> (1977, 11)

Here, the speaker focuses almost clinically on a narration of the details of the scene: the wallet on the bureau, the boots moored under the bed, the blood. But Tony Lopez exists only as a "Pusher Who Went Too Far." He is not presented to serve either as a role model or as a catalyst for change. His community is absent except for the final action in which we see the traces of an absent mother and sense the racial blood which he closed his eyes to. The poem's speaker does not articulate the event in its representative dimensions, but rather in its idiosyncratic force. That "Lopez" is a Spanish surname is the only link to a recognizable social milieu. His death becomes a general metaphor of violence in which community and any notion of redress is distanced and abstracted. Similarly, in "History," a poem in the same volume, *The Elements of San Joaquin,* the speaker details his grandmother in all her particularity, "Loose skin of belly and breasts" (Soto 1977, 41). But most important, he articulates a severance from the "events" of her life and the community which she represented: "I do not know why / Her face shines / Or what goes beyond this shine, / Only the stories / That pulled her / From Taxco to San Joaquin, / Delano to Westside, / The places / In which we all begin" (41). The "event," or the "social drama or stories about them," to borrow Turner's phrase, are no longer immediate; they are representative only by nature of their abstraction. "The places in which we all begin" is a metaphorical declaration not based on immediate event or experience. Here there is no "other" which causes a breach between the grandmother and the speaker, only time which allows no redress. The shift from "event" poetry to "poetry of abstraction," for lack of a better term, does not necessarily imply privilege of one form over the other. Rather, I contend that the movement out of event, out of the social drama mode and into a more abstract response to our communal reality goes beyond a reframing of the "other" and becomes a qualitative redefinition of self and of history.

The folklore, the *corrido,* and the stories have become abstracted and have changed in both functional and, perhaps, aesthetic value, although we are not necessarily concerned with value in this discussion. This process of abstraction is not limited to Mexicano/Chicanos, in fact it has been noted and commented upon by many from Ortega y Gasset to Irving Howe. Recently, Gerald Graff has offered a provocative observation of the situation in *Literature Against Itself* when he declares his "sympathy with the view that literature ought to play an adversary role in society. But recent social developments have opened up difficult questions about the adequacy of our ways of conceiving 'adversariness' " (1979, 2). To further illustrate his point, he draws on the ideas of Hans Magnus Enzensberger:

> The capacity of the capitalist society to reabsorb, suck up, swallow, 'cultural goods' of widely varying digestibility has enormously increased. Today the political harmlessness of all literary, indeed, all artistic products, is clearly evident: the very fact that they can be defined as such neutralized them. Their claim to be enlightening, their utopian surplus, their critical potential has shrivelled to mere appearance . . . sooner or later, and usually sooner, by way of detours via advertising, design, and styling, the inventions become part and parcel of the consumer sphere. (1974, 90–91)

These are suggestive notions for what we encounter in this discussion. What then is at stake when resistance-based forms become mere conventions? What shift in values occurs and what implications does this shift hold for the future of the "adversariness" of Chicano literature? It also appears that certain questions arise regarding the development of Chicano poetry out of the folk base. The first has to do with narrativity and the importance of consensual values in the creation of communitas. As poetry increasingly ceases to revolve around the politico-laden event, will communitas survive? But the most important issue has to do with the disappearance of the "other" and its effects on the distinction and raison d'être of Chicano poetry as it has developed through the various manifestations of the Mexicano/Chicano social drama.

If we consider the following poem, "With a Polka in his Hand," by Evangelina Vigil, the prospects of the creative force of transformation are bright. She aptly dedicates the poem to Don Américo Paredes:

> tired out de todo el día
> me senté a pistearme
> una cuba libre
> in a classy joint
>
> with delicately leaved green plants
> blossoming in all directions
> and picturesque windows
> brilliant mirrors
> and a polished wooden antique bar
>
> and I gazed out
> through elongated window structures
> framing like a picture
> el patio en el mercado:
> white, sun-bleached ladrillos cuadrados
> whereupon
> just one drink ago
> troteaban los pies indios clad in dusty shoes
> de aquel viejito
> que se atravesaba en frente de la puerta
> de la cantina cara y gringa—
> yo
> por un instante
> esperando que él pasara
> y él

contenido
en sus pensamientos claros
pushing with strong weathered brown arm
an ancient wooden cart
y en su mano izquierda
un radio de transistor
aventando acordeón

and amazed
while just beginning to feel the buzz and warmth
I utter to myself out loud
"He's carrying a polka in his hand!"
and the anglo client seated next to me
glances over uncomprehendingly
and I think about Gregorio Cortez
and Américo Paredes
y en que la defensa cultural es permitida
and that calls for another drink
and another toast
y yo le digo a mí por el espejo
"¡ay, nomás!"
y me echo el trago.
(1985, 25)

The observation which Vigil draws from Paredes's work on the *corrido* is a significant one. That "la defensa de la cultura es permitida" (defense of the culture is permitted) is a defiant stance against those who deny our culture permission to exist. Her scenario is a fitting analogue to the larger social drama we have been discussing. In this small drama an old man is framed in the doorway of "la cantina cara y gringa" (a costly Anglo-American bar). In that liminal space a polka bursts from the high-tech transistor radio he carries with him. The polka, a derivative form of Texas-Mexican folk song, resonates back to the early forms of the *corrido* and to those forms of cultural resistance which survive as the contiguous agonistic relationship of the Mexican and Anglo-American "other" continues to the present day; Cortez used a pistol, Rito Canales used a pen and the old man a radio to express their resistance. As the old man is framed, so too is the *corrido* reframed in that oppositional image of him in the doorway of the Anglo-American bar. There is no audience to support and applaud the speaker's story, just a mirror to which she lifts her glass and makes her toast. Consequently, it is only her own image reflected in the mirror which assents in return. Despite the solitary image with which Vigil's poem ends, it appears that the transformation of the drama out of the classic border *corrido* to the María Córdova poem in *El Grito del Norte* continues to be positive, creative, and generative.

Yet, Vigil's whimsical poem with its positive attitude about cultural resistance is not the rule in contemporary Chicano poetry. The following lines from Lorna Dee Cervantes's "Visions of Mexico While Attending a Writing Symposium in Port Townsend, Washington," perhaps more aptly express the tension and agony which many other contemporary poets face when trying to plumb the cultural space that has been bequeathed to them:

> I don't want to pretend I know more
> and can speak all the names. I can't.
> My sense of this land can only ripple through my veins
> like the chant of an epic corrido.
> I come from a long line of eloquent illiterates
> whose history reveals what words don't say.
> Our anger is our way of speaking,
> the gesture is an utterance more pure than word.
> We are not animals
> but our senses are keen and our reflexes,
> accurate punctuation.
> All the knifings in a single night, low-voiced
> scufflings, sirens, gunnings . . .
> We hear them
> and the poet within us bays.
> (1981, 45–46)

The attitude of resistance which is a key ingredient of the social drama as it developed historically is called upon here to anchor the poet's inspiration. The dramatistic elements of the politically keyed situation are absent and the "other" is undefined, but the rage remains and, therefore, the poetic impulse survives.

What happens when these elements are gone? Lentricchia remarks that the ideological struggle at the level of discourse can lead to a "new organic ideology, where it might serve a different collective will" (1983, 34). If this redefinition of the collective will is at the core of the transformation of symbols, metaphors, and genres of cultural performance, then we might deduce, as does Lentricchia, that "the fluidity, or undecidability, of the symbol is not, therefore, the sign of its social and political elusiveness but the ground of its historicity and of its flexible but also specific political significance and force" (1983, 34). The answers to the questions which are posed by these considerations are not now mine to give; they can only be borne out by time. All that we can do at this point is to recognize and to reaffirm the force and importance of "event" in forging the uniqueness of Chicano literature as it has been underscored through history. As usual this affirmation is best given voice by a poet. In "Puente de cristal" Lucha Corpi writes of the influence which the life and death of her friend and mentor, the political activist Magdalena Mora, had on her work. She declares: "Y por primera vez / dejé que mi palabra / apuntara hacia esenciales" (And for the first time / I let my words / point to the essentials) (1980, 80). For this poet the choice is a conscious one—to let words point to the essential issues of communal existence or not. When and how, and if, this choice occurs forms the basis for an understanding of the evolution of Chicano poetry.

Notes

1. McKenna, Teresa, Parto de Palabra: Essays on Chicano Literature in Process, unpublished manuscript (Department of English, University of Southern California, 1987).

2. Limón's periodization of the second phase of his Mexicano/Chicano social drama corresponds roughly to the temporal divisions of "Chicano movement" and "post-movement" which were mentioned at the beginning of this discussion. The social drama framework, however, supercedes these kinds of divisions because it permits discussion of political/cultural action on more fruitful theoretical and practical rhetorical considerations.

3. See *Raíz fuerte que no se arranca*, memorial volume dedicated to Magdalena Mora (Los Angeles: Editorial Prensa Sembradora, 1983).

4. I reproduce the *corrido* as it appeared in print without any corrections.

5. We need not recapitulate here all of the literature on the classic border *corrido* form. We should note, however, that like the ballad, the *corrido* tells a story which usually has a beginning, a middle, and an end. In addition, the *corrido* is usually composed in octosyllabic quatrains and is sung in ¾ or ⁶⁄₈ meter. As in most oral and epic poems, moreover, the memory of the performer is assisted by formulaic phrases, formal introductions and closings, and is structured in the common a b c b rhyme pattern.

6. Turner describes three types of communitas: "1) existential or spontaneous communitas, the direct, immediate, and total confrontation of human identities . . . ; 2) normative communitas, where, under the influence of time, the need to mobilize and organize resources to keep the members of a group alive and thriving . . . the original existential communitas is organized into a perduring social system . . . ; 3) ideological communitas, which is a label one can apply to a variety of utopian models or blueprints of societies believed by their authors to exemplify or supply the optimal conditions for existential communitas" (1974, 169). I would argue that Mexican/Chicano cultural performance, for the most part, operates within either normative or ideological communitas, but I will reserve discussion of this issue for another time.

7. Chicano cultural production appears to operate in a creative liminal space in which communitas is generated. When cultural production ceases to proceed out of anti-structure, it could be argued, the activity loses its liminality and becomes increasingly separate from communitas.

8. Turner also explains that "because of the action of root paradigms in people's heads . . . (they) . . . become objectified models for future behavior in the history of collectives such as churches or nations" (1974, 96). Mexicano/Chicanos may not comprise a church or a nation in themselves, but because they are identified as a distinct racial/ethnic group within a larger dominant culture, their status as a collective holds true, as does this action of root paradigms within their collective behavior.

Sonia Saldívar-Hull

Feminism on the Border: From Gender Politics to Geopolitics

Is it possible for Chicanas to consider ourselves part of this "sister-hood" called feminism? Can we assume that our specific interests and problems will be taken care of by our Marxist compañeros? In her essay, "Feminism, Marxism, Method, and the State," Catharine MacKinnon decrees that "[s]exuality is to feminism what work is to marxism: that which is most one's own yet most taken away" (1982, 515). MacKinnon argues that while we can draw parallels between Marxist and feminist methodologies, we must remember not to conflate these two "theories of power and its distribution" (1982, 516), that one theory must not be subsumed into the other. She continues:

> What if the claims of each theory are taken equally seriously, each on its own terms? Can two social processes be basic at once? Can two groups be subordinated in conflicting ways, or do they merely crosscut? Can two theories, each of which purports to account for the same thing—power as such—be reconciled? Or, is there a connection between the fact that the few have ruled the many and the fact that those few have been men? (517)

But to the Chicana, a woman with a specific history under racial and sexual and class exploitation, it is essential that we further problematize the feminist/Marxist discussion by adding the complication of race and ethnicity. Our feminist sisters and Marxist compañeros/as urge us to take care of gender and class issues first and race will naturally take care of itself. Even MacKinnon, as thorough as she is, constantly watching that she herself does not recreate a monolithic "woman," uses footnotes to qualify the difference between the white woman's and the black woman's situations. She claims to have checked her statements "to see if women's condition is shared, even when contexts or magnitudes differ" (520, note 7). If her check system fails, then "the statement is simply wrong and will have to be qualified or the aspiration (or the theory) abandoned" (520, note 7).

My project does not suggest that we abandon the aspiration nor the theory. It does insist, however, that our white feminist "sisters" recognize their own blind spots. When MacKinnon uses the black woman as her sign for all dispossessed women, we see the extent to which Chicanas, Asian-American, Native American, or Puerto Rican women, for example, have been rendered invisible in a discourse whose explicit agenda is to expose ideological erasure. Chicana readings of color *blindness* instead of color consciousness in "politically correct" feminist essays indicate the extent to which the issues of race and ethnicity are ignored in feminist and Marxist theories. Theorists such as Rosaura Sánchez, Alma Gómez, Cherríe Moraga, Mariana Romo-Carmona, Gloria Anzaldúa, and Helena María Viramontes, working collectively as in *Cuentos* (Gómez, Moraga, and Romo-Carmona, 1983) and individually as in *Borderlands* (Anzaldúa 1987), insist on illuminating the complications and intersections of the multiple systems of exploitation: capitalism, patriarchy, and white supremacy.

As Chicanas making our works public—publishing in marginalized journals and small, underfinanced presses and taking part in conferences and workshops—we realize that the "sisterhood" called feminism professes an ideology that at times comes dangerously close to the phallocentric ideologies of the white male power structure against which feminists struggle. In her essay, "Ethnicity, Ideology, and Academia," Rosaura Sánchez reminds us of the ideological strategies that the dominant culture manipulates in order to mystify "the relation between minority cultures and the dominant culture" (1987, 80). She points out that U.S. cultural imperialism extends beyond the geopolitical borders of the country, "but being affected, influenced, and exploited by a culture is one thing and sharing fully in that culture is another" (1987, 81). If we extend the analogy to feminism and the totalizing concept of sisterhood, we begin to understand how the specific interests of Anglo-American and other European feminists tend to erase the existence of Chicana, Puerto Rican, Native American, Asian-American, and other Third World feminisms. Indeed, feminism affects and influences Chicana writers and critics, but feminism as practiced by women of the hegemonic culture oppresses and exploits the Chicana in both subtle and obvious ways.

When white feminists begin to categorize the different types of feminisms, we in turn can begin to trace the muting of issues of race and ethnicity under other feminist priorities. Elaine Showalter in *A Literature of Their Own* charts the "stages" of writing by women into the categories of "feminine, feminist, and female" (1977, 13). She first establishes that *all* "literary subcultures, such as black, Jewish, Canadian, Anglo-Indian, or even American," go through phases of imitation, internalization, protest, and finally self-discovery (1977, 13). In addition to the misrepresentation of what "literary subcultures" write, Showalter creates an ethnocentric, Euro-centric, middle-class history of women's writing.

Her penchant for creating literary history, however, does not stop with British women. In "The Feminist Critical Revolution," she again maps out "phases," this time of feminist criticism (1985). Feminist criticism, in Showalter's program, progresses from critiques of sexist texts by men, to the rediscovery of the female literary tradition, then finally, and presumably most advanced, to the revision of literary theories to take into account women's own interpretations, a type of essentialism that assumes the universality of Woman's experience. When we look at a Chicana literary project like Helena María Viramontes's "The Cariboo Cafe" (1985), published at the same historical moment as Showalter's essay, however, we can see how her model does not contain Chicana writers or our agendas.

Liberal, Anglo-American feminists are not alone in the recreation and representation (colonization) of women's literary history. In "Women's Time" (1981) Julia Kristeva also defines the phases of feminism. Sounding alarmingly like a version of racist anthropologist Lewis Henry Morgan's (1877) categories of savagery, barbarism, and civilization, which structure the evolution of societies, Kristeva sets up her own hierarchies. The most "primitive" would be the position that women in the United States would call liberal feminism. While not denying the political importance of this phase, the struggle for universal suffrage, equal pay for equal work, abortion rights, and so on, Kristeva nonetheless sees the limits of this ahistorical, universalist, globalizing stage. Next on the evolutionary scale is the radical feminist phase, a reductive, essentialist feminism where women "demand recognition of an irreducible identity, without equal in opposite sex and, as such, exploded, plural, fluid" (1981, 19). A mixture of these two feminisms, Kristeva explains, constitutes the dominant European feminism. For Kristeva it is the final "signifying space" that she privileges. Sounding extremely premature in her optimism that there has been a real change in sexist institutions of power, she is ready to abandon "the very dichotomy man/woman as an opposition between two rival entities" (1981, 33). This dichotomy, she claims, belongs to the metaphysical. "What can 'identity,' even 'sexual identity,' mean in a new theoretical and scientific space where the very notion of identity is challenged?" (1981, 33–35).

While the first three categories Kristeva outlines are defined politically, the category she advocates for herself is dangerously apolitical as well as ahistorical. Even if we accept that Kristeva specifies European feminisms, her own category assumes a universalist privilege. Nowhere in Kristeva's essay do we get a sense that she even considers women of color in her theories.

Toril Moi, in a text that unfortunately is beginning to be used as the textbook for introductory feminist theory courses, polarizes Anglo-American feminism against European feminism. She goes to great lengths to critique various Anglo-American feminists, often citing that they have not gone far enough in their politics: "The central paradox of Anglo-American feminist criticism is thus that despite its often strong, explicit political engagement, it is *in the end* not quite political enough; not in the sense that it fails to go *far* enough along the political spectrum, but in the sense that its radical analysis of sexual politics still remains entangled with depoliticizing theoretical paradigms" (1985, 87–88). Only one paragraph earlier, however, Moi has just issued an apologia for omitting "black or lesbian (or black-lesbian) feminist criticism in America" (1985, 87). Not only does she assume that she can conflate the concerns of all women of color in the United States as "black" or "lesbian" or a reductionist combination of the two, but she continues to show her bias against non-European feminist theory by stating that "*in so far as textual theory is concerned* there is no discernible difference between these three fields [Anglo-American, black, and lesbian criticism]" (1985, 86). After homogenizing all women of color as black and/or lesbian, and doing it all in a single paragraph, Moi takes this opportunity to further chastise Anglo-American, heterosexual, middle-class women who have made their own concerns universal. Moi's own neglect of race or ethnic specificity in the United States mirrors the way that white supremacy institutes its racist ideology. Clearly, Chicana feminists cannot look to their Eurocentric "sister" for discussions of our specific positions.

In our search for a feminist critical discourse that adequately takes into account our position as women under multiple oppressions we must turn to our own "organic intellectuals." But because our work has been ignored by the men and women in charge of the modes of cultural production, we must be innovative in our search. Hegemony has so constructed the idea of method and theory that often we cannot recognize anything that is different from what the dominant discourse constructs. We have to look in nontraditional places for our theories: in the prefaces to anthologies, in the interstices of autobiographies, in our cultural artifacts, our *cuentos*, and if we are fortunate to have access to a good library, in the essays published in marginalized journals not widely distributed by the dominant institutions. While Chicana academics do publish feminist essays in journals such as *Crítica*,

The Americas Review (formerly *Revista Chicano-Riqueña*), and *Third Woman*, I will focus on one specific type of Chicana feminism that deconstructs the borders erected by Eurocentric feminism.

The prefatory *testimonio* to *Cuentos: Stories by Latinas* (1983)—collectively written by the editors Alma Gómez, Cherríe Moraga, and Mariana Romo-Carmona—offers such a site of radical Chicana and Latina theory. The editors identify themselves as "U.S. Third World women," writers who want to break the tradition of silence imposed upon them by the pressures of the dominant culture which works against the viability of an oral tradition. The realities of women of color under capitalism in the United States urge the Latina woman to write. The material realities of life in the urban barrio or ghetto cannot sustain, in the authors' words, "a tradition which relies so heavily on close family networks and [is] dependent upon generations of people living in the same town or barrio" (1983, vii).

The Gómez, Moraga, and Romo-Carmona project explodes all of Showalter's assumptions about women's writing. As women whose daily existence confronts institutionalized racism, class exploitation, sexism, and homophobia, the U.S. Third World woman does not enjoy the luxury to privilege one oppression over another. While recognizing that Latinos are not a homogeneous group, the editors acknowledge that "as Latinas in the U.S., our experience is different [from that of white people]. Because living here means throwing in our lot with other people of color" (1983, x). Unlike Anglo-American and European feminists, Gómez, Moraga, and Romo-Carmona reject Eurocentrism and "claim 'la mezcla,' la mestiza, regardless of each author's degree of indio, africano, or european blood" (1983, x).

While Showalter's model insists that the first stage of feminist criticism looks back to find a literary tradition, the collaborators of *Cuentos* believe that in order to forge a new affiliation among working-class people of color in the United States who share a kinship of exploitation, looking to a romanticized past is a luxury in which we cannot indulge. Instead, the stories they present are tied to the specific historical imperatives of the woman of color.

By the time Cherríe Moraga and Gloria Anzaldúa each writes her own foreword to the second edition of their breakthrough anthology, *This Bridge Called My Back* (1983), their feminism on the border, or bridge feminism, can issue a full-fledged manifesto for their brand of radical feminism. Moraga also begins to bridge the chasm between radical women and oppressed men, acknowledging that if the volume were written in 1983 rather than in the original 1979, "it would speak much more directly now to the relations between women and men of color, both gay and heterosexual" (Moraga, foreword to the second edition, n.p.). In the four years between editions she envisions a more internationalist *Bridge* that would affirm the connections between U.S. people of color and other "refugees of a world on fire."

As Moraga elaborates her feminist agenda, the many ways in which this feminism differs from the Showalter, Moi, and Kristeva versions of feminism become clear. The Chicana feminist does not present "signifying spaces," but material geopolitical issues that redirect feminist discourse. No longer limiting the feminist agenda to issues of race, class, ethnicity, and sexual orientation, Moraga expresses solidarity with the Third World people struggling against the hegemony of the United States. The issues that Moraga presents in 1983 remain urgent in 1988:

> The U.S. is training troops in Honduras to overthrow the Nicaraguan people's government.
> Human rights violations . . . on a massive scale in Guatemala and El Salvador (and as in this country those most hard-hit are often the indigenous peoples of those lands).
> Pinochet escalates political repression in Chile.
> The U.S. invades Grenada.
> Apartheid continues to bleed South Africa.
> Thousands of unarmed people are slaughtered in Beirut by Christian militia men and Israeli soldiers.
> Aquino is assassinated by the Philippine government.
> And the U.S.? The Reagan administration daily drains us of nearly every political gain made by the feminist, Third World, and anti-war work of the late 60's and early 70's. (Moraga, foreword to the second edition, n.p.)

In the same way that we must break with traditional (hegemonic) concepts of genre to read Chicana feminist theory, working-class women of color in other Third World countries articulate their feminisms in nontraditional ways and forms. The Chicana feminist acknowledges the often vast historical, class, racial, and ethnic differences among women living on the border, but the nature of hegemony practiced by the united powers of patriarchy, capitalism, imperialism, and white supremacy promotes an illusion of an irreconcilable split between feminists confined within national borders. We must examine and question the First versus Third World dichotomy before we accept the opposition as an inevitable fissure that separates women politically committed in different ways from any common cause.

In her testimony, *Let Me Speak* (1978), Bolivian activist Domitila Barrios de Chungara acknowledges the separation between "First" and "Third World feminists: "Our Position is not like the feminists' position. We think our liberation consists primarily in our country being freed forever from the yoke of imperialism and we want a worker like us to be in power and that the laws, education, everything, be controlled by this person. Then, yes, we'll have better conditions for reaching a complete liberation, including a liberation as women" (Barrios 1978, 41). Her statement, however, is problematized by her occasion for speaking. As a participant at the UN-sponsored International Year of the Woman Conference held in Mexico City in 1975, Barrios witnessed co-optation of "feminism" by governments which use women and women's issues to promote their own political agendas. Barrios observed Imelda Marcos, Princess Ashraf Pahlevi, and Jihan Sadat as some of the conference's "official" Third World representatives. We begin to reformulate the dichotomy when we no longer choose to see these representatives as "Third World feminists," but as agents of their respective governments: agents of patriarchy, capitalism, and imperialism. Suddenly the First World/Third World dichotomy emerges as the arena where the split between the ruling class and the working class, between those in power and the disenfranchised, is exposed.

When Barrios disassociates herself from "feminism," she means feminism as defined by women and men of the dominant class. In the paragraph immediately following the one cited above, Barrios speaks as a working-class, socialist-feminist, affiliating herself with border feminists like Moraga and Anzaldúa. Unlike feminists whose political considerations must take into account their positions in an academic institution, Moraga, Anzaldúa, and Barrios consider themselves community activists first and, in the case of Moraga and Anzaldúa, academics second. Indeed, the tension between academic and community pressures erupts in Anzaldúa's own text, *Borderlands/La Frontera* (1987), in a mixture of autobiography, poetry, identity politics, and academic footnotes.

Barrios, for her part, speaks as the union organizer of the Bolivian tin miner's wives, the Housewife Committee of Siglo XX. "For us," she asserts,

> the important thing is the participation of the compañero and the compañera together . . . if women continue only to worry about the house and remain ignorant of the other parts of our reality, we'll never have citizens who'll be able to lead our country. . . . And if we think of the central role played by women as the mothers who have to forge future citizens, then, if they aren't prepared they'll only forge mediocre citizens who are easily manipulated by the capitalist, by the boss. (1978, 41)

While she echoes the rhetorical strategy of the nineteenth-century U.S. feminist, Margaret Fuller (1845), who also argued that women be given equal education in order to teach the children, what to Fuller may have been a conscious rhetorical strategy is to Barrios a cultural imperative as a working-class woman in Bolivia.

If Barrios's point of reference is that of a heterosexual woman who does not question woman's role as mother, we must remember her historical context as a working-class woman in Bolivia, the poorest country in South America. History forces her to accept her position as primary nurturer, as the one who will teach the children about the struggle. History, however, also forces her to act in untraditional ways that ultimately place her in the middle of social and political involvement and in the hands of the Bolivian torturers. Considering the historical and economic realities of Barrios's position as a Bolivian woman, her own discourse echoes Moraga's internationalist agenda:

We know there's a long struggle ahead, but that's what we're all about. And we aren't alone. How many peoples are in the same struggle! And, why not say it? Every people needs the solidarity of others, like us, because our fight is big. So we have to practice proletarian internationalism that many people have sung about, and many countries have followed. Many other countries suffer persecutions, outrages, murders, massacres, like Bolivia. (1978, 42)

While the publication date of Showalter's *A Literature of Their Own* (1977) coincides with Barrios's experiences at the Woman's Year Conference in 1975, the two women's concerns and contexts allow for little else in common. Likewise, Kristeva's deconstruction of the metaphysical constitution of masculine and feminine offer few solutions to the issues that concern women like Barrios and the other border feminists. Moi's admitted ignorance of the existence of any other marginalized women in the United States speaks for itself. MacKinnon's pledge to accept her premises as "simply wrong" if they do not apply to racial complications at least places her feminism closer to that of Barrios, Anzaldúa, Moraga, Gómez, and Romo-Carmona.

But what is "border feminism," which I have begun to use to specify as a type of Chicana feminism? Is it a new discursive practice or methodology that would legitimize the specificity of Chicana/black/lesbian . . . feminisms in Moi's eyes? Or is it simply a rearticulation of Anglo-American feminism with the added twist of color consciousness?

In *Borderlands/La Frontera* (1987) Gloria Anzaldúa examines the dynamics of race, class, gender, and sexual orientation. Whereas Barrios's historical context does not permit her to recognize lesbian issues as valid political concerns, women like Anzaldúa insist on complicating what at first appear as simple, clear-cut issues. For Anzaldúa feminism emerges as the force that gives voice to her origins as "the new *mestiza.*" This "new *mestiza*" is a woman alienated from her own, often homophobic culture, as well as from the hegemonic culture. She envisions the new *mestiza* "caught between *los intersticios,* the spaces between the different worlds she inhabits" (1987, 20). If compañeras like Barrios cannot allow themselves the luxury of bourgeois feminism, a possible alternative is this "bridge feminism" that deconstructs geopolitical boundaries. Anzaldúa's "feminism on the border" begins to do just that. It is a feminism that exists in a borderland not limited to geographic space, a feminism that resides in a space not acknowledged by hegemonic culture. Its inhabitants are what Anzaldúa calls "*Los atravesados* . . . : squint-eyed, the perverse, the queer, the troublesome, the mongrel, the mulato, the half-breed, the half-dead; in short, those who cross over, pass over, or go through the confines of the 'normal' " (1987, 3). By invoking racist, homophobic epithets, Anzaldúa explodes the power that the dominant culture holds over what is "normal" or acceptable.

Whereas the earlier works of women like Angela de Hoyos articulate Tejana feminist issues, Anzaldúa makes the leap from the history of colonization by the United States to the history of colonization as a *mestiza,* a Native American woman. And although some Chicana critics reject the internal colony model because, as María Linda Apodaca states, "when the land was conquered the Mexican population in the Southwest was small given the total land mass" (1986, 110), the specific history of the Tejano/Tejana urges us to remember that there is not one single Chicano/Chicana experience in the United States. Apodaca's assumptions neglect to acknowledge historical specificity of the Tejanas/Tejanos who were forced to live under a reign of terror in post–1845 Texas.

In the poem "Hermano," Angela de Hoyos taunts the Anglo usurper by reminding him of his own immigrant status. He is told to "scare up your little 'Flor de Mayo'—/ so *we* can all sail back / to where we came from" (1975, 13, emphasis added). While De Hoyos identifies with her European heritage, the Pinta, the Niña, and the Santa María of the Spanish conquerors, Anzaldúa, in opposition, insists on identifying with the indigenous Indian tribes as well as with the African slaves who mixed with the conquerors resulting in the *mestizo.* She bases her political, feminist position on the Chicana's history within multiple cultures: indigenous Mexican, African, and always "grounded on the Indian woman's history of resistance" (1987, 21).

Anzaldúa's text is itself a *mestizaje:* a postmodernist mixture of autobiography, historical document, and poetry collection. Like the people whose lives it chronicles, *Borderlands* resists genre boundaries as well as geopolitical borders. The text's opening epigraph is an excerpt from a song by the *norteño* conjunto band, Los Tigres del Norte. But if Anzaldúa's historical ties are closer to the *corrido* tradition than to the historical imperatives of postmodern theory, hers is the new *corrido* of the *mestiza* with a political analysis of what it means to live as a woman in a literal and figurative Borderland. She tells us that "The U.S.-Mexican border *es una herida abierta* (is an open wound) where the Third World grates against the first and bleeds. And before a scab forms it hemorrhages again, the lifeblood of two worlds merging to form a third country—a border culture" (3). Through issues of gender politics Anzaldúa locates personal history within a history of the border people. Legitimacy belongs to the Anglo hegemony, the indigenous population is nothing more than an aberrant species. To the white power structure the *mojado* (wetback) is the same as the *mexicano de este lado* (Mexican from the U.S. side). As she chronicles the history of the new *mestiza*, Anzaldúa explores issues of gender and sexual orientation that Chicano historians like David Montejano, Arnoldo De León, and Rodolfo Acuña have not adequately addressed. Presenting this other history of Texas that Anglo-Texans like J. Frank Dobie (1936) and Walter Prescott Webb (1935) never mention, Anzaldúa further merges autobiography with historical document. Her family history becomes the history of the Chicana/o experience in south Texas after colonization and occupation by U.S. forces. Those who dared resist were lynched by the Texas Rangers. "My grandmother," Anzaldúa informs us, "lost all her cattle / they stole her land" (8). The history of dispossession is transmitted orally from one generation to the next; Anzaldúa's mother tells the story of *her* widowed mother who was cheated by the Anglo usurper: "A smart *gabacho* lawyer took the land away *mamá* hadn't paid taxes. No *hablaba inglés*, she didn't know how to ask for time to raise the money" (8).

Autobiography for the new *mestiza is* the history of the colonization of indigenous Southwestern peoples by Anglo-American imperialists intent on their manifest destiny. Texas history, in Anzaldúa's revision, is incomplete without the presentation of the Mexican woman who dares to cross the border. She is the one who is the most easily exploited, physically as well as sexually. The *coyote* can enslave her after raping her. If she is lucky enough to make it to the U.S. side, she can look forward to laboring as a maid "for as little as $15 dollars a week" (12).

Once she establishes a working definition of the *mestizo* border culture with which she identifies, Anzaldúa begins her internal critique of that world. Because she is so much a part of this world, she can penetrate its inner dynamics and understand the oppressions that it in turn uses to control women within the culture. When Anzaldúa tells us how she rebelled, we can see the intense power that the Chicano culture holds over women: "*Repele, Hable pa' 'tras. Fuí muy hocicona. Era indiferente a muchos valores de mi cultura. No me deje de los hombres. No fuí buena ni obediente*" (I argued. I talked back. I was quite a bigmouth. I was indifferent to many of my culture's values. I did not let the men push me around. I was not good nor obedient) (15, my translation). The ideal woman for the people of the borderland is one who stands behind her man in silence and passivity. If she refuses her female role as housekeeper, she is considered "lazy." To study, read, paint, write are not legitimate choices for the *mestiza*. Her testimony rings true for many Chicanas who struggle against their gender indoctrination. That her history exists for us to study is a testament to her resistance: "Every bit of self-faith I'd painstakingly gathered took a beating daily. Nothing in my culture approved of me. Había agarrado malos pasos [I had taken the wrong path]. Something was 'wrong' with me. *Estaba más allá de la tradición* [I was beyond the tradition]" (16, my translation).

"Cultural tyranny" for the Chicana feminist imposes an additional hegemonic power against which she must struggle. She must not only contend with the racism of the dominant Anglo-American restraints, she must also resist the oppressive yoke of the sexist Chicano culture:

> Culture is made by those in power—men. Males make the rules and laws; women transmit them. How many times have I heard mothers and mothers-in-law tell their sons to beat their wives for not obeying them, for being *hociconas* (big mouths), for being *callejeras* (going to visit and gossip with neighbors), for expecting their husbands to help with the rearing of children and the housework, for wanting to be something other than housewives?" (16)

Anzaldúa's gender politics are always aware of the women who are agents of the patriarchy.

In addition, Anzaldúa understands that for the new *mestiza* an education is imperative for liberation. But the realities of living in a borderland, a muted culture in the midst of the hegemonic power of the United States, the chances are slim that a Chicana will survive the battle against the combined forces of a sexist Chicano culture and the racist power of the dominant culture. Furthermore, economic exploitation ensures that Chicanas stay in their place because "as working class people our chief activity is to put food in our mouths, a roof over our heads and clothes on our backs" (17).

Anzaldúa's project problematizes further still the traditions of Chicanismo, when, as a lesbian Chicana, she forces the homophobes of the Chicano community to see their prejudice. If the heterosexual Chicana is ostracized from her culture for transgressing its rules of behavior, for the

Chicana lesbian "the ultimate rebellion she can make against her native culture is through her sexual behavior" (19). She makes the "choice to be queer" and as a result feels the ultimate exile from her homeland, cultural as well as geographic. She transforms the bourgeois concept of "safety" and "home" to concepts she can carry with her along with her political commitments. As a Chicana "totally immersed" in her culture, she can choose to reject the crippling aspects of traditions that oppress women and silence homosexual men and women. Her refusal to "glorify those aspects of my culture which have injured me and which have injured me in the name of protecting me" signals the agenda for the new *mestiza*, the border feminist (22). The border feminist that Anzaldúa presents is a woman comfortable with new affiliations that subvert old ways of being, rejecting the homophobic, sexist, racist, imperialist, and nationalist.

In addition to gender transgressions that Anzaldúa's new *mestiza* introduces, new subject matter for poetry is another "aberration" that the Chicana feminist presents. African-Americanists from Ida B. Wells (1969) to Hazel Carby (1985) and Wahneema Lubiano (1987) have explored the terroristic method by which the dominant culture kept the black people under control: the law of the rope. Likewise, Chicanos, particularly in Texas, have lived under the threat of lynching. But while historian Arnoldo De León investigates lynching as an institutionalized threat against Tejanos, it takes Anzaldúa's poem, "We Call Them Greasers," to flesh out the ramifications of the lynch law to Chicanas. In the poem whose title pays tribute to De León's history, *They Called Them Greasers* (1983), the connection between the history of oppression of nineteenth-century African slaves and ex-slaves and nineteenth-century *mestizos*/Chicanos emerges. Narrated by the Anglo-American usurper, this example of what Barbara Harlow (1987) has called resistance poetry speaks of how tejanos lost their lands and often their lives. The Anglo narrator assumes the role of deity as he forces the Tejanos to place their hats "over their hearts" and lower their eyes in his presence. He rejects their collective farming techniques, cultural remnants of indigenous tribal traditions of the *mestizo*. He sneers, "they didn't even own the land but shared it." The Tejano "troublemakers" who actually have "land grants and appeal to the courts" are called laughingstocks, "them not even knowing English" (134). For the Anglo-American imperialist literacy in Spanish or any other nonstatus language is by their definition illiteracy. The women, in particular, suffer an additional violence before they are murdered by the gringo.

While Chicano (male) historians have done much to expose the realities of violent acts against the Tejanos, they have, to a great extent, been reluctant to voice the perhaps unspeakable violence against Tejanas. Even

Américo Paredes in his breakthrough text, *"With His Pistol in His Hand"* (1958), cannot articulate the violence that Gregorio Cortez's wife, Leonor Díaz Cortez, must have suffered in the four months that she spent in a Texas jail, incarcerated for her husband's alleged crime (87). During the Ranger's manhunt for Cortez, a Mexican woman is alleged to have given information to the sheriff leading to Cortez's capture. Paredes states: "The woman, whoever she was, at first refused to talk, but 'under pressure' told Glover where Cortez was going. . . . What sort of pressure Glover used, whether it was physical or psychological, there is no way of telling" (1958, 68). Precisely because "there is no way" for a male historian to tell the history of the Chicana, it takes Anzaldúa's voice to articulate the violence against nineteenth-century Tejanas. In "We Call Them Greasers" she finds the words that acknowledge the history of violence against the Tejana. This history includes rape as institutionalized strategy in the war to disempower Chicano men. While the Tejano is tied to a mesquite tree, the Chicano version of the African-American hanging tree, the gringo rapes the Tejana.

> She lay under me whimpering.
> I plowed into her hard
> kept thrusting and thrusting
> felt him watching from the mesquite tree
> heard him keening like a wild animal
> in that instant I felt such contempt for her
> round face and beady black eyes like an Indian's.
> Afterwards I sat on her face until
> her arms stopped flailing,
> didn't want to waste a bullet on her.
> The boys wouldn't look me in the eyes.
> I walked up to where I had tied her man to the
> tree and spat in his face. Lynch him, I told the
> boys. (134–35)

Once the rapist gains total control over the Tejano through the violation of his woman, the rapist can feel only contempt for her. Within the hierarchy of powerlessness the woman occupies a position below the already inferior brown man. While De León chronicles how Anglo-American occupiers made their conquests and massacres more bearable by comparing their victims to animals, similarly, by emphasizing the *mestiza*'s "Indian" features, the Anglo-American imperialist further relegates the Chicana to the savagery of the Indian (1983, 14–23). Anzaldúa's reluctance to condemn the passive observers, "the boys," in the poem is not because of a misguided loyalty to the gringo, but an implicit recognition of the power of the class structure even in nineteenth-century Texas where the rich land barons controlled all their workers, regardless of race or ethnicity.

In poems like "sus plumas el viento," "Cultures," and "sobre piedras con lagartijos," Anzaldúa reasserts her solidarity with the exploited men and women along the border. "El sonavabitche" protests the exploitation of undocumented farm workers in places like Muncie, Indiana. Her poetry exposes the methods by which unscrupulous farmers create a modern-day slave system. Hiring undocumented Mexican laborers to work their fields, they tip off the Immigration and Naturalization Service (INS) for a raid before pay day. The Chicano narrator expresses solidarity with his undocumented compañeros when he refuses to work for the *sonavabitche* who has used the INS tactic "three times since we've been coming here / *Sepa dios* [God knows] how many times in between. / Wets, free labor, *esclavos* [slaves]. / *Pobres jijos de la chingada* [Poor sons of whores]. / This is the last time we work for him / no matter how *fregados* [desperate] we are" (126–27, my translation).

Finally, it is in the poem "To live in the Borderlands Means You" that Anzaldúa sums up her definition of the new *mestiza*, the feminist on the border. She is one who "carries five races" on her back, not Hispanic, Indian, black, Spanish, or Anglo, but the mixture of the five which results in the *mestiza, mulata*. She's also "a new gender," "both woman and man, neither" (194). While not rejecting any part of herself, Anzaldúa's new *mestiza* becomes a survivor because of her ability to "live *sin fronteras* [without borders] / be a crossroads" (195).

While Anzaldúa transgresses aesthetic boundaries in her text, transgresses gender boundaries in her "choice" to be a lesbian, transgresses ethnicity and race in her formulation of the new *mestiza* combining Native American, Spanish, African, and even Anglo "blood" to form a *mestizaje*, her project is nonetheless articulated within the vital history of the Texas Chicana. If history is what forces Anzaldúa's escape into what Jenny Bourne (1987) has called "identity politics" in her essay, "Homelands of the Mind," it is because the only history for the Chicana is the history of the *mestiza*'s colonization by both the Spanish conquerors and the Anglo-American imperialists in their conquest of south Texas. Once Anzaldúa establishes a history of the border people who "were jerked out by the roots, truncated, disemboweled, dispossessed, and separated from [their] identity and [their] history," (8) the Chicana feminist can turn to other concerns. Patricia Fernández-Kelly's *For We Are Sold, I and My People* (1983) presents a history of the *mestiza* laboring in the exploitative *maquiladora* (factory) system that Anzaldúa alludes to in her own work. In addition, Anzaldúa calls attention to the unwritten history of the *mestizas* in the *colonias* of south Texas and the border cities like El Paso and Ciudad Juárez, homelands of contemporary victims of U.S. multinational corporations. These people are being poisoned by the water they are forced to store in chemical drums that once held carcinogens. (*Austin American Statesman*, 27 March 1988).

The Chicana feminist's theory and methodology are ideological analysis, materialist, historical research, as well as race, class, and gender analysis. It is never an ahistorical "politics of equal oppressions" (Bourne 1987, 16) because Chicana feminism develops from an awareness of specific material experience of the historical moment. Unlike the feminism of sisterhood, "feminism which is separatist, individualistic and inward-looking" (Bourne 1987, 2), Chicana feminists look "inward" in moments of self-exploration and see themselves as daughters of non-Western, indigenous tribes. Anzaldúa's feminist discourse leads her to look inward only for a deeper understanding of a larger erased history.

Anzaldúa's text can be seen as a bridge that forms a continuum between her collaboration with Moraga in *This Bridge Called My Back* (1983) and Helena María Viramontes's "The Cariboo Cafe" in her collection, *The Moths and Other Stories* (1985). One of the Chicana contributors to the *Cuentos* anthology (Gómez, Moraga and Romo-Carmona 1983), Viramontes continues the internationalist connection with women in Latin America and other Third World countries. If Anzaldúa's antihegemonic strategy is to recreate border history for the *mestiza*, in "The Cariboo Cafe" Viramontes's strategy is to expose the extent of the political power of the United States. Viramontes presents the oppression of the reserve army of laborers that the United States creates and then designates as "other," the "illegal" immigrants. In this story Viramontes shows us that we *can* combine feminism with race and class consciousness, even if we recognize the fallacies of an all-encompassing "sisterhood." In this Chicana political discourse Viramontes commits herself to a transnational solidarity with other working-class people who like all nonindigenous tribes are immigrants to the United States. In *The Political Unconscious* Fredric Jameson has said that "history is what hurts" (1981, 102). For the most recent wave of brown immigrants who come to the United States in search of political freedom, the pain intensifies when they realize that for the brown, black, and Asian races, the suppressed history of the United States is the history of exploitation as well as racism.

"They arrived in the secrecy of night, as displaced people often do, stopping over for a week, a month, eventually staying a lifetime" (Viramontes 1985, 61). So Viramontes begins her history of the displaced immigrants of the eighties. They are the "illegal aliens," the racist label by which the U.S. government designates an exploited subculture it has created. As

James Cockcroft asks: "if so many employers and all consumers depend so heavily on these people, then why is it that they are viewed as a "problem" or as "illegals"? Human beings can *do* illegal things, but can a human being actually *be* illegal? Moreover, since when under capitalism is it an illegal act to sell one's labor power for a low wage to an employer engaged in a socially approved business?" (Cockcroft 1986, 64).

In "The Cariboo Cafe" Viramontes interweaves narrative voices to give the history of the undocumented worker in the United States. Viramontes gives the story of the killing of an undocumented female worker wider political significance in the heteroglossic versions (see Bakhtin 1981, 263) of life at the borders, at the periphery of North American society.

The Cariboo Cafe is the center around which Viramontes constructs her revision of history. The cafe, a sleazy diner on the wrong side of the tracks, attracts the outcasts of late capitalism. Burned-out drug addicts, prostitutes, and undocumented workers frequent the place run by a petty bourgeois man who becomes the mouthpiece of the dominant society. While his speech places him in the working class, he spouts the ideology of the dominant class. What to him are unexamined platitudes, "family gotta be together" (73), are for outsiders like the undocumented workers ideologically charged, an ideology that Viramontes resists and unmasks in her tale. Viramontes transforms this cynical short-order cook with a grease-stained apron into a grotesque Uncle Sam, a living contradiction of core and periphery. The great irony here is that this man is almost as much a victim of the capitalist system as are the undocumented workers. If the new immigrants are exploited by capital as they labor in the sweatshops of the garment warehouses, this Anglo-American has been similarly victimized by the imperialistic urges of a U.S. government that led the country into a war in Southeast Asia. We learn that the man's only son is dead; it still haunts him that he will never know "what part of Vietnam JoJo is all crumbled up in" (73).

The owner of what the workers call the "zero zero place" is able to voice the dominant ideology not because of a class privilege, but because of his privilege as a white man. It is here that Viramontes exposes how the hegemonic forces of race, class, and gender intersect and collide. When she gives equal weight to the voices of the young daughter of undocumented workers and to a Salvadoran political refugee, Viramontes gives voice to the counterhegemonic.

The first voice we hear in the story is that of Sonya; we see the urban landscape through her eyes. Both her parents work so that the family may one day have a "toilet [of] one's own." For the feminist reader this turn of phrase resonates of Virginia Woolf's desire for financial independence for the woman writer, but it also reminds us of the vast difference between the concerns of bourgeois feminists and border feminists. Sonya is a latchkey child whose duties as a female include caring for her younger brother, Macky. The children lose the key to their apartment and get lost trying to find their way to safety. A premise for survival in hostile territory for these children is never to trust the police; the "polie" is "La Migra in disguise and thus should always be avoided" (61). Lost, the children see "a room with a yellow glow, like a beacon light at the end of a dark sea" which Sonya thinks will be a sanctuary from the alleys and the dead ends of the urban barrio. Ironically, the beacon is the "zero, zero place" (64).

In the "double zero cafe" we hear the story of the children's fate in flashback. The cafe owner tells his version as if he were on trial. Indeed, Viramontes *is* putting U.S. immigration policies and ideology on trial. The man constantly presents himself as honest, yet in the same breath he admits to lacing his hamburgers with something that is "not pure beef." He thinks that he redeems himself when he proclaims, at least "it ain't dog-meat" (64). The he remembers the basic contradiction of the "American" ideal: "It never pays to be honest." He continues his version of how it came to be that a Salvadoran refugee was killed in his cafe. When he first saw "that woman," he immediately labeled her as Other: "Already I know that she's bad news because she looks street to me. Round face, burnt toast color, black hair. . . . Weirdo" (65). Through his voice we hear the articulation of the dominant race's rationale for excluding brown races from integration into the U.S. society. Because immigrants of different skin color belie the melting-pot myth, it is harder for them to be accepted in the same way that European emigrants have been accepted in the history of U.S. colonization. When the woman speaks Spanish to the children with her, he states: "Right off I know she's illegal, which explains why she looks like a weirdo" (66). Here Viramontes unmasks how the dominant marginalize on the basis of color and language.

Only when we get the third voice does Viramontes allow us to realize what has happened to the lost children of the first section. They have been taken by a Salvadoreña who mistakes Macky for her missing son. This woman is a modern day *llorona* (the wailing woman of *mestizo* folklore) who has fled her country after her own child was murdered by the right-wing, U.S.-backed government. The child is one of the countless *desaparecidos* in those countries whose dictators the U.S. government keeps in power.

The Salvadoreña tells her story and, indeed, becomes the modern-day wailing woman; in this version she represents all women who are victimized by conquering races and classes. The Salvadoreña represents all women "who come up from the depths of sorrow to search for their children; . . . [she] hear[s] the wailing of the women and know[s] it to be [her] own (68–69). In his essay "On Language as Such and on the Language of Man," Walter Benjamin argued that the lament "is the most undifferentiated, impotent expression of language; it contains scarcely more than the sensuous breath" (1978, 329). Viramontes uses the lament motif in this story not only to expose the socially sanctioned, passive roles for women within the patriarchy, but to show the powerlessness of the victims of repressive governments, and thus, the lament contains much more than Benjamin would have it contain.

In her abjection the Salvadoreña believes Macky is her son. She cares for him and cannot understand why the cafe owner would call her act a kidnapping. For her, as for the children, the police here are no different from the police in the country she has fled. They will take her son away from her. She resists arrest and throws boiling coffee at the man pointing a gun at her forehead. With the Salvadoreña's final act of resistance Viramontes explodes the boundaries of family, of safety, and of home.

From Anzaldúa's important revision of Texas history to the theoretical proclamations by the collective voices of Moraga, Gómez, and Romo-Carmona to Viramontes's questioning the constitution of family, Chicana feminism challenges boundaries defined by the hegemony. When Eurocentric, liberal feminists define "theory" and "methodology," they become part of the hegemonic power that constructs the idea of "method" and "theory"; they cannot recognize racial or ethnic difference. Chicana feminism, both in its theory and method, is tied to the material world. When feminist anthologizers like Toril Moi cannot recognize Chicana theory, it is because Chicanas ask different questions which in turn ask for a reconstruction of the very premises of "theory." Because the history of the Chicana experience in the United States defines our particular *mestizaje* of feminism, our theory cannot be a replicate of white feminism nor can it be only an academic abstraction. The Chicana feminist looks to her history (to paraphrase Bourne's plea for feminist praxis) to learn how to transform the present. For the Chicana feminist it is through our affiliation with the struggles of other Third World people that we find our theories and our methods.

José E. Limón

Dancing with the Devil: Society, Gender, and the Political Unconscious in Mexican-American South Texas

"¡Es puro pedo de viejas!" ("It's all women's crap!) Mendieta told me as we sat at the bar in the mostly empty dance hall on a Monday morning in the summer of 1979. We were effectively alone as we each sipped a late morning beer, save for an elderly janitor cleaning up after the Sunday *tardeada* (the Sunday afternoon dance). Mendieta, part owner of this slightly decrepit dance hall, continued to talk: "Mira, Limón, el pedo pasó allá" (Look Limón, the shit happened over there), motioning toward the far corner of the dance floor; "pero, pa mí . . . que un vato le metió mano a la ruca" (but, if you ask me, some dude grabbed the broad's ass), telling me this with a yellowed toothy grin while grabbing a hammy handful of air. He paused and leaned toward me. "¡Pero eso que dicen del diablo . . . es puro pedo! ¡Pedo de viejas!" (But all that stuff they're saying about the devil is just a lot of crap! Women's crap!) "Y si quieres saber la verdad, anda ver a la ruca; se llama Sulema y es mesera en el restaurante San Miguel" (And, if you want to know the truth, go see the broad, her name is Sulema and she's a waitress at San Miguel's restaurant). "¿Quieres otra vironga, carnal?" (Would you like another beer, *bro?*), he asked, and without waiting for my answer, he half waddled to the other side of the bar and pulled another two out of the ice dismissing my effort to pay with a wave and a flash of a ring-laden hand. However, he was only part-owner of *El Cielito Lindo* (the Beautiful Little Heaven) dance hall, so, from a well-loaded money clip extracted with some difficulty from a deep pocket of his yellow matching leisure suit pants, he peeled off a couple of dollars and put them in the cash register taking his change as well. One beer and a few pleasantries later, I was off to San Miguel's restaurant in search of Sulema and the devil, but not without Mendieta's parting shot, "No se te olvide, Limón, es puro pedo" (And don't forget . . . it's just a lot of crap).[1]

In the early summer of 1979 I had returned to my native, hot, poverty-stricken south Texas from cool, distant, hip Westwood, California, where I had been spending a postdoctoral year at UCLA. I had gone to UCLA as a cultural anthropologist interested in folklore, particularly Mexican-American folklore, but I had spent the year fighting traffic and reading in political economy and Marxist cultural theory and historiography. Gramsci, E. P. Thompson, Peter Burke, Genovese, Gutman, Stuart Hall, Raymond Williams, all these and others swam into my ken, but particularly Gramsci and his discussions of the relationship between folklore and class resistance. These I now brought home with me to southern Texas and the folklore of its racially and class-dominated Mexican-Americans. I was interested in testing this theoretical outlook against the ballads, dances, legends, food rituals, folk speech of this my native class and cultural community. But where to begin?

Shortly before leaving Texas, I had begun to gather data on a devil figure that had recurrently appeared among Mexican-Americans in south Texas since the mid-seventies and, I soon discovered, had not disappeared during my absence. Why not here? A relative had told me about one of many reported recent appearances, this one at *El Cielito Lindo* dance hall in a medium-sized town (population 90,000) in deep south Texas that I shall fictitiously call *Limonada* (Lemonade) since so many of my relatives live there.

Now, as I finished a delicious *fritada* (goat blood pudding) at San Miguel's restaurant, Sulema, to whom I had briefly introduced myself already, was done with the lunch rush hour, and she had a little time to come over and talk to me during her own thirty-minute lunch break. While Señor San Miguel checked his Rolex and eyed us both suspiciously, she munched her tacos, sipped her *tamarindo* (tamarind) water, and began to tell me about the devil.

As it turned out, according to her, Mendieta was mistaken. Nothing, she said, had actually happened to *her*. It was some other *muchacha* (girl), though she knew her. "Nos salimos de high school al mismo tiempo, hace seis años" (We dropped out of high school about the same time, six years ago), she added, with only the slightest trace of embarrassment crossing her face which looked older than the twenty-four to twenty-seven years of age I now calculated her to be. But how did she know about the incident? Well, while she wasn't involved in it, she had been at the dance at *El Cielito Lindo* the night it happened. "Tocaron Shorty y los Corvettes y andaba con mis amigas" (Shorty and the Corvettes played that night and I was with my girlfriends). But did she actually *see* the devil, I asked, in a silly, too hurried anthropologically adolescent fashion. "Pos, no, pero una de mis amigas lo vio" (Well, no, but one of my girlfriends saw him). "Yo nomás sé lo que dice la gente" (I only know what people say).

I was about to ask her just what it was that people say, but our lunch time had run out and Sr. San Miguel and dirty dishes waited. Could I see her again, and, perhaps her girlfriends, I inquired? Long pause . . . and I knew. I had made another mistake. She didn't have to say it; her long hesitation said it all: "Familia? ¿Quién eres tú? ¿y qué quieres de deveras?" (Family? Who are you? and what do you really want?), and, the ultimate deep normative structure of greater Mexico, "¿Qué va a decir la gente?" (What will people say?). I pulled back slightly in silence as we stood at the restaurant door. Perhaps sensing my discomfort, she quickly and expertly negotiated this tricky cultural terrain for both of us. Well, she said, she lived with her parents since she was single, so she wasn't so sure about my coming to their house, since they didn't *know* me nor, we had established earlier, did they know my relatives well, although one of her brothers had known my cousin, Tony, in high school before he was killed in Vietnam. There was the restaurant as a place to meet like today, but there was only the lunch period like today . . . and then there was Sr. San Miguel. As for some other place . . . after hours . . . well, ¿qué va a decir la gente? She didn't have to say it.

Then she had a bright thought. Could we meet Wednesday night at the Denny's Restaurant on the highway? She and her friends went there almost every Wednesday night for lemon meringue pie and coffee. Good pie, she assured me. I couldn't at least not this Wednesday. I was on a preliminary field scouting trip, making initial contacts such as these and establishing a place to live for the summer. And I had to return to Austin for the rest of the week, but I would be back on Friday—I explained to Sulema and I would see her at the Denny's the following Wednesday. She had another bright thought. There was a dance at *El Cielito Lindo* this Friday night, and, if I liked dances, maybe I could come and maybe she and her friends would be there and maybe we could talk. "A la mejor, ¿quién sabe?" (Maybe, who knows?). San Miguel glared and waited impatiently. His $2.50 an hour was being used up with no labor in return. Later, I would also discover that he, in his married state, periodically tried to get Sulema to go to bed with him. "I'll see you there," I said. As we parted, she told me with a smile, "¡Y no se preocupe del diablo, nomás se le aparece a las mujeres!" (And don't worry about the devil, he only appears to women!).

That Friday night, after paying my $10.00 admission, being frisked for concealed weapons, and making my way past a huge bouncer who wholly engulfed the stool he was sitting on, I met Sulema and her friends, Ester, Blanca, and Dolores or Lola. I politely asked if I could join them, and there were introductions all around with Sulema prefacing the whole thing with a "this is the professor I told you about, es anthropologist y quiere saber del diablo (He's an anthropologist and he wants to know about the devil). Ester, a hairdresser, wanted to know what that had to do with digging up old bones, since the local newspaper had run a story about a team of anthropologists who had a dig going near the town. (Damn those archaeologists I thought to myself, they always get the headlines!) On the other subdisciplinary hand, Lola, a salesperson at Woolworth's, wanted to know was it really true that anthropologists could teach monkeys to speak English like she had read in the *Time* magazine in the beauty shop. Blanca, who worked at the ticket window of the local theater, made a joke that such anthropologists should come to south Texas if they really wanted a challenge. Everyone laughed. I mumbled something about the different kinds of anthropologists and somehow explained my interest by saying in not too convincing fashion then that cultural anthropology is something like history.

Throughout the evening we talked when *Los Cadetes de Linares* (the Cadets from Linares) weren't playing a particularly loud polka or between their sets. We drank a little; me, to keep a clear head; they, perhaps as well and as a matter of social discretion. One would inevitably run into cousins. I had beer while they shared one purse-sized pint bottle of Bacardi rum (bought for them by Blanca's older brother, just recently released from prison). They passed the bottle around either under or flat across the table and carefully poured tiny amounts into mostly Coca-Cola and ice-filled cups. With a small penknife Ester cut up slices of Mexican lemons since the establishment did not provide any with their setups. (This also led to the usual conventional personal joke about not cutting up Limón).

We danced. By dancing with each of them and moving myself around the table each time, we returned from the floor; I tried to solve a probable cultural problem. I wanted other men to feel quite free to come up to ask any of them to dance, the ostensible reason everyone was here. However, I suspected that I had produced another possible cultural problem for myself. After all, I was just one guy dancing with four women. I could just hear the men, particularly the large group of unaccompanied men gathered around the bar saying, "O es muy chingón, o es joto" (Either he's a big fucker or he's a fag), that dark fate that haunts so many men at the edge of their masculine consciousness. In terms of the local principles of homosexuality I'm sure my slight build, buttoned-down shirt, and glasses didn't help. (I was reminded of the times when I visit my parents and go out to drink and shoot pool with my 200-pound, working-class brother. "Damn it," he says after a few beers, "why don't you get some fucking contact lenses?") At any rate I negotiated myself past this possible dark fate throughout the night with only occasional slightly amused glances and, perhaps, paradoxically with

Mendieta's unsolicited help. He was serving behind the crowded bar re-
splendent in another, this time light blue, leisure suit. As I came up to get
another beer and a second setup for the women, he gestured "hello," with
outstretched hands, rolled his eyes and head toward the women, and, in
front of all the men, made an obscene gesture with his hand suggesting
sexual intercourse.

But amidst drink, dance, and talk, I was after the devil and he indeed
appeared, not in any visible dramatic form, but as the principal figure in a
collective narrative produced by the women that night and reproduced in
varying versions throughout my summer. Amidst moments of intense concentration, nervous laughter, and occasional glances toward the dance floor,
this is how I came to know the devil. I offer it as a general dialogue of voices
including my own.

Dice la gente [people say], that sometimes at night when a Mexican-
American dance is in full swing in southern Texas as so many are, especially
on weekend nights; as couples glide in almost choreographed fashion coun-
terclockwise around the floor to the insistent, infectious rhythm of conjunto polka music; as men, women, and music and not small amounts of
liquor all blend in heightened erotic consciousness, it is then that the devil
may appear.

He comes in the form of a well-dressed, quite handsome man. "Estaba
bien cute" (He was real cute), says Blanca, but hastens to add that she didn't
really see him, this is what she was told by a female cousin. The devil is tall
and strong in appearance. "Con shoulders así" (With shoulders like this),
demonstrates Ester with outstretched fingers. Sulema cannot resist. "¿Estás
segura que nomás los shoulders?" (Are you sure you're only talking about
the shoulders?). Laughter. Embarrassed looks and glances. It's a few moments before we can continue and they can look at me again without
laughing. What does he look like? How is he dressed I ask? "¡Muy elegante,
con suit y todo!" (Very elegant with a suit and everything!). "Es güero, así
como Robert Redford" (He's blond, like Robert Redford). I think of Robert
Redford, as I take note of the young Mexican-American men around me, at
best, one or two in inexpensive suits, most with thick dark hair and shirts
open to mid-chest or lower revealing on some, the Virgin of Guadalupe
resting on Indian bare, brown skin.

The narrative stops, perhaps because I have been looking away. So what
else happens, I finally ask. Is that it? A handsome guy appears? Oh no, then
comes the good part, Ester continues. They say that after he came in right
over there, motioning to the entrance to *El Cielito Lindo*, a girl sitting with
her friends spots him and she really wants to dance with him. Blanca
interrupts. "Well, everyone does!" "I know," Ester replies, "pero ésta le hace

ojos" (But this one makes eyes at him). I ask them to slow down as I try to jot down at least the main points of the story and their reactions. So, Ester continues, she makes eyes at him, and he comes over to ask her to dance. In parody and with a laugh, Lola flicks her own heavily made-up eyelids quickly up and down. So he asks her, y salen a bailar [and they go out to dance]. At this point Sulema covers her eyes. Blanca whispers, "this is the good part, this is the good part," and gets a *Shhh!* from Lola.

Up on the bandstand *Los Cadetes de Linares* are coming back from their break and around us men, very occasionally a woman, walk by carrying beers and setups to their tables. The few all-female groups like the one I am with will try to get a male friend or relative to bring them beer and setups to avoid going up to the male-crowded bar. And so, Ester continues, "as they're dancing, la girl le mira los feet y tiene feet de chicken!" (the girl looks down at his feet and he has chicken feet!). "Goat! goat!" Sulema says loudly trying to correct her. Clearly exasperated, Ester sharply replies, "¡Chingado, lo que sea!" (Godamnit, whatever!), and apologizes for using a bad word. On my small pad I scribble as fast as I can, missing a lot but concentrating on the narrators. Ester continues: "Y cuando le vio los feet, la girl gritó" (And when she saw his feet, the girl screamed). "And then she faints right there on the floor," Sulema quickly adds and gets a dirty look from Ester for her unsolicited contribution. "And then she fainted, Mr. Limón," Ester continues (who can't seem to call me José), "and he ran to that corner over there and disappeared in a puff of smoke!" Lola adds a denouement. "My brother says that he was in that corner that night but he only heard the scream, he didn't see smoke or nothing. ¿Quién sabe?" (Who knows?). A puzzle remains. I say to them: Sulema told me that one of you did see the devil. Which one was it? "¡Qué liar, Sulema!" (What a liar!), Blanca exclaims. You told us that *you* saw him when you were going to the ladies room. Sulema looks embarrassed. In the final analysis, however, the issue is not really that important, and I decide to leave it alone as well as the true identity of the woman who encountered the devil on the dance floor.

The Devil and the Varieties of Reading

What is important is that a recurrent belief exists in the form of an emergent collective narrative, that it exists for these women and, to judge from other less systematic data, for women like these throughout south Texas including San Antonio and the extensions of Texas everywhere, for the devil has also been reported in the agriculture labor camps of California and Wisconsin. In another fashion it exists for men as well, as I will show in a moment, but first let me say a bit more about these women and their interpretive perceptions of the devil as I continued to engage them in later conversations principally over too many lemon meringue pies at Denny's. What is the devil all about; what does it mean, if any, for you? Why do you think such an unusual thing happens? Why does the devil appear to women like yourselves at dances? Before answering me directly, they first summarize what la gente dice (people say) which really turns out to be, as I will demonstrate below, synonymous with what the elders say. However, in more extended conversation, it turns out that Sulema, Ester, Blanca, and Lola have their own distinctive consensus perception of this figure and its relation to their lives. Ester: "I don't know. . . . I kind of like him!" Why? (I feign surprise.) He's a devil isn't he? "Sí, pero, he's so *different!*" (Different from what I think to myself? Do I need to really ask or having met Mendieta is the answer evidently clear?) "Está bien *chulo*" (He's so cute, attractive), Ester continues. Lola adds, "I once met a guy like that in Houston." What do you think he would be like, I mean, as a person? I ask. "Te apuesto que es bien suave" (I bet he's real kind, soft, sweet, suave). But he's a devil! I insist in mock argument. What about the goat's feet? "Ay, who cares?" says Sulema. And with this gesture, Blanca adds, with a nice laugh, "¡Nomás le pones zapatitos!" (You just need to put little shoes on him!).

But there are other perceptions of the devil in this community. Let me briefly summarize three others. For example, there are the elderly, both male and female. Here, I talked to eight people. The devil, they say, comes because today things are out of hand. Girls go out to dances by themselves. En nuestro tiempo, no se vía eso (In our time you didn't see that). There is too much drinking. Outside the dances and even inside, you see *marijuanos* (marijuana smokers). A seventy-year-old man tells me. "La última vez que fui, tuve que ir al escusado, y allí estaban los cabrones fumando mugrero" (The last time I went to a dance, I went to a rest room and there were the bastards smoking trash). "And the music is so loud," says another, "con todos esos aparatos (With all those electronic things). And, for all this, they charge so much! ¡Se imagina usted señor Limón diez dólares! ¡Ni que fuéranos ricos!" (Can you imagine Mr. Limón, ten dollars! As if we were rich!) "Ya no son como los bailes de antes (They are not like dances used to be [in our time]). Por eso viene el diablo" (That's why the devil comes).

I carried my same questions to another social scene; the daily afternoon, all male, quiet slow drinking scene at the bar at Mendieta's place. Here is another view more or less shared by the married and the single men who drink there. Like Mendieta, they think of the story as women's noise, chatter, crap, and, they claim, they do not go around telling the story, although they've heard it from women. Nonetheless, what do they think the devil is all about?

They seem to see it as women imagining what they think the women would like to have but can't or shouldn't have. To some extent the single men see the issue in more sexual terms but with an element of race. "Las viejas quieren vatos así, tú sabes, vatos gabachos" (Broads want guys like that, you know, like Anglos). It is the married guys at the bar who offer a more extended analysis. "Women," you know, "always want more of everything. They're never satisfied." "It's like my wife," one tells me, "Cómprame esto, cómprame el otro" (Buy me this, buy me that). "Se vuelven locas con las credit cards" (They go crazy with credit cards). "Chingue, chingue, con que vamos al mall, vamos al mall" (Nag, nag, let's go to the mall, let's go to the mall), says another.

I don't quite see the connection. What does that have to do with the devil? "It's like the church says, like Eve," tells another one, "quería la pinche manzana" (she wanted the damn apple!). "So this rich *white* guy, real high society, appears and he tempts them but he disappears pa que aprendan que no pueden tener todo" (so that they learn they can't have everything). "But they think they can or they want to, por eso se imaginan todo ese pedo" (so that is why they imagine all that shit).

Finally and frankly, here my data is weakest for it comes from a few married women and ample access to them required delicate negotiations so that I really wound up talking to very few wives of relatives and close friends. What do they think? The devil is moral retribution, they tell me, God's way of punishing all those loose women who try to entice men. "You see how she made eyes at him in the story right, José?" a married cousin asks me. "They shouldn't be at the dances out like that. The girls who go to the nightclub at the Holiday Inn are even worse. They're just out to get men." (The Holiday Inn nightclub is where my cousin's husband does his drinking, by the way.) "They should stay at home," she continues. "If the devil appears, quien les manda que anden allí?" (who forced them to be there?). "¡Viejas feas!" (Dirty broads!).

Having set out these different gender-keyed perspectives on the devil in southern Texas, let me now return to the interpretive mission that had brought me in search of the devil in the first place: the desire to begin to understand how such folkloric symbolic phenomena could be integrated into an interpretive account of political economy, an account of race and class domination. And, once interpretively integrated, how should this ethnography—this people writing—be written? How, and to what purpose and end? This interpretive integration and writing finally, of course, turning out to be one and the same thing.

My field notes and memories remained largely unwritten for two or three years after that summer of 1979, although through recurring reports I continued to verify the periodic reappearance of the devil indeed until this past fall. But at that time I did not write. In September 1979 I was beginning my first semester as a new, quite junior assistant professor at the University of Texas at Austin where I had also taken my Ph.D. New classes, new graduate students asking scary intelligent questions, the watchful presence of my mentor, Américo Paredes, and other former professors, all of these marked and accentuated the normal case of APFA—assistant professor fear and anxiety—and absorbed my attention, not to mention my desire to finish older lingering projects and to spend some time with a special person, now my wife, whom I had just met at the anthropology beginning-of-the-year party.

Yet, in a way all of this proved to be a fortunate delay in my writing. For in the interval between then and almost now I had at least two major intellectual experiences that have been critical in shaping this manuscript as it is now developing. The first was my exposure to a relatively new and disturbing concern then at the margins of anthropology with issues of reflexivity and textuality in ethnographic writing as well as a closely re-lated concern with the ethnographic fit between the analytically but only analytically separable notions of political economy and cultural practice. The recent writings of Marcus, Fischer, Boon, and Clifford, among others, seem to be moving these questions to the center of anthropology where they belong. A principal issue that has emerged in these new writings is how to write ethnography particularly in articulating the fit between "polit-ical economy" and local "cultural practice." Marcus and Fischer put the matter this way:

> Most local cultures worldwide are products of a history of appropria-tions, resistances, and accommodations. The task for this subtrend in the current experimental moment is thus to revise conventions of ethnographic description away from a measuring of change against some self-contained, homogeneous, and largely ahistoric framing of the cultural unit toward a view of cultural situations as always in flux, in a perpetual historically sensitive state of resistance and accommoda-tion to broader processes of influence that are as much inside as outside the local context. (1986, 78)

These authors point to various ethnographic experiments in such writ-ing, and I would like to think that my on-going effort is another one. As such I take as my principal task in writing the problem of how to make evident political and economic domination in the lives of my subjects in the detail of everyday life without having to do a formal and fundamentally "false" section showing statistically and otherwise how domination has occurred in south Texas (Foley 1977; de León 1983; Montejano 1987). I have not fully solved this problem yet, but what you have read is my most current effort.

The second experience is closely related to the first and concerns the important influence on my career 1979–81 of a critical intellectual group composed mostly of graduate students from anthropology and literature, called the "social theory group," where in critical dialogue I refined what I had been reading in Marxist cultural theory, tested some ideas on paper, and acquired new sources. Among these new sources were the writings of Michael Taussig, particularly his obviously relevant, *The Devil and Commodity Fetishism in South America* (1980), and Fredric Jameson, *The Political Unconscious* (1981). These I will particularly draw on in my analysis.

It remains to be seen how, to pose my original question in Marxist terms, this symbolic construction speaks to this lived race and class domination and in terms that are open to Marxist cultural criticism even while preserving and not diminishing the local, call them "native" if you will, categories of interpretation. As I noted earlier, I had been introduced to the Marxist literary criticism of Fredric Jameson, and it is to his theoretical framework that I now turn even as I will also suggest its critical revision and expansion in the light of my data. Who is the devil in Mexican American southern Texas that appears and reappears to haunt the imaginations of this historically and contemporarily dominated people?

For Jameson the largest critical project is to discover how any given symbolic act embedded in capitalism, particularly any given narrative— *Heart of Darkness, Light in August,* or the devil at the dance—becomes a part of what he, and I agree with him, takes to be the master narrative of world history. Such narratives

> can recover their original urgency for us only if they are retold within the unity of a single great collective story; only if, in however disguised and symbolic a form, they are seen as sharing a single fundamental theme,—for Marxism, the collective struggle to wrest a realm of Freedom from a realm of Necessity; but only if they are grasped as vital episodes in a single vast, unfinished plot. (1981, 19)

"It is," he continues, "in detecting the traces of that uninterrupted narrative, in restoring to the surface of the text the repressed and buried reality of this fundamental history, that the doctrine of a political unconscious finds its function and necessity" (20).

For Jameson each narrative (and for that matter any symbolic production) is open to an analysis which will restore its "repressed and buried reality," its "traces," into a relationship of meaning with the master narrative. To this analytical end he proposes a threefold model of analysis which demonstrates a narrative's meaning in increasingly wider social contexts of "horizons." These are first that of "political history, in the narrow sense of punctual event and a chronicle-like sequence of happenings in time" (75).

Here Jameson seems to suggest that texts can be read politically but in fairly direct and literal manner. Whatever the ultimate sources of conflict and domination, the text is interpreted by the reader in an explicit representational manner. Thus, in the present case we might say that the social contradictions generated by advanced capitalism are presented to and read by the two sets of women as explicit issues of gender. Specifically, the single women seem to propose a solution to social contradiction by reading the text in the explicit relatively unmediated language of an attractive man, an attractive and presumably manageable man, a man quite unlike those everyday men of prey who fill and dominate their social existence. Against the Mendietas and San Miguels and the male dancers with, according to Blanca, "only one thing on their mind," they project Robert Redford, "con suit y todo, bien suave." Similarly, though in what I shall call a politically negative reading, the younger married women also read the devil but in the most conventional literal terms of Christianity.

It is Evil that appears at the dance, but it does so to punish those women who pose the most direct threat to the achieved security of the married women. Again, the image is read at the most literal level to provide a minimalist and negative solution to the gender experience of the larger social contradiction. It is the impersonal Marxist forces that have set in motion the lived problem of having few marriageable men in the immediate environment. I refer to the married women's solution as negative politics because whereas the single women project a utopian solution through what Richard Flores has called the logic of hope, the married women "solve" the problem by castigating their fellow women through their literal reading of the narrative (Flores, n.d.). At this first level or horizon shared by both sets of women, we might say in Jameson's terms that the aesthetic act as read by those women is providing a symbolic resolution to a felt gender-mediated social contradiction in turn generated by the larger political economy.

Unfortunately, Jameson does leave the impression that this horizon of reading is somehow more limited and not as important as the second and third levels which I shall describe shortly. The relatively unreflective, literal readings at the first level might imply a lack of wider social vision on the part of these women. However, let me suggest an alternative which would acknowledge the explicitness of these women's commentary even while arguing for the comparable importance of the first horizon, thus perhaps revising Jameson. If their readings are indeed literal, it is perhaps because it is precisely these women who live out the most intense and degrading experiences of the social contradiction of capitalism on a daily basis. Intensely caught between the traditional demands of an orthodox capitalist cultural order and the new sexually charged demands of a new advanced capitalism, they, especially the single women, project the only viable solution in fantasy. It is only a greater distance from the intensity of everyday domination that might permit a more abstract though more bloodless interpretive exercise. This is what we find the men doing consistent with Jameson's second horizon of interpretation.

This second interpretive horizon, which Jameson calls the "social," becomes operative "only at the moment in which the organizing categories of analysis become those of social class," more particularly the antagonistic and active relationships between "a dominant and a laboring class" whose ideologies and symbolic acts are also involved in an active, dialectical, and antagonistic relationship (83).

In this kind of class-based analysis "the individual utterance or text is grasped as a symbolic move in an essentially polemic and strategic ideological confrontation between classes." It is, however, an uneven symbolic confrontation from the perspective of global power. Because of the class nature and authority of writing, Jameson implies (echoing Foucault) that "the cultural monuments and masterworks that have survived tend necessarily to perpetuate only a single voice in this class dialogue, the voice of a hegemonic class." What is required at this level of analysis is the interpretive reconstruction of the voice of the dominated, "a voice for the most part stifled and reduced to silence, marginalized, its own utterances scattered to the winds, or reappropriated in their turn by hegemonic culture" (85). At this interesting juncture in his exposition Jameson subconsciously recognizes the power of what so many of us call *folklore* although he cannot name it, an interesting historical repression in itself. It is in this "framework" he tells us,

> in which the reconstruction of so-called popular cultures must properly take place—most notably, from the fragments of essentially peasant cultures: folksongs, fairy tales, popular festivals, occult or oppositional systems of belief such as magic and witchcraft; . . . only an ultimate rewriting of these utterances in these terms of their essentially polemic and subversive strategies restores them to their proper place in the dialogic system of social class. (85–86)

At this level symbolic acts, particularly folkloric symbolic acts, may be understood as expressive diagnostic instruments for making evident the social forces that dominate and for critiquing them, much as the men do in the bar setting.

By experiencing only the everyday domination of race and class but not of gender, the men have the privilege, as it were, of interpreting this narrative in terms of race/class relations. It is they who seem to understand Robert Redford not as utopian hope but as the Anglo who comes to further dominate through gender or the "Anglo" political economy, which again sets in motion commodity consumption which they project onto their wives. While ostensibly a "wider" reading, we can see nonetheless, how it is possibly limited by a sexist perception of their wives as the entry point for the penetration of advanced capitalism through women's perceived intense commodity fetishism, *Vamos al mall, vamos al mall.*

Finally, Jameson suggests a third horizon of reading, one in which the ultimate Marxist historical category of the modes of production is invoked. For Jameson symbolic narratives may also be read at this ultimate level. Here he would suggest that a narrative read at this wider horizon may express, though in a deeply disguised and quite indirect way, the conflict between wholly different cultural periods or modes of production; a narrative may evidence "that moment in which the coexistence of various modes of production becomes visibly antagonistic, then contradiction moving to the very center of political, social and historic life" (95). The narrative is now to be read as "a field of force in which the dynamics of sign systems of several distinct modes of production can be registered and apprehended" (98). However, Jameson also wants to suggest that at this level this registering and apprehension of conflict between different modes of production occurs not so much through a reading of the symbolic "contents" of the narrative as is the case at the other two levels. At the third horizon, he argues, *form* becomes the focus of the interpretive move. We want to concern ourselves with the way the ideology associated with a particular mode of production is captured not in context but in form, we are concerned with what Jameson calls the "ideology of form" (99).

Let me suggest that it is the elders who come closest to reading the devil in this manner. For while they, like others, depart from the contents of the narrative to offer their reading, it is only they who seem to be concerned with form, though not with form in any conventional sense but rather with social form, with the form of society, with their folk sense of the modes of production. The narrative for them signifies not sexual competition nor even antagonistic class relation but something more historically embracing, namely, the perceived long-term changes in their lives as they have undergone conflict and change in what they perceive from a folk perspective as shifts and overlaps in the modes of production. To speak of *los tiempos de antes* is to invent a tradition, for in the historical lives of the elder they, in fact, experienced a more virulent and intense race and class domination both in Mexico and in Texas: strict codes of racial segregation, lynchings, hurrying to step off the sidewalk when an Anglo approached, picking cotton at dirt wages from sunup to sundown, unchecked diseases treated only by largely ineffective *curanderos* because no Anglo doctor would accept Mexican patients. These were the conditions experienced by these elders. Yet as they speak of the past, they invent a tradition, for amidst intense domination they developed a moral economy based on a number of moral principles and an etiquette, both of which were in evident display at the dances they remember. For all its hardship *era bonita la vida* (life was lovely), and the dance is always used as a signifier of this illustration. This tradition of moral economy associated with an orthodox stage of agriculture capitalism is brought to bear on the present moment of advanced capitalism in which domination continues in covert forms *and* in which the critical moral economy is, in the eyes of the elders, rejected by the young who have given way to the psychology penetration of advanced capitalism. "Estos huercos cabrones," says an old man, "toman lo peor de los gringos [These brats, they take the worst of the gringos]."

In setting out these multiple readings and glossing them in Jameson's Marxist terms—as horizons of reading, all occasioned, in the final analysis, by capitalist race domination, I have tried to suggest how it is that folklore can, in its most disguised and symbolic form, speak critically to such domination.

Folklore, however, and the social nature of the folkloric performance also afford us an opportunity to critically revise Jameson's theory. I have already suggested how his levels and concentric circles tend to delegitimize the immediate and concrete and, therefore in this case, the intense lived experience of women in favor of the "under" and more abstract. However, let me point to another problem. Even as Jameson takes note of the power of folklore, he misses the folk and their interpretive power. For Jameson, as with so many literary critics (though not all), there is always the assumption of the ideal individual reader/critic. He or she who consciously or unconsciously reads and registers at the three levels of analyses. There is in such a model the hegemonic internalization of individualism—capitalism's construct of the individual—as the proper stance for all reading. In contrast, we have the shared, collective model I have proposed here, where a community takes multiple readings of the same text and in doing so produces and enhances their collectivity even while allowing their different perspectives.

This notion of collectivity and difference leads us to a critical comparative account of another anthropological understanding of a devil who in the Latin American world also responds to capitalism. For Michael Taussig the devil as it appears to peasants and proletarians in Colombia and Bolivia stands as a critique of the commodity fetishism in advanced capitalism (1980). I find this reading wholly persuasive save in one point and that is the homogeneous nature of this peasant interpretation as Taussig interprets it. Lapsing into conventional ethnography, Taussig posits the homogeneous community, all of who, it is presumed, share this understanding of the devil. Perhaps it is so, but I seriously doubt it. If Mexican-Americans are more heterogeneous as I have suggested, perhaps, they are so because, unlike South American peasants, advanced capitalism has almost wholly enveloped their lives.

Conclusion

Who or what is the devil who haunts the folk imagination of Mexican-American south Texas? Unlike Michael Taussig's devil in South America, this devil does not speak only to a homogeneous, largely male peasantry or only about class interests and encroaching capitalism. As I have suggested in Mexican-American south Texas, the devil is a site for multiple perspectives and cultural contradictions occasioned by the social contradictions generated by capitalism, and while revising Jameson, I have tried to show how these multiple perspectives may be consonant with a Marxist reading of symbolic action in capitalism.

But, as I close, I must note that in Mexican-American south Texas, the devil also appears in another social sector that I have wholly neglected up until now, namely among the *mexicanitos*, the children.

In Mexican-American south Texas, if a child drops a special object of desire, perhaps a piece of candy on the ground, another child may cry out, "¡Lo besó el diablo!" (The devil has kissed it!). At that point the child may do one of two things if he wishes to retrieve the object. She or he may pick it up and spit on the spot where the candy fell or she or he may make a *crucita* (a little cross) with his or her foot. And the devil, it is believed, will go away. In Mexican-American south Texas the future belongs to these children. Perhaps someday they really *will* make the devil go away.

Notes

1. All names and field site references are fictitious.

Works Cited

Acuña, Rodolfo.

1981   *Occupied America: A History of Chicanos.* 2d ed. New York: Harper & Row.

Alarcón, Justo.

1979   "Consideraciones sobre la literatura y crítica chicanas." *La Palabra* 1, no. 1:3–21.

Alarcón, Norma.

1985   "What Kind of Lover Have You Made Me, Mother?: Towards a Theory of Chicanas' Feminism and Cultural Identity Through Poetry." In *Women of Color: Perspectives on Feminism and Identity,* ed. Audrey T. McKloskey, 85–110. Women's Studies Program Occasional Papers Series, Indiana University, vol. 1, no. 1.

Aldridge, A. Owen.

1982   *Early American Literature: A Comparatist Approach.* Princeton: Princeton University Press.

Almaguer, Tomás.

1974   "Historical Notes on Chicano Oppression: The Dialectics of Race and Class Domination in North America." *Aztlán* 5, no. 1–2:27–54.

Althusser, Louis.

1971   *Lenin and Philosophy and Other Essays.* Translated by Ben Brewster. London: Monthly Review Press, NLB.

1977   "From *Capital* to Marx's Philosophy." In Louis Althusser and Etienne Balibar, *Reading Capital,* 11–69. London: NLB.

Anderson, Perry.

1983   *In the Tracks of Historical Materialism.* London: Verso.

Anonymous.

1983   *Raíz fuerte que no se arranca.* Los Angeles: Editorial Prensa Sembradora.

Anzaldúa, Gloria.

1987   *Borderlands/La Frontera: The New Mestiza.* San Francisco: Spinsters/Aunt Lute.

Apodaca, María Linda.

1986   "A Double Edge Sword: Hispanas and Liberal Feminism." *Crítica* 1, no. 3:96–114.

Arac, Jonathan, Wlad Godzich, and Wallace Martin, eds.

1983   *The Yale Critics: Deconstruction in America.* Minneapolis: University of Minnesota Press.

Argueta, Manlio.

1983   *One Day of Life.* Translated by Bill Brow. New York: Pantheon.

1987   *Cuzcatlán Where the Southern Sea Beats.* Translated by Bill Brow. New York: Pantheon.

Austin, Mary.

1930   *The American Rhythm.* Boston: Houghton Mifflin.

1932   *Earth Horizon: Autobiography.* Boston: Houghton Mifflin.

Baca Zinn, Maxine, et al.

1986   "The Costs of Exclusionary Practices in Women's Studies." *Signs* 11, no. 4:290–303.

Baker, Jr., Houston A.

1986   "Caliban's Triple Play." In *"Race," Writing, and Difference,* ed. Henry Louis Gates, Jr., 381–96. Chicago: University of Chicago Press.

1987   *Modernism and the Harlem Renaissance.* Chicago: University of Chicago Press.

Bakhtin, M. M.

1981   *The Dialogic Imagination: Four Essays.* Edited by Michael Holquist. Translated by Caryl Emerson and Michael Holquist. Austin: University of Texas Press.

Barrios de Chungara, Domitila.

1978   *Let Me Speak! Testimony of Domitila, a Woman of the Bolivian Mines.* With Moema Viezzer. New York: Monthly Review Press.

Bateson, Gregory.

1972   *Steps to an Ecology of Mind: Collected Essays in Anthropology, Psychiatry, Evolution, and Epistemology.* San Francisco: Chandler Publishing.

Beauvoir, Simone de.

1974   *The Second Sex.* New York: Vintage Books.

239   Works Cited

Benhabib, Seyla.

1987   "The Generalized and the Concrete Other: The Kohlberg-Gilligan Controversy and Feminist Theory." In *Feminism as Critique*, ed. Seyla Benhabib and Drucilla Cornell, 77–95. Minneapolis: University of Minnesota Press.

Benjamin, Walter.

1978   "On Language as Such and on the Language of Man." In *Reflections: Essays, Aphorisms, Autobiographical Writings*, ed. Peter Demetz, 314–32. New York: Harcourt Brace Jovanovich.

Bercovitch, Sacvan.

1981   "The Rites of Assent: Rhetoric, Ritual, and the Ideology of American Consensus." In *The American Self: Myth, Ideology, and Popular Culture*, ed. Sam B. Girgus, 5–42. Albuquerque: University of New Mexico Press.

1986   "The Problem of Ideology in American History." Paper presented at the Graduate Conference on Literary History and Ideology, University of Texas at Austin, 4 February.

Bercovitch, Sacvan, ed.

1986   *Reconstructing American Literary History.* Cambridge: Harvard University Press.

Bourne, Jenny.

1987   "Homelands of the Mind: Jewish Feminism and Identity Politics." *Race and Class* 29, no. 1:1–24.

Broyles, Yolanda Julia.

1986   "Women in El Teatro Campesino: ¿Apoco Estaba Molacha La Virgen de Guadalupe?" In *Chicana Voices: Intersections of Class, Race, and Gender*, ed. Ricardo Romo, 162–87. Austin: Center for Mexican American Studies Publications.

Bruce-Novoa, Juan.

1975   "The Space of Chicano Literature." *De Colores* 1, no. 4:22–42.

1980   *Chicano Authors: Inquiry by Interview.* Austin: University of Texas Press.

1982   *Chicano Poetry: A Response to Chaos.* Austin: University of Texas Press.

1982–83 "La crítica literaria de Luis Leal." *La Palabra* 4–5, no. 1–2:25–40.

Bruss, Elizabeth.

1982   *Beautiful Theories: The Spectacle of Discourse in Contemporary Criticism.* Baltimore: Johns Hopkins University Press.

Butler, Judith.

1987   "Variations on Sex and Gender: Beauvoir, Wittig, and Foucault." In *Feminism as Critique*, ed. Seyla Benhabib and Drucilla Cornell, 128–42. Minneapolis: University of Minnesota Press.

Cabeza de Baca, Fabiola.

1954   *We Fed Them Cactus.* Albuquerque: University of New Mexico Press.

Calderón, Héctor.

1983 "To Read Chicano Narrative: Commentary and Metacommentary." *Mester* 13, no. 2:3–14.

1985 "On the Uses of Chronicle, Biography and Sketch in Rolando Hinojosa's *Generaciones y semblanzas*." In *The Rolando Hinojosa Reader*, ed. José David Saldívar, 133–42. Houston: Arte Público Press.

1986 "Rudolfo A. Anaya's *Bless Me, Ultima*. A Chicano Romance of the Southwest." *Crítica* 1, no. 3:21–47.

1987 *Conciencia y lenguaje en el "Quijote" y "El obsceno pájaro de la noche."* Madrid: Editorial Pliegos.

Callinicos, Alex.

1985 *Marxism and Philosophy.* Oxford: Oxford University Press.

Campa, Arthur L.

1933 "The Spanish Folksong in the Southwest." *University of New Mexico Bulletin* 4, no. 2.

Carby, Hazel V.

1985 " 'On the Threshold of Woman's Era': Lynching, Empire and Sexuality in Black Feminist Theory." *Critical Inquiry* 12:262–77.

1987 *Reconstructing Womanhood: The Emergence of the Afro-American Woman Novelist.* New York: Oxford University Press.

Cárdenas, Reyes.

1987 *I Was Never a Militant Chicano.* Austin: Relámpago Books Press.

Castillejo, Irene Claremont de.

1974 *Knowing Woman: A Feminine Psychology.* New York: Harper & Row.

Castillo, Ana.

1986 *The Mixquiahuala Letters.* Binghamton, N.Y.: Bilingual Press/Editorial Bilingüe.

Cervantes, Lorna Dee.

1981 *Emplumada.* Pittsburgh: University of Pittsburgh Press.

Chan, Jeffery Paul, et al.

1982 "An Introduction to Chinese-American and Japanese-American Literatures." In *Three American Literatures: Essays in Chicano, Native American, and Asian-American Literature for Teachers of American Literature*, ed. Houston A. Baker, Jr., 197–228. New York: MLA.

Chávez, Denise.

1986 *The Last of the Menu Girls.* Houston: Arte Público Press.

Chawaf, Chantal.

1980　"Linguistic Flesh." In *New French Feminisms,* ed. E. Marks and I. de Coutivron, 177–78. Amherst: University of Massachusetts Press.

Cisneros, Sandra.

1988　*The House on Mango Street.* 2d rev. ed. Houston: Arte Público Press.

Cixous, Hélène.

1980　"The Laugh of Medusa." In *New French Feminisms,* ed. E. Marks and I. de Coutivron, 245–64. Amherst: University of Massachusetts Press.

Cixous, Hélène, and Catherine Clément.

1986　*The Newly Born Woman.* Translated by B. Wing. Minneapolis: University of Minnesota Press.

Clarke, Colin, David Ley, and Ceri Peach, eds.

1984　*Geography and Ethnic Pluralism.* London: George Allen and Unwin.

Clifford, James.

1986　"Introduction: Partial Truths." In *Writing Culture: The Poetics and Politics of Ethnography,* ed. James Clifford and George E. Marcus, 1–27. Berkeley: University of California Press.

Cockcroft, James D.

1986　*Outlaws in the Promised Land: Mexican Immigrant Workers and America's Future.* New York: Grove Press.

Corpi, Lucha.

1980　*Palabras de mediodía: Noon Words.* Translated by Catherine Rodríguez-Nieto. Berkeley: El Fuego de Aztlán Publications.

Cott, Nancy F.

1986　"Feminist Theory and Feminist Movements: The Past Before Us." In *What is Feminism?: A Re-Examination,* ed. Juliet Mitchell and Ann Oakley, 49–62. New York: Pantheon Books.

Cuéllar, José.

1971　"Toward the Study of Chicano Urban Adaptation." *Aztlán* 2, no. 1:37–65.

Culler, Jonathan.

1982　*On Deconstruction: Theory and Criticism after Structuralism.* Ithaca: Cornell University Press.

Davidson, R. Theodore.

1974　*Chicano Prisoners: The Key to San Quentin.* New York: Holt, Rinehart & Winston.

Davies, Miranda.

1987   *Third World: Second Sex.* London: Zed Books.

Davis, Mike.

1985   "Urban Renaissance and the Spirit of Postmodernism." *New Left Review* 151:106–13.

De Hoyos, Angela.

1975   "Hermano." In *Chicano Poems: For the Barrio*, 12–13. San Antonio: M & A Editions.

De Lauretis, Teresa.

1986   "Feminist Studies/Critical Studies: Issues, Terms, and Contexts." In *Feminist Studies/Critical Studies*, ed. Teresa de Lauretis, 1–19. Bloomington: Indiana University Press.

1987   *Technologies of Gender.* Bloomington: Indiana University Press.

De León, Arnoldo.

1983   *They Called Them Greasers: Anglo Attitudes toward Mexicans in Texas, 1821–1900.* Austin: University of Texas Press.

De Man, Paul.

1984   "Phenomenality and Materiality in Kant." In *Hermeneutics: Questions and Prospects*, ed. Gary Shapiro and Alan Sica, 121–44. Amherst: University of Massachusetts Press.

Derrida, Jacques.

1976   *Of Grammatology.* Translated by Gayatri Chakravorty Spivak. Baltimore: Johns Hopkins University Press.

Dobie, J. Frank.

1936   *The Flavor of Texas.* Dallas: Dealy and Lowe.

Eagleton, Terry.

1976   *Criticism and Ideology: A Study in Marxist Literary Theory.* London: NLB.

1983   *Literary Theory: An Introduction.* Minneapolis: University of Minnesota Press.

Eco, Umberto.

1979   *The Role of the Reader: Explorations in the Semiotics of Texts.* Bloomington: Indiana University Press.

Edwards, Richard.

1979   *Contested Terrain: The Transformation of the Workplace in the Twentieth Century.* New York: Basic Books.

Eliot, T. S.

1962   "The Love Song of J. Alfred Prufrock." In *The Waste Land and Other Poems*, 3–9. New York: Harcourt, Brace & World.

El Saffar, Ruth S.

1974   *From Romance to Novel: A Study of Cervantes's "Novelas ejemplares."* Baltimore: Johns Hopkins University Press.

Elshtain, Jean Bethke.

1982   "Feminist Discourse and Its Discontents: Language, Power, & Meaning." *Signs* 7, no. 3:603–21.

Enzensberger, Hans Magnus.

1974   *The Consciousness Industry: On Literature, Politics and the Media.* New York: Seabury Press.

Epple, Juan Armando.

1983   "Literatura chicana y crítica literaria." *Ideologies & Literature,* 4, no. 16:149–71.

Ercilla y Zúñiga, Alonso de.

1569–89 *La araucana.* Primera parte. Madrid: Pierres Cossin, 1569; Segunda parte, 1578; Tercera parte, 1589.

Espinel, Luisa.

1946   *Canciones de Mi Padre: Spanish Folksongs from Southern Arizona Collected by Luisa Espinel from Her Father Don Federico Ronstadt y Redondo. University of Arizona Bulletin* 17, no. 1.

Espinosa, Aurelio M.

1915   "Romancero Nuevomejicano." *Revue Hispanique* 33, no. 84:446–560.

1917   "Romancero Nuevomejicano." *Revue Hispanique* 40, no. 97:215–227; 41, no. 100:678–80.

Fernández-Kelly, María Patricia.

1983   *For We Are Sold, I and My People: Women and Industry in Mexico's Frontier.* Albany: State University of New York Press.

Fernández-Retamar, Roberto.

1989   *Caliban and Other Essays.* Trans. Edward Baker. Foreword by Fredric Jameson. Minneapolis: University of Minnesota Press.

First, Ruth.

1983   *Black Gold: The Mozambican Miner, Proletarian and Peasant.* New York: St. Martin's Press.

Fischer, Michael M. J.

1986   "Ethnicity and the Post-Modern Arts of Memory." In *Writing Culture: The Poetics and Politics of Ethnography,* ed. James Clifford and George E. Marcus, 194–233. Berkeley: University of California Press.

Flax, Jane.

1987   "Postmodernism and Gender Relations in Feminist Theory." *Signs* 12, no. 4:621–43.

Flores, Lauro.

1981   "Notas básicas para la literatura chicana." *La Palabra* 3, no. 1–2:21–29.

Flores, Richard.

n.d.   "Resistance, Change, and the Logic of Hope." Unpublished manuscript. Department of Anthropology, University of Texas, Austin.

Foley, Douglas, et al.

1977   *From Peones to Politicos: Ethnic Relations in a South Texas Town.* University of Texas, Center for Mexican-American Studies.

Foucault, Michel.

1972   "The Discourse on Language." In *The Archaeology of Knowledge,* trans. A. M. Sheridan, 215–37. New York: Pantheon Books.

Fox-Genovese, Elizabeth.

1986   "The Claims of Common Culture: Gender, Race, Class and the Canon." *Salmagundi* 72:131–43.

Fredrickson, George.

1981   *White Supremacy: A Comparative Study of American and South African History.* New York: Oxford University Press.

Frye, Northrop.

1957   *Anatomy of Criticism: Four Essays.* Princeton: Princeton University Press.

1976   *The Secular Scripture: A Study of the Structure of Romance.* Cambridge: Harvard University Press.

Fuller, (Sarah) Margaret (marchesa d'Ossoli).

1845   *Woman in the Nineteenth Century.* New York: Greely & McElrath; New York: W. W. Norton, 1971.

Furman, Necah.

1983   "Walter Prescott Webb: Pioneer of the Texas Literary Tradition." In *The Texas Literary Tradition: Fiction, Folklore, History,* ed. Don Graham et al., 26–36. Austin: Texas Historical Association.

Galarza, Ernesto.

1964   *Merchants of Labor: The Mexican Bracero Story.* Santa Barbara, Calif.: McNally and Loftin.

Gallop, Jane.

1982   *The Daughter's Seduction: Feminism and Psychoanalysis.* Ithaca: Cornell University Press.

Garzón, Luz.

1979   "Going for a Ride." In *Requisa Treinta y Dos: Bilingual Short Story Collection*, ed. Rosaura Sánchez, 165–67. La Jolla: Chicano Research Publications.

Gates, Jr., Henry Louis, ed.

1984   *Black Literature and Literary Theory*. New York: Methuen.

1986   *"Race," Writing, and Difference*. Chicago: University of Chicago Press.

Geertz, Clifford.

1973   *The Interpretation of Cultures*. New York: Basic Books.

Gómez, Alma, Cherríe Moraga, and Mariana Romo-Carmona, eds.

1983   *Cuentos: Stories by Latinas*. New York: Kitchen Table: Women of Color Press.

González, Jovita.

1930   "Social Life in Cameron, Starr, and Zapata Counties." Master's thesis, University of Texas, Austin.

1954   "Mexican Tales: Stories of My People." In *Texas Folk and Folklore*, ed. Mody C. Boatright, Wilson M. Hudson, and Allen Maxwell, 19–24. Dallas: Southern Methodist University Press.

González-Echevarría, Roberto.

1984   "*Cien años de soledad:* The Novel as Myth and Archive." *Modern Language Notes* 99, no. 2:358–80.

Graff, Gerald.

1979   *Literature Against Itself: Literary Ideas in Modern Society*. Chicago: University of Chicago Press.

Gramsci, Antonio.

1971   *Selections from the Prison Notebooks*, ed. Quintin Hoare and Geoffrey Nowell Smith. New York: International Publishers.

Greenblatt, Stephen.

1980   *Renaissance Self-Fashioning: From More to Shakespeare*. Chicago: University of Chicago Press.

Gubar, Susan.

1981   "'The Blank Page' and the Issues of Female Creativity," *Critical Inquiry* 8:243–63.

Habermas, Jürgen.

1972   *Knowledge and Human Interests*. Boston: Beacon Press.

Hall, Stuart.

1977   "Culture, the Media and the 'Ideological Effect'." In *Mass Communication and Society*, ed. J. Curran et al., 315–48. London: Arnold.

Harding, Sandra.

1986   "The Instability of the Analytical Categories." *Signs* 11, no. 4:645–64.

Harlow, Barbara.

1987   *Resistance Literature.* New York: Methuen.

Harss, Luis, and Barbara Dohmann.

1967   *Into the Mainstream: Conversations with Latin-American Writers.* New York: Harper & Row.

Hebdige, Dick.

1979   *Subculture: The Meaning of Style.* London: Methuen.

Herrera-Sobek, María, ed.

1985   *Beyond Stereotypes: The Critical Analysis of Chicana Literature.* Binghamton, N.Y.: Bilingual Press/Editorial Bilingüe.

Herrera-Sobek, María, and Helena María Viramontes, eds.

1988   *Chicana Creativity and Criticism: Charting New Frontiers in American Literature.* Houston: Arte Público Press.

Higham, John.

1974   "Hanging Together: Divergent Unities in American History." *Journal of American History* 61:10–18.

Hinojosa, Rolando.

1973   *Estampas del valle y otras obras.* Berkeley: Quinto Sol Publications.

1976   *Klail City y sus alrededores.* La Habana: Casa de las Américas.

1977a   *Generaciones y semblanzas.* Berkeley: Editorial Justa.

1977b   *Korean Love Songs.* Berkeley: Editorial Justa.

1981   *Mi querido Rafa.* Houston: Arte Público Press.

1982   *Rites and Witnesses.* Houston: Arte Público Press.

1985   *Partners in Crime.* Houston Arte Público Press.

1986   *Claros varones de Belken/Fair Gentlemen of Belken County.* Tempe, Ariz.: Bilingual Press/Editorial Bilingüe.

Hirst, Paul Q.

1979   *On Law and Ideology.* London: Macmillan.

Hull, Gloria T., Patricia Bell Scott, and Barbara Smith.

1982   *All the Blacks are Men, All the Women are White, But some of us are Brave.* Westbury, N.Y.: Feminist Press.

Hutcheon, Linda.

1985   *A Theory of Parody: The Teachings of Twentieth-Century Art Forms.* New York: Methuen.

Independent Commission on International Humanitarian Issues.

1986   *Refugees.* London: Zed Books.

Iser, Wolfgang.

1974   *The Implied Reader: Patterns of Communication in Prose Fiction from Bunyan to Beckett.* Baltimore: Johns Hopkins University Press.

1978   *The Act of Reading: A Theory of Aesthetic Response.* Baltimore: Johns Hopkins University Press.

Islas, Arturo.

1984   *The Rain God: A Desert Tale.* Palo Alto: Alexandrian Press.

Jaggar, Alison M.

1983   *Feminist Politics and Human Nature.* Totowa, N.J.: Rowan & Allanheld.

Jameson, Fredric.

1971   *Marxism and Form: Twentieth-Century Dialectical Theories of Literature.* Princeton: Princeton University Press.

1981   *The Political Unconscious: Narrative as a Socially Symbolic Act.* Ithaca: Cornell University Press.

1983   "Postmodernism and Consumer Society." In *The Anti-Aesthetic: Essays on Postmodern Culture,* ed. Hal Foster, 111–25. Port Townsend, Wash.: Bay Press.

1984   "Foreword," to Jean-François Lyotard, *The Postmodern Condition: A Report on Knowledge,* vii–xxi. Minneapolis: University of Minnesota Press.

Jaramillo, Cleofas.

1939a   *Cuentos del Hogar.* El Campo, Tex.: Citizens Press.

1939b   *The Genuine New Mexico Tasty Recipes.* Santa Fe: Seton Village Press.

1941   *Shadows of the Past/Sombras del Pasado.* Santa Fe: Seton Village Press.

1955   *Romance of a Little Village Girl.* San Antonio: Naylor.

Katsiaficas, George.

1987   *The Imagination of the New Left: A Global Analysis of 1968.* Boston: South End Press.

Khalifeh, Sahar.

1985   *Wild Thorns.* Translated by Tevor LeGassick and Elizabeth Fernea. London: al-Saqi Books.

Kristeva, Julia.

1979   *Folle vérité.* Paris: Seuil.

1981   "Women's Time." *Signs* 7, no. 1:13–35.

Krupat, Arnold.

1989   *The Voice in the Margin: Native American Literature and the Canon.* Berkeley: University of California Press.

Lacan, Jacques.

1968   *Ecrits*. Paris: Seuil.

Lattin, Vernon E., ed.

1986   *Contemporary Chicano Fiction: A Critical Survey.* Binghamton, N.Y.: Bilingual Press/Editorial Bilingüe 1986.

Leal, Luis.

1973   "Mexican-American Literature: A Historical Perspective." *Revista Chicano-Riqueña* 1, no. 1:32–44.

1980   "Cuatro siglos de prosa aztlanense." *La Palabra* 2, no. 1:2–12.

Leal, Luis, and Pepe Barrón.

1982   "Chicano Literature: An Overview." In *Three American Literatures: Essays in Chicano, Native American, and Asian-American Literature for Teachers of American Literature*, ed. Houston A. Baker, Jr., 9–32. New York: MLA.

Lears, T. J. Jackson.

1985   "The Concept of Cultural Hegemony: Problems and Possibilities." *American Historical Review* 90, no. 3:567–93.

Lenin, V. I.

1968   *La literatura y el arte*. Moscú: Editorial Progreso.

Lentricchia, Frank.

1981   *After the New Criticism*. Chicago: University of Chicago Press.

1983   *Criticism and Social Change*. Chicago: University of Chicago Press.

Limón, José E.

1978   "Agringado Joking in Texas Mexican Society: Folklore and Differential Identity." In *New Directions in Chicano Scholarship*, ed. R. Romo and R. Paredes, 33–50. Chicano Studies Monograph Series. La Jolla: Chicano Studies Program, University of California, San Diego.

1980   "Américo Paredes: A Man from the Border." *Revista Chicano–Riqueña* 8, no. 3.

1986a   "Mexican Ballads, Chicano Epic: History, Social Dramas and Poetic Persuasions." SCCR Working Paper No. 14. Stanford: Stanford Center for Chicano Research.

1986b   "The Return of the Mexican Ballad: Américo Paredes and His Anthropological Text as Persuasive Political Performance." SCCR Working Paper no. 16. Stanford: Stanford Center for Chicano Research.

Lizárraga, Sylvia.

1982   "Observaciones acerca de la crítica literaria chicana." *Revista Chicano-Riqueña* 10, no. 4:55–64.

Lomelí, Francisco.

1980   "Eusebio Chacón: Eslabón temprano de la novela chicana." *La Palabra* 2, no. 1:45–55.

Lotman, M. Iurii, and Boris A. Uspenskii.

1985   "Binary Models in the Dynamics of Russian Culture." In *The Semiotics of Russian Cultural History*, ed. Alexander D. Nakhimovsky and Alice Stone Nakhimovsky, 30–66. Ithaca: Cornell University Press.

Lubiano, Wahneema.

1987   "The Harlem Renaissance and the Roots of Afro-American Literary Modernism." In *Messing with the Machine: Four Afro-American Novels and the Nexus of Vernacular, Historical Constraint, and Narrative Strategy*, 44–87. Ph.D. dissertation, Stanford University, Stanford, Calif.

Lucero, Judy.

1980   "Jail-Life Walk" and "I Speak in an Illusion." In *The Third Woman: Minority Women Writers of the United States*, ed. Dexter Fisher, 395, 396. Boston: Houghton Mifflin.

Lummis, Charles F.

1891   *A New Mexico David and Other Stories and Sketches of Southwest*. New York: Charles Scribner's Sons.

1893a   *The Land of Poco Tiempo*. New York: Charles Scribner's Sons.

1893b   *The Spanish Pioneers*. Chicago: Charles McClurg.

1925   *Mesa, Cañon and Pueblo; Our Wonderland of the Southwest; Its Marvels of Nature; Its Pageant of Earth Building; Its Strange Peoples; Its Centuried Romance*. New York: Century.

1952   *The Land of Poco Tiempo*. Albuquerque: University of New Mexico Press.

MacDonell, Diane.

1986   *Theories of Discourse: An Introduction*. New York: Basil Blackwell.

McDowell, John.

1981   "The Corrido of Greater Mexico as Discourse, Music, and Event." In *"And Other Neighborly Names": Social Process and Cultural Image in Texas Folklore*, ed. Richard Bauman and Roger D. Abraham, 44–75. Austin: University of Texas Press.

Macherey, Pierre.

1978   *A Theory of Literary Production*. Translated by Geoffrey Wall. London: Routledge & Kegan Paul.

McKenna, Teresa.

         "Immigrants in Our Own Land: A Chicano Literature Review." In *ADE Bulletin*, forthcoming.

MacKinnon, Catherine.

1982   "Feminism, Marxism, Method and the State: An Agenda for Theory." *Signs* 7, no. 3:515–44.

Mailloux, Steven.

1985   "Reading *Huckleberry Finn:* The Rhetoric of Performed Ideology." In *New Essays on Adventures of Huckleberry Finn,* ed. Louis J. Budd, 107–33. New York: Cambridge University Press.

Major, Mabel.

1938   *Southwest Heritage: A Literary History with Bibliography by Mabel Major, Rebecca W. Smith and T. M. Pearce.* Albuquerque: University of New Mexico Press.

Marcus, George E., and Michael M. J. Fischer.

1986   *Anthropology as Cultural Critique: An Experimental Moment in the Human Sciences.* Chicago: University of Chicago Press.

Martínez, Lorri.

1982   *Where Eagles Fall.* Brunswick, Minn.: Blackberry.

Marx, Karl.

1973   *Grundrisse. Foundations of the Critique of Political Economy.* New York: Random House.

1974   *Capital. Volume I.* New York: International Publishers.

Marx, Karl, and Friedrich Engels.

1932   *The German Ideology* (1845–46). In *The Marx Engles Reader,* 2d ed., ed by Robert C. Tucker. New York: W. W. Norton.

Mathiessen, F. O.

1941   *American Renaissance: Art and Expression in the Age of Emerson and Whitman.* Oxford: Oxford University Press.

Mattelart, Armand.

1986   "Communicating in Nicaragua Between War and Democracy." In *Communicating in Popular Nicaragua,* ed. Armand Mattelart, 7–27. New York: International General.

Meese, Elizabeth.

1986   *Crossing the Double-Cross: The Practice of Feminist Criticism.* Chapel Hill: University of North Carolina Press.

Menefee, Seldon C.

1974   *Mexican Migratory Workers of South Texas.* Washington, D.C.: United States Government Printing Office, 1941; rpt. in *Mexican Labor in the United States.* New York: Arno Press.

Meyer, Doris.

1978   "Felipe Maximiliano Chacón: A Forgotten Mexican-American Author." In *New Directions in Chicano Scholarship*, ed. R. Romo and R. Paredes, 111–26. Chicano Studies Monograph Series. La Jolla: Chicano Studies Program, University of California, San Diego.

Miller, Wayne Charles.

1981   "Cultural Consciousness in a Multi-Cultural Society: The Uses of Literature." *MELUS* 8, no. 3:29–44.

Moi, Toril.

1985   *Sexual/Textual Politics: Feminist Literary Theory.* London: Methuen.

Montejano, David.

1987   *Anglos and Mexicans in the Making of Texas, 1836–1986.* Austin: University of Texas Press.

Montoya, José.

1972   "El Louie." In *Aztlán: An Anthology of Mexican American Literature*, ed. Luis Valdez and Stan Steiner, 333–37. New York: Random House, Vintage Books.

Mora, Pat.

1986   *Borders.* Houston: Arte Público Press.

Moraga, Cherríe.

1983   *Loving in the War Years: Lo que nunca pasó por sus labios.* Boston: South End Press.

Moraga, Cherríe, and Gloria Anzaldúa.

1983   *This Bridge Called My Back: Writings by Radical Women of Color.* Kitchen Table: Women of Color Press.

Morgan, Lewis Henry.

1877   *Ancient Society or, Researches in the Line of Human Progress from Savagery through Barbarism to Civilization.* New York: H. Holt; ed. Eleanor Burke Leacock. Rev. ed. Cleveland: World Publishing, 1963.

New Mexico Folklore Society.

1955   *The New Mexico Folklore Record.*

Niggli, Josephina.

1945   *Mexican Village.* Chapel Hill: University of North Carolina Press.

Olmsted, Frederick Law.

1857   *A Journey through Texas: Or, a Saddle-Trip on the Southwestern Frontier.* New York: Dix, Edwards.

Ordóñez, Elizabeth.

1985   "Introduction." In Villanueva, A. *Life Span*, v. Austin: Place of Herons Press.

Ostriker, Alicia.

1980   "Body Language: Imagery of the Body in Women's Poetry." In *The State of Language,* ed. L. Michaels and C. Ricks, 247–63. Berkeley: University of California Press.

Otero de Warren, Nina.

1936   *Old Spain in Our Southwest.* New York: Harcourt, Brace.

Padilla, Genaro.

1984   "A Reassessment of Fray Angélico Chávez's Fiction." *MELUS* 5, no. 4:31–45.

Paredes, Américo.

1958   *"With His Pistol in His Hand": A Border Ballad and Its Hero.* Austin: University of Texas Press.

1964   "Some Aspects of Folk Poetry." *Texas Studies in Literature and Language* 6, no. 2:213–25.

1976   *A Texas-Mexicano Cancionero: Folkways of the Lower Border.* Urbana: University of Illinois Press.

1979   "The Folk Base of Chicano Literature." In *Modern Chicano Writers,* ed. Joseph Sommers and Tomás Ybarra-Frausto, 4–17. Englewood Cliffs, N.J.: Prentice-Hall.

1982   "Folklore, Lo Mexicano and Proverbs." Special Issue on Mexican Folklore and Folk Art in the United States, *Aztlán* 13, no. 1–2:1–11.

Paredes, Raymund A.

1978   "The Evolution of Chicano Literature." *MELUS* 5, no. 2:71–110.

1982   "The Evolution of Chicano Literature." In *Three American Literatures: Essays in Chicano, Native American, and Asian-American Literature for Teachers of American Literature,* ed. Houston A. Baker, Jr., 33–79. New York: MLA.

Paredes, Raymund A., and Américo Paredes, eds.

1972   *Mexican-American Authors.* Boston: Houghton Mifflin.

Pêcheux, Michel.

1982   *Language, Semantics and Ideology.* New York: St. Martin's Press.

Peña, Manuel.

1982   "Folk Song and Social Change: Two Corridos as Interpretive Forces." Special Issue on Mexican Folklore and Folk Art in the United States, *Aztlán* 13, no. 1–2:13–41.

1985   *The Texas-Mexican Conjunto: History of a Working-Class Music.* Austin: University of Texas Press.

Pérez de Villagrá, Gaspar.

1900   *Historia de la Nueva México (1610).* Alcalá: Luis Martínez Grande; rpt. 2 vols. ed. by Luis González Obregón. México: Museo Nacional de México.

Pérez-Firmat, Gustavo, ed.

1990   *Do the Americas Have a Common Literature?* Durham, N.C.: Duke University Press.

Pierce, Donna, ed.

1985   *Vivan Las Fiestas.* Santa Fe: Museum of New Mexico Press.

Portales, Marco A.

1984   "Literary History, a 'Usable Past,' and Space." *MELUS* 11, no. 1:97–102.

Pratt, Mary Louise.

1981   "The Short Story: The Long and the Short of It." *Poetics* 10:175–94.

1986   "Fieldwork in Common Places." In *Writing Culture: The Poetics and Politics of Ethnography,* ed. James Clifford and George E. Marcus, 27–51. Berkeley: University of California Press.

Quintana, Alvina E.

1988   "Challenge & Counter-Challenge: Chicana Literary Motifs." In *Intersections: Studies in Ethnicity, Gender, and Inequality,* ed. Jennie Curry and Sucheng Chen, 197–221. Pullman: Washington State University Press.

Rebolledo, Tey Diana.

1987   "Tradition and Mythology: Signatures of Landscape in Chicana Literature." In *The Desert Is No Lady,* ed. Vera Norwood and Janice Monk, 96–124. New Haven: Yale University Press.

Reilly, John M.

1978   "Criticism of Ethnic Literature: Seeing the Whole Story." *MELUS* 5, no. 1:2–13.

Rich, Adrienne.

1977   *Of Woman Born: Motherhood as Experience and Institution.* New York: W. W. Norton.

1979   *On Lies, Secrets, and Silence.* New York: W. W. Norton.

Ridd, Rosemary.

1987   "Introduction." In *Women and Political Conflict: Portraits of Struggle in Times of Crisis,* ed. Rosemary Ridd and Helen Callaway, 1–24. New York: New York University Press.

Ríos, Alberto.

1984   *The Iguana Killer: Twelve Stories of the Heart.* New York: A Blue Moon and Confluence Press Book.

Rivera, Tomás.

1971   *"Y no se lo tragó la tierra"/"And the Earth Did Not Part."* Berkeley: Publicaciones Quinto Sol, S. A./Quinto Sol Publications.

1975   "Recuerdo, Descubrimiento y Voluntad." Translated by Gustavo Valadez. *Atisbos,* no. 1:66–77.

1982   "Chicano Literature: The Establishment of a Community." In *A Decade of Chicano Literature (1970–1979): Critical Essays and Bibliography*, ed. Luis Leal et al., 9–17. Santa Barbara, Calif.: Editorial La Causa.

1984   "Richard Rodriguez' *Hunger of Memory* as Humanistic Antithesis." *MELUS* 11, no. 4:5–13.

Robinson, Cecil.

1963   *With the Ears of Strangers.* Tucson: University of Arizona Press.

Rodríguez, Juan, comp.

1982   *Crónicas diabólicas de "Jorge Ulica"/Julio G. Arce.* San Diego: Maize Press.

Roffe, Reina.

1973   *Juan Rulfo: Autobiografía armada.* Buenos Aires: Ediciones Corregidor.

Rosaldo, Renato.

1978   "Lope as a Poet of History: History and Ritual in *El Testimonio Vengado*." In *Perspectivas de la comedia: Ensayos sobre la comedia del Siglo de Oro. Vol. 1*, ed. Alva V. Ebersole, pp. 9–32. Estudios de Hispanófila. Colección Siglo de Oro, no. 6. Valencia: Albatros Ediciones Hispanófila.

1985   "Chicano Studies, 1970–1984." *Annual Review of Anthropology* 14:405–27.

1986   "Ilongot Hunting as Story and Experience." In *The Anthropology of Experience*, ed. Victor Turner and Edward Bruner, 97–138. Urbana: University of Illinois Press.

1987   "Politics, Patriarchs, and Laughter." *Cultural Critique* 6:65–87.

Roudiez, L.

1980   "Introduction." In Kristeva, J., *Desire in Language: A Semiotic Approach to Literature and Art*, 1–20, trans. T. Gora, A. Jardine, and L. Roudiez. New York: Columbia University Press.

Ryan, Michael.

1982   *Marxism and Deconstruction: A Critical Articulation.* Baltimore: Johns Hopkins University Press.

Sagar, Keith.

1982   *D. H. Lawrence and New Mexico.* Salt Lake City: Peregrine Smith.

Said, Edward.

1977   "Roads Taken and Not Taken in Contemporary Criticism." In *Directions for Criticism: Structuralism and Its Alternatives*, ed. Murray Krieger and L. S. Dembo, 33–54. Madison: University of Wisconsin Press.

1983   *The World, the Text, and the Critic.* Cambridge: Harvard University Press.

Salazar Parr, Carmen.

1977   "Current Trends in Chicano Literary Criticism." *Latin American Literary Review* 5, no. 10:8–15.

1982   "Literary Criticism." In *A Decade of Chicano Literature (1970–79): Critical Essays and Bibliography*, ed. Luis Leal et al., 65–72. Santa Barbara, Calif.: Editorial La Causa.

Saldívar, José David.

1985   "The Ideological and the Utopian in Tomás Rivera's 'Y no se lo tragó la tierra' and Ron Arias's *The Road to Tamazunchale*." *Crítica* 1, no. 2:100–14.

1986   "Towards a Chicano Poetics: The Making of the Chicano-Chicana Subject." *Confluencia* 1, no. 2:10–17.

Saldívar, José David, ed.

1985   *The Rolando Hinojosa Reader: Essays Historical and Critical*. Houston: Arte Público Press.

Saldívar, Ramón.

1979   "A Dialectic of Difference: Towards a Theory of the Chicano Novel." *MELUS* 6, no. 3:73–92.

1983   "The Form of Texas-Mexican Fiction." In *The Texas Literary Tradition: Fiction, Folklore, History*, ed. Don Graham et al., 139–44. Austin: Texas State Historical Association.

1984   *Figural Language in the Novel: The Flowers of Speech from Cervantes to Joyce*. Princeton: Princeton University Press.

1985   "Ideologies of Self: Chicano Autobiography." *Diacritics* 15, no. 3:25–34.

1990   *Chicano Narrative: The Dialectics of Difference*. Madison: University of Wisconsin Press.

Saldívar-Hull, Sonia.

    "Helena María Viramontes." In *Dictionary of Literary Biography: Chicana Writers*. Forthcoming.

Salinas, Raúl.

1980   *Un Trip through the Mind Jail y Otras Excursions*. San Francisco: Editorial Pocho-Che.

Sánchez, George I.

1934   *The Education of Bilinguals in a State School System*. Berkeley: University of California Press.

1940   *Forgotten People: A Study of New Mexicans*. Albuquerque: University of New Mexico Press.

Sánchez, Marta Ester.

1985   *Contemporary Chicana Poetry: A Critical Approach to an Emerging Literature*. Berkeley: University of California Press.

Sánchez, Rosaura.

1977   "The Chicana Labor Force." In *Essays on La Mujer*, ed. Rosaura Sánchez and Rosa Martínez Cruz, 3–15. Los Angeles: Chicano Studies Center UCLA.

1979   "The Ditch." In *Requisa Treinta y Dos: Bilingual Short Story Collection*, ed. Rosaura Sánchez, 182–84. La Jolla: Chicano Research Publications.

1983   *Chicano Discourse: Socio-Historic Perspectives*. Rowley, Mass.: Newbury House.

1985a   "From Heterogeneity to Contradiction: Hinojosa's Novel." In *The Rolando Hinojosa Reader*, ed. José David Saldívar, 44–63. Houston: Arte Público Press.

1985b   "Voces, códigos y cronotopos en la literatura chicana." *Revista Chicano-Riqueña* 13, no. 1:54–63.

1987   "Ethnicity, Ideology and Academia." *The Americas Review* 15, no. 1:80–88.

Showalter, Elaine.

1977   *A Literature of Their Own: British Women Novelists from Brontë to Lessing*. Princeton: Princeton University Press.

1985   "The Feminist Critical Revolution." In *The New Feminist Criticism: Essays on Women, Literature and Theory*, ed. Elaine Showalter, 3–17. New York: Pantheon Books.

Sollors, Werner.

1986a   *Beyond Ethnicity: Consent and Descent in American Culture*. New York: Oxford University Press.

1986b   "A Critique of Pure Pluralism." In *Reconstructing American Literary History*, ed. Sacvan Bercovitch, 250–79. Cambridge: Harvard University Press.

Sommers, Joseph.

1977   "From the Critical Premise to the Product: Critical Modes and Their Application to a Chicano Literary Text." *New Scholar* 6:34–50.

Sommers, Joseph, and Tomás Ybarra-Frausto, eds.

1979   *Modern Chicano Writers: A Collection of Critical Essays*. Englewood Cliffs, N.J.: Prentice-Hall.

Soto, Gary.

1977   *The Elements of San Joaquin*. Pittsburgh: University of Pittsburgh Press.

Spivak, Gayatri Chakravorty.

1985   "Three Women's Texts and a Critique of Imperialism." *Critical Inquiry* 12, no. 1:243–61.

Standiford, Lester A.

1982   "Worlds Made of Dawn: Characteristic Image and Incident in Native American Imaginative Literature." In *Three American Literatures: Essays in Chicano, Native American and Asian-American Literature for Teachers of American Literature*, ed. Houston A. Baker, Jr., 168–96. New York: MLA.

Stepto, Robert B.

1986   "Distrust of the Reader in Afro-American Narratives." In *Reconstructing American Literary History*, ed. Sacvan Bercovitch, 300–22. Cambridge: Harvard University Press.

Strathern, Marilyn.

1984 "Dislodging a World View: Challenge and Counter-Challenge in the Relationship Between Feminism and Anthropology." Lecture at the Research Center for Women's Studies, University of Adelaide, July 4, 1984.

Suárez, Mario.

1947 "El Hoyo," "Señor Garza," "Cuco Goes to a Party," and "Kid Zopilote." *Arizona Quarterly* 3, no. 2:112–15, 115–20, 121–27, 130–37.

1948 "Southside Run" and "Maestria." *Arizona Quarterly* 4, no. 4:362–68, 368–73.

1950 "Mexican Heaven." *Arizona Quarterly* 6, no. 4:310–15.

Tatum, Charles.

1982 *Chicano Literature.* Boston: Twayne.

Taussig, Michael.

1980 *The Devil and Commodity Fetishism in South America.* Chapel Hill: University of North Carolina Press.

Therborn, Göran.

1980 *The Ideology of Power and the Power of Ideology.* London: NLB.

Thompson, E. P.

1978 "Folklore, Anthropology, and Social History." *Indian Historical Review* 3, no. 2:247–66.

Treichler, Paula.

1986 "Teaching Feminist Theory." In *Theory in the Classroom,* ed. Cary Nelson, 57–128. Urbana: University of Illinois Press.

Turner, Victor.

1974 *Dramas, Fields and Metaphors: Symbolic Action in Human Society.* Ithaca: Cornell University Press.

1981 "Social Dramas and Stories About Them." In *On Narrative,* ed. W. J. T. Mitchell, 137–64. Chicago: University of Chicago Press.

Vigil, Evangelina.

1985 *Thirty an' Seen a Lot.* Houston: Arte Público Press.

Villanueva, Alma.

1985 *Life Span.* Austin: Place of Herons Press.

n.d. "Women's Spirituality and Sexuality in Contemporary Women's Literature." Unpublished master's thesis.

Villarreal, José Antonio.

1959 *Pocho.* Garden City, N.Y.: Doubleday Anchor Books.

Viramontes, Helena María.

1985   *The Moths and Other Stories.* Houston: Arte Público Press.

Vizenor, Gerald, ed.

1988   *Narrative Chance: Postmodern Discourse on Native American Literatures.* Albuquerque: University of New Mexico Press.

Vološinov, V. N.

1973   *Marxism and the Philosophy of Language.* New York: Seminar Press.

Vygotsky, L. S.

1978   *Mind in Society: The Development of Higher Psychological Processes.* Cambridge: Harvard University Press.

Wald, Alan.

1986   "Virtue in Dissensus." Review of Bercovitch *Reconstructing American Literary History. New York Times Book Review* 35 (28 September).

Wallerstein, Immanuel.

1974   *The Modern World System: Capitalist Agriculture and the Origins of the European World-Economy in the Sixteenth Century.* New York: Academic Press.

Webb, Walter Prescott.

1935   *The Texas Rangers: A Century of Frontier Defense.* Boston: Houghton Mifflin.

Wellek, René, and Austin Warren.

1949   *Theory of Literature.* New York: Harcourt, Brace.

Wells, Ida B.

1969   *On Lynching.* New York: Arno Press and New York Times.

West, Cornel.

1988   "Marxist Theory and the Specificity of Afro-American Oppression." In *Marxism and the Interpretation of Culture,* ed. Lawrence Grossberg and Cary Nelson, 17–29. Urbana: University of Illinois Press.

Williams, Raymond.

1977   *Marxism and Literature.* Oxford: Oxford University Press.

Wolf, Eric R.

1982   *Europe and the People Without History.* Berkeley: University of California Press.

Woolf, Virginia.

1957   *A Room of One's Own.* London: Harcourt Brace Jovanovich.

Wright, Erik Olin.

1973   *The Politics of Punishment: A Critical Analysis of Prisons in America.* New York: Harper & Row.

Writers' Program of the Work Projects Administration in the State of New Mexico.

1940   *New Mexico: A Guide to the Colorful State.* Sponsored by the Coronado Cuarto Centennial and the University of New Mexico. New York: Hastings House.

Ybarra-Frausto, Tomás.

1978   "The Chicano Movement and the Emergence of a Chicano Poetic Consciousness." In *New Directions in Chicano Scholarship,* ed. R. Romo and R. Paredes, 81–109. Chicano Studies Monograph Series. La Jolla, Calif.: Chicano Studies Program, University of California, San Diego.

Zamora, Emilio.

1983   "Mexican Labor Activity in South Texas, 1900–1920." Ph.D. dissertation, University of Texas, Austin.

Zavella, Patricia.

1987   *Women's Work and Chicano Families: Cannery Workers of the Santa Clara Valley.* Ithaca: Cornell University Press.

A Selected and Annotated Bibliography of Contemporary Chicano Literary Criticism

The following works were selected by the editors with the assistance of Roberto Trujillo, curator of Mexican American Collections for Stanford University Libraries. They represent a comprehensive search and review of Chicano materials through December 1990 based on the MLA Bibliography and the Research Libraries Information Network databases, various reference guides including Ernestina N. Eger's *A Bibliography of Contemporary Chicano Literature*, Trujillo and Rodriguez's *Literatura Chicana: Creative and Critical Writings Through 1984*, Julio A. Martínez and Francisco Lomelí's *Chicano Literature: A Reference Guide*, Julio A. Martínez's *Chicano Scholars and Writers: A Bio-Bibliographical Directory*, and volumes of the *Chicano Periodical Index*. Ultimately, the criteria for selection, which were to offer to the widest interested audience a basic knowledge of the field of Chicano literary criticism, rested with the editors. Thus we chose works of different critical tendencies on literary history and theory, on literary and performance genres, as well as important collections, bibliographies, and reference guides.

Alarcón, Norma. "Chicanas' Feminist Literature: A Re-Vision Through Malinntzin/or Malintzin: Putting Flesh Back on the Object." In *This Bridge Called My Back: Writings by Radical Women of Color*, ed. Cherríe Moraga and Gloria Anzaldúa, 182–90. New York: Kitchen Table/Women of Color Press, 1983.

An essay examining the traditional image of Malintzin in Chicano culture and its recuperation by Chicana writers.

———. "Making *Familia* From Scratch: Split Subjectivities in the Work of Helena María Viramontes and Cherríe Moraga." In *Chicana Creativity and Criticism: Charting New Frontiers in American Literature*, ed. María Herrera-Sobek and Helena María Viramontes, 147–59. Houston: Arte Público Press, 1988.

Alarcón explores the refusal to speak as woman (wife/mother) and the crisis of meaning that this position engenders for two Chicana writers.

———. "Traddutura, Traditora: A Paradigmatic Figure of Chicana Feminism." *The Construction of Gender and Modes of Social Division*, ed. Donna Przybylowicz, Nancy Hartsock, and Pamela McCallum. Special issue of *Cultural Critique*, no. 13 (Fall 1989):57–87.

An overview of the Malinche figure drawn from both Mexican and Chicana creative and critical traditions.

———. "What Kind of Lover Have You Made Me Mother?: Towards a Theory of Chicana's Feminism and Cultural Identity Through Poetry." In *Women of Color: Perspectives* on *Feminism and Identity*, ed. Audrey T. McCluskey, 85–110. Bloomington: Indiana University, Women's Studies Program Occasional Papers Series, vol. 1, no. 1, 1985.

In this essay Alarcón maps the emergence of Chicana poetry in Evangelina Vigil, Lorna Dee Cervantes, Cherríe Moraga, Carmen Tafolla, Pat Mora, Barbara Brinson Curiel, and Sandra Cisneros by focusing on how the intimate relations with mothers and lovers are interconnected in ways that help define the daughter.

Alurista (Alberto Urista). "Cultural Nationalism and Chicano Literature During the Decade of 1965–1975." *MELUS: The Journal of the Society for the Study of the Multi-Ethnic Literature of the United States* 8, no. 2 (Summer 1981):22–34.

An explication of the sociopolitical factors contributing to the emergence of a poetic consciousness and nationalism as manifest in Chicano narrative, poetry, and drama.

Bardeleben, Renate von, et al., eds. *Missions in Conflict: Essays on U.S.-Mexican Relations and Chicano Culture*. Tübingen: Narr, 1986.

Includes twenty-six essays from scholars both in Europe and the United States on Chicano culture and literature; specifically Chicano poetry, fiction, theater, and criticism; as well as language, education, and the impact of Chicano culture in American discourse. The essays were presented at the First International Symposium on Chicano Culture in 1984 at the University of Mainz at Germersheim, Germany.

Bassnett, Susan. "Bilingual Poetry: A Chicano Phenomenon." *Revista Chicano-Riqueña* 13, no. 3–4 (1985):137–47.

A survey exploring the history, influences, polemics, and characteristics of Chicano poetry as an emergent phenomenon in contemporary literature.

Bauder, Thomas A. "The Triumph of White Magic in Rudolfo Anaya's *Bless Me, Ultima*." *Mester* 14, no. 1 (Spring 1985):41–54.

A thorough analysis of Christian cosmology, pre-Columbian myth, and Nahuatl Indian magic in Anaya's novel.

Binder, Wolfgang. "Die Lyrik der Chicanos seit den sechziger Jahren: Sprache als soziokulturelle Bestandsaufnähme und emanzipatorisches Verfahren." *Die Legitimation der Alltagssprache in der modernen Lyrik: Antworten aus Europa und Lateinamerika*. Erlangen: Universitätsbund Erlangen-Nürnberg, (1984):85–111.

A study of the evolution and importance of Chicano poetry since the 1960s, exploring language as a sociocultural factor; examines the work of Juan Rodríguez, Lucha Corpi, Américo Paredes, José Montoya, Luis Valdez, Rodolfo Gonzales, Alurista, Raúl Salinas, Lorna Dee Cervantes, and Tino Villanueva, among others.

Bruce-Novoa, Juan. *Chicano Authors: Inquiry by Interview*. Austin: University of Texas Press, 1980.

Interviews with fourteen Chicano authors and their opinions and beliefs within the context of Chicano letters.

———. *Chicano Poetry: A Response to Chaos*. Austin: University of Texas Press, 1982.

A formalist analysis of Chicano poetry including critical applications and explications of the works of José Montoya, J. L. Navarro, Abelardo Delgado, Raúl Salinas,

Rodolfo Gonzales, Alurista, Sergio Elizondo, Miguel Méndez, Tino Villanueva, Ricardo Sánchez, Bernice Zamora, and Gary Soto.

———. *RetroSpace: Collected Essays on Chicano Literature, Theory and History.* Houston: Arte Público Press, 1990.

A collection of mostly previously published essays on literary space with a critical bibliography.

———. "The Space of Chicano Literature." *De Colores* 1, no. 4 (1975):22–42.

An explication of the polemics of Chicano literary space and the critical implications of nothingness, chaos, unity, and universality in Chicano literature.

Calderón, Héctor. "At the Crossroads of History, on the Borders of Change: Chicano Literary Studies Past, Present, and Future." In *Left Politics and the Literary Profession,* ed. Lennard J. Davis and M. Bella Mirabella, 211–35. New York: Columbia University Press 1990.

Calderón argues that Chicano literature should be seen as a branch of American literature that offers in its literary pursuits a valid picture of the history and politics of the Southwest. With this in mind Calderón goes on to give an overview of the institutional history of Chicano literary studies.

———. "On the Uses of Chronicle, Biography and Sketch in Rolando Hinojosa's *Generaciones y semblanzas.*" *The Rolando Hinojosa Reader: Essays Historical and Critical,* ed. José David Saldívar, 133–42. Houston: Arte Público Press, 1985.

A look at Hinojosa's formal and thematic use of the Spanish Medieval and Renaissance forms of the chronicle, biography, and sketch as narrative strategies to represent a collective Texas-Mexican character.

———. "Rudolfo Anaya's *Bless Me Ultima.* A Chicano Romance of the Southwest." *Crítica* 1, no. 3 (Fall 1986):21–47.

Calderón argues that the romance genre is possible during periods of cultural transformation, and that the reading and critical interpretation of Anaya's novel follows that paradigm.

———. "To Read Chicano Narrative: Commentary and Metacommentary." *Mester* 11, no. 2 (1983):3–14.

An interpretation of Chicano narrative genres based on Fredric Jameson's dialectical criticism, Northrop Frye's theory of genres, and Wolfgang Iser's theory of aesthetic response with particular attention to romance in Rudolfo Anaya's *Bless Me, Ultima* and satire in Oscar Zeta Acosta's *Autobiography of a Brown Buffalo.*

Candelaria, Cordelia. *Chicano Poetry: A Critical Introduction.* Westport, Conn.: Greenwood Press, 1986.

A critical and interpretive guide of Chicano poetry from 1967–present; the critical theories and methodologies used in interpreting Chicano verse; and the application of bilingual, multicultural perspectives to the Chicano literary movement.

Carrasco, David. "A Perspective for the Study of Religious Dimensions in Chicano Experience: *Bless Me, Ultima* as Religious Text." *Aztlán* 13, no. 1–2 (Spring–Fall 1982):195–221.

A study of the quasireligious dimensions of Anaya's novel with special attention to shamanism, landscape sacrality, etc. and these implications in the Chicano experience and imagination.

Chabram, Angie. "Chicano Critical Discourse: An Emerging Cultural Practice." *Aztlán* 18, no. 2 (Fall 1987):45–90.

An examination and an assessment of both the internal and external factors that have shaped Chicano literary criticism since its inception in the sixties. The essay also charts out the role of Chicano literary critics with respect to mainstream criticism.

Chabram, Angie, and Rosalinda Fregoso, eds. *Chicana/o Cultural Representations: Reframing Critical Discourses*. Special Issue of *Cultural Studies* 4, no. 3 (1990).

Nine essays examining the field of Chicano studies, its past and future, through cultural institutions and practices, educational and critical theory, and cultural forms in literature, theater, film, and ethnography. The collection features art by Malaquías Montoya.

Cisneros, Sandra. "Cactus Flowers: In Search of Tejana Feminist Poetry." *Third Woman* 3, no. 1–2 (1986):73–80.

A critical introduction to the varied and rich voices of sexual politics, oppression and identity in Tejana feminist poetry; featuring the poets Angela de Hoyos, Pat Mora, Rosemary Catacalos, et al.

Cota-Cárdenas, Margarita. "The Chicana in the City as Seen in Her Literature." *Frontiers: A Journal of Woman Studies* 6, no. 1–2 (Spring–Summer 1981):13–18.

A critical survey of contemporary urban Chicana poets and their issues; e.g., self-awareness, identity formation, and dissatisfaction with imposed stereotypes and roles.

Eger, Ernestina N. *A Bibliography of Criticism of Contemporary Chicano Literature*. Berkeley: Chicano Studies Library Publications, University of California, 1982. (Chicano Studies Library Publications Series, No. 5.)

An exhaustive compilation and index of over two thousand critical citations in contemporary Chicano literature.

Elizondo, Sergio D. "A Question of Origins and Presence in Chicano Literature." *Latin American Literary Review* 11, no. 21 (Fall–Winter 1982):39–43.

Stressing dialectics of authenticity, legitimacy, autochthony, quality, and cultural verisimilitude, the author traces the history of Chicano literature as well as proposes criteria for future criticism.

Epple, Juan Armando. "Literatura Chicana y Crítica Literaria." *Ideologies & Literature: A Journal of Hispanic and Luso-Brazilian Studies* 4, no. 16 (1983):149–71.

A reevaluation of the sociohistoric parameters of Chicano literary criticism.

Fabre, Geneviève, ed. *European Perspectives on Hispanic Literature of the United States*. Houston: Arte Público Press, 1988.

A collection of essays presented at the 1986 conference "Hispanic Cultures and Identities in the United States" at the University of Paris; includes essays on Chicano writers Rudolfo Anaya, Alurista, Lorna Dee Cervantes, Sandra Cisneros, and Rolando Hinojosa by European and American critics.

Fischer, Michael M. J. "Ethnicity and the Post-Modern Arts of Memory." *Writing Culture: The Poetics and Politics of Ethnography: A School of Research Advanced Seminar,* ed. James Clifford and George E. Marcus, 194–233. Berkeley: University of California Press, 1985.

An intertextual analysis of the dynamics of contemporary ethnic autobiography; includes references to the works of Chicano writers Sandra Cisneros, Alurista, Rolando Hinojosa, Bernice Zamora, José Montoya, Rudolfo Anaya, et al.

Flores, Lauro. "Narrative Strategies in Rolando Hinojosa's *Rites and Witnesses.*" *The Rolando Hinojosa Reader: Essays Historical and Critical,* ed. José David Saldívar, 170–79. Houston: Arte Público Press, 1985.

Flores argues that Hinojosa's narrative project is based on the dynamics between individual and collective history.

———. "Notas básicas para la crítica literaria chicana." *La Palabra: Revista de Literatura Chicana* 3, no. 1–2 (Spring–Autumn 1981):21–29.

Basic definitions of the limitations and polemics needed to critically approach Chicano literature.

Flores, Lauro, and Mark McCaffrey. "Miguel Méndez: El subjetivismo frente a la historia." *De Colores* 3, no. 4 (1977):46–57.

An explication of Méndez's poetry and his use of the historical-generational metaphor of experience.

González-Berry, Erlinda, and Tey Diana Rebolledo. "Growing Up Chicano: Tomás Rivera and Sandra Cisneros." *International Studies in Honor of Tomás Rivera,* ed. Julián Olivares, 109–19. Houston: Arte Público Press, 1985.

A comparative analysis of the Chicano *bildungsroman* through the short-story cycles of Rivera and Cisneros.

Gonzales-Berry, Erlinda, ed. *Pasó por Aquí: Critical Essays on the New Mexican Literary Tradition.* Albuquerque: University of New Mexico Press, 1989.

Sixteen thematic essays distributed among five historical divisions from the Spanish chroniclers to the contemporary period. The collection also includes a selected bibliography of New Mexican Hispanic literature.

González-T., César A., ed. *Rudolfo A. Anaya: Focus on Criticism.* La Jolla: Lalo Press, 1990.

Fifteen essays, a few previously published, on *Bless Me, Ultima, Heart of Aztlán, Tortuga,* and themes in Anaya's work. In addition the volume includes a brief autobiography, a selected bibliography, and interviews with Anaya.

Grajeda, Rafael. "The Pachuco in Chicano Poetry: The Process of Legend-Creation." *Revista-Chicano-Riqueña* 8, no. 4 (1988):45–59.

Grajeda traces the historical creation of the Pachuco as myth and its subsequent manifestations in contemporary Chicano poetry.

Hernández, Guillermo. "El México de fuera: notas para su historia cultural." *Crítica* 1, no. 3 (1986):61–80.

A study of the sociocultural and historical problematics of what literary tradition Chicano letters belong to: Mexican-Latin American or Anglo American? Can Chicano literature be considered an independent corpus?

———. "On the Theoretical Bases of Chicano Literature." *De Colores* 5, no. 1–2 (1980):5–18.

Hernández argues for the necessity of establishing a coherence of Chicano literature independent from strict geopolitical and linguistic considerations that are based on a Chicano historical foundation.

Herrera-Sobek, María. "Chicano Literary Folklore." *Chicano Studies: A Multidisciplinary Approach*, ed. E. García, et al., 151–70. New York: Teachers Collective Press, 1984.

An analysis of the cultural phenomenon of Chicano folklore including: (1) prose narratives, (2) folk songs, (3) folk speech, (4) proverbs and proverbial expressions, (5) folk drama, (6) children's songs and games, (7) riddles, and (8) beliefs and folk medicine.

Herrera-Sobek, María, ed. *Beyond Stereotypes: The Critical Analysis of Chicana Literature*. Binghamton, N.Y.: Bilingual Press/Editorial Bilingüe, 1985.

A collection of six critical essays concerning Chicana prose and poetry; topics include: the Chicana fictive voice, the female hero, the personal vision, humor, and the search for feminine identity.

Hinojosa-Smith, Rolando R. "This Writer's Sense of Place." *The Texas Literary Tradition: Fiction, Folklore, History*, ed. Don Graham et al., 120–24. Austin: College of Liberal Arts, University of Texas at Austin, Texas State Historical Association, 1983.

Essay discusses the importance of the perception of literary place and its essential role in Chicano letters.

Huerta, Jorge A. *Chicano Theater: Themes and Forms*. Ypsilanti, Mich.: Bilingual Press/Editorial Bilingüe, 1982. (Studies in Language and Literature of United States Hispanics.)

A thorough study of the history, themes, and contemporary forms in Chicano drama.

Jiménez, Francisco, ed. *The Identification and Analysis of Chicano Literature*. New York: Bilingual Press/Editorial Bilingüe, 1979.

A series of previously published essays examining the origins of Chicano literature, as well as the development of critical trends and their applications in specific works. Features essays by Tomás Rivera, Rolando Hinojosa, Luis Leal, et al.

Kanellos, Nicolás. *The History of Hispanic Theatre in the United States: Origins to 1940*. Austin: University of Texas Press, 1990.

Kanellos situates the book around the cities where Hispanic theatre flourished: Los Angeles, San Francisco, Tucson, Laredo, San Antonio, New York, and Tampa. From vaudeville and tent theatre to an examination of the individual careers of actors, writers, and directors, Kanellos charts the rise of Hispanic theatre in the United States. Includes photographs.

————. *Mexican American Theater: Then and Now.* Houston: Arte Público Press, 1983. (*Revista Chicano-Riqueña* 11, no. 1 [Spring 1983].)

A collection of sketches, essays, and interviews conveying the breadth of Mexican American theater.

Lattin, Vernon E., ed. *Contemporary Chicano Fiction: A Critical Survey.* Binghamton, N.Y.: Bilingual Press/Editorial Bilingüe, 1986.

Survey contains four chapters each containing mostly previously published essays, including: (1) critical overviews; (2) the early writers in English: Villarreal, Acosta, Barrio; (3) Tomás Rivera and the Spanish language novel; and (4) the accomplished voices, essays on Hinojosa, Anaya, Méndez, Arias, Portillo Trambley, et al.

Leal, Luis. *Aztlán y México: Perfiles literarios e históricos.* Binghamton, N.Y.: Bilingual Press/Editorial Bilingüe, 1985.

This collection brings together both new and previously published essays on both Chicano and Mexican literature and culture. Essays on literary history and folklore are distributed between the two major divisions for the volume, Aztlán and México.

————. "Cuatro siglos de prosa aztlanense." *La Palabra: Revista de Literatura Chicana* 2, no. 1 (Spring 1980):2–15.

Leal leads a survey cataloging four decades of prose in Aztlán, with special emphasis on the didactic forms which prevailed in early writings; those being, *memorias, diarios, viajes, crónicas, relaciones,* and *cartas.*

————. "Literary Criticism and Minority Literatures: The Case of the Chicano Writer." *Confluencia: Revista Hispánica de Cultura y Literatura* 1, no. 2 (Spring 1986):4–9.

Leal argues for the integration and legitimization of Chicano literature into the mainstream of American literature by literary historians.

————. "Mexican-American Literature: A Historical Perspective." *Revista Chicano-Riqueña* 1, no. 1 (Spring 1973):32–44.

A study of the emergence of Chicano literature through successive historical periods: Hispanic to 1821; Mexican 1821–1848; transition 1848–1910; interaction 1910–1942; and the Chicano period 1943 to the present.

————, and Pepe Barrón. "Chicano Literature: An Overview." *Three American Literatures: Essays in Chicano, Native American, and Asian-American Literature for Teachers of American Literature,* ed. Houston A. Baker, Jr., 9–32. New York: Modern Language Association, 1982.

A historical survey of the genesis, context, characteristics, and roots of Chicano literature, specifically: pre-Chicano literature to 1884; literature of transition 1848–1910; emergence of a group consciousness 1910–1943; and literature of confrontation 1943–1981.

Lewis, Marvin A. *Introduction to the Chicano Novel.* Houston: Arte Público Press, 1984.

A brief analysis outlining the historical, environmental, migratory, and sociomythical realities as found in the Chicano novel.

Lizárraga, Sylvia. "Observaciones acerca de la crítica literaria chicana." *Revista Chicano-Riqueña* 10, no. 4 (Fall 1982):55–64.

A critical evaluation of Juan Bruce-Novoa's theory of literary space.

Lomeli, Francisco A. "En torno a la literatura de la frontera: ¿Convergencia o divergencia?" *Plural: Revista Cultural de Excelsior* 15, no. 11 (August 1986):24–32.

This essay explores the cultural milieu of the border and how this area is manifest in the sociological, interlingual, and intersymbolic relationships between Chicano and Mexican literature.

———. "An Overview of Chicano Letters: From Origins to Resurgence." *Chicano Studies: A Multidisciplinary Approach,* ed. E. García et al., 103–19. New York: Teachers Collective Press, 1984.

An overview of the history of Chicano literature, as well as an analysis of the stigmas and misperceptions that hinder its inclusion into mainstream American literature and canon.

———, and Donaldo W. Urioste. *Chicano Perspectives in Literature: A Critical and Annotated Bibliography.* Albuquerque: Pajarito, 1976.

An extensive annotated bibliography with citations in poetry, novel, short fiction, theater, anthology, literary criticism, oral tradition in print, journal, and "literatura Chicanesca." Also illustrated by José Antonio Burciaga.

Madrid-Barela, Arturo. "Identidad y creatividad chicana." *Ideologies & Literature: A Journal of Hispanic and Luso-Brazilian Studies* 2, no. 10 (1979):36–44.

Madrid traces the historical, geographical, economic, and cultural vitality found in Chicano literature.

———. "In Search of the Authentic Pachuco." *Aztlán* 4, no. 1 (Spring 1973):31–60.

A study of the mythical and cultural dimensions of the Pachuco and its significance in Chicano poetry, art, drama, film, etc.

———. "La problemática de la experiencia y la literatura chicana." *Casa de las Américas* 114 (1979):60–63.

Examines the problems of the Chicano condition and Chicano literature as a historical-dialectical process of the search for identity between the Anglo and Mexican cultures.

Márquez, Antonio C. "Richard Rodriguez' *Hunger of Memory* and the Poetics of Experience." *Arizona Quarterly* 40, no. 2 (Summer 1984):130–41.

Márquez explores the development of a shift in modern autobiography, that of historiography to literature in Rodriguez's prose.

Martínez, Julio A., and Francisco A. Lomelí. *Chicano Literature: A Reference Guide.* Westport, Conn.: Greenwood Press, 1985.

This guide includes comprehensive information on authors; pivotal articles on the history of the literature, as well as three literary genres (the novel, poetry, and theater), Chicano children's literature, and Chicano philosophy; and a chronology of Chicano literature and glossary of useful terms.

Méndez M., Miguel. *La Palabra: Revista de Literatura Chicana* 3, no. 1–2 (1981):3–120. Thematic issue of *La Palabra*.

Special issue of *La Palabra* focusing on the work of Miguel Méndez M.; includes an interview with Méndez, a collection of critical writings on his work (especially *Peregrinos de Aztlán*), and several of his poems and short stories.

Monsiváis, Carlos. "Literatura comparada: literatura chicana y literatura mexicana." *Fomento Literario* 1, no. 3 (1983):42–49.

Monsiváis establishes the validity of a parallelism between Chicano and Mexican literatures and points out the seminal differences.

Olivares, Julián, ed. *International Studies in Honor of Tomás Rivera.* Houston: Arte Público Press, 1986.

The collection includes ten essays by Rivera's colleagues and friends on his life and work plus six others on Chicano and Hispanic literature of the United States.

———. *U.S. Hispanic Autobiography.* Special issue of *The Americas Review* 16, no. 3–4 (1988).

Thematic issue containing essays on Anthony Quinn, Gary Soto, Oscar Zeta Acosta, border narratives, and nineteenth-century narratives by women.

Ordóñez, Elizabeth J. "Chicana Literature and Related Sources: A Selected and Annotated Bibliography." *Bilingual Review* 7, no. 2 (May–August 1980):143–64.

An exhaustive annotated compilation of critical essays, bibliographies, anthologies, poetry, and prose focusing on or written by Chicana authors.

———. "The Concept of Cultural Identity in Chicana Poetry." *Third Women* 2, no. 1 (1984):75–82.

Ordóñez critically evaluates the quest for and definition of Chicana cultural identity through Chicana poetry. Essay focuses on poetry by Lucha Corpi, Lorna Dee Cervantes, Alma Villanueva, et al.

———. "Sexual Politics and the Theme of Sexuality in Chicana Poetry." *Women in Hispanic Literature: Icons and Fallen Idols,* ed. Beth Miller, 316–39. Berkeley: University of California Press, 1983.

A study of the Chicana feminist polemic relevant to the sexual politics of the Chicano movement, with specific attention to the poetry of Lorna Dee Cervantes, Evangelina Vigil, Bernice Zamora, et al.

Ortego, Philip D., and David Conde, eds. *The Chicano Literary World 1974: Proceedings of the National Symposium on Chicano Literature and Critical Analysis, November 1974.* Las Vegas, N.M: New Mexico Highlands University, 1975. 94 leaves.

Papers stress the themes of national character and identity through literary "space," as well as satire and humor in Chicano literature.

Padilla, Genaro M. "The Recovery of Nineteenth-Century Chicano Autobiography: 'tis not vengeance, it is regaining a loss,'" *American Quarterly* 40, no. 3 (1988): 286–307.

An exploration of autobiography as a rhetorical response to the threat of cultural, social, and historical effacement after the Mexican-American War of 1846–48 with a focus on Mariano Guadalupe Vallejo's "Recuerdos históricos de alta California."

————. "The Self as Cultural Metaphor in Acosta's *Autobiography of a Brown Buffalo.*" *Journal of General Education* 35, no. 4 (1984):242–58.

Padilla argues that the genre of autobiography, in particular Acosta's work, can stand as a faithful documentary record of the Chicano's search for cultural identity, political consciousness, and struggle for dignity in face of assimilation.

————. "'Yo Sola Aprendí': Mexican Women's Nineteenth-Century California Personal Narratives." *Revealing Lives: Autobiography and Gender,* ed. Marilyn Yalom and Susan Groag Bell, 115–31. Albany: State University of New York Press.

A group of narratives by California women originally collected by Hubert H. Bancroft is read to reveal a critique of the patriarchy as well as a subversion of the transcription process.

Paredes, Américo. "El folklore de los grupos de origen mexicano en Estados Unidos." *Folklore Americano* 14, no. 14 (1964):146–63.

A look at Mexican-American folklore as an expression of historical conflict of cultures.

————. "The Folk Base of Chicano Literature." *Modern Chicano Writers: A Collection of Critical Essays,* ed. Joseph Sommers and Tomás Ybarra-Frausto, 4–17. Englewood Cliffs, N.J.: Prentice-Hall, 1979.

A translated, abbreviated version of the above article.

————. "Nearby Places and Strange-Sounding Names." *The Texas Literary Tradition: Fiction, Folklore, History,* ed. Don Graham et al. 130–38. Austin: College of Liberal Arts, University of Texas at Austin, Texas State Historical Association 1983.

Paredes analyzes the persistent stereotypes, the uses of bilingualism, and sense of place in the realm of Chicano literature.

————. *"With His Pistol in His Hand": A Border Ballad and Its Hero.* Austin: University of Texas Press, 1958.

The seminal study of the *corrido* of Gregorio Cortez against the history of cultural conflict in the Río Grande Valley of Texas.

Paredes, Raymund A. "The Evolution of Chicano Literature." *Three American Literatures: Essays in Chicano, Native American, and Asian-American Literature for Teachers of American Literature,* ed. Houston A. Baker, Jr., 33–79. New York: Modern Language Association, 1982.

An historical account of the development of Chicano literature from folklore and the birth of the *corrido* to its manifestations in the contemporary Chicano novel and poetry.

Pino, Frank, Jr. "A Chicano Perspective on American Cultural History." *Journal of Popular Culture* 13, no. 3 (1980):488–500.

Pino argues that American historians must undertake a broader interpretive approach including the history of the Mexican-American for a more accurate account of this nation's history.

Rebolledo, Tey Diana. "The Maturing of Chicana Poetry: The Quiet Revolution of the 1980's." *For Alma Mater: Theory and Practice in Feminist Scholarship*, ed. Paula A. Treichler et al., 143–58. Urbana: University of Illinois Press, 1985.

An essay asserting the emergence of Chicana poetry as a genre and discussing the various themes it expresses, for example, growing up, self-identity, search for myth, social criticism, and sexuality.

———. "Witches, Bitches and Midwives: The Shaping of Poetic Consciousness in Chicana Literature." *The Chicano Struggle: Analyses of Past and Present Efforts*, ed. John A. García, 166–77. Binghamton, N.Y.: Bilingual Review/Press, 1984.

This critical essay explores the unique and powerful poetic voices and consciousnesses of Chicana poets, specifically the processes of creation linked to motherhood, midwifery, and tale spinning, as well as witchery and magic.

Rebolledo, Tey Diana, Erlinda Gonzales-Berry, and Teresa Márquez, eds. *Las Mujeres Hablan: An Anthology of Nuevo Mexicana Writers*. Albuquerque: El Norte Publications, 1989.

Varied works of poetry, short fiction, artwork, folklore, and *testimonios* in English, Spanish, and bilingual combinations by forty-four Chicanas from New Mexico. The collection emphasizes daily activities as lived by women.

Rivera, Tomás. "Chicano Literature: Life in Search of Form." *Bridging Two Cultures: Multidisciplinary Readings in Bilingual Bicultural Education*, ed. Martha Cotera and Larry Hufford, 333–41. Austin: National Educational Library, 1980.

An inquiry into literary form as a unique reflection of Chicano life as manifest in the Chicano novel, poetry, and the essay.

———. "Mexican-American Literature: The Establishment of Community." *The Texas Literary Tradition: Fiction, Folklore, History*, ed. Don Graham et al., 124–30. Austin: College of Liberal Arts, University of Texas at Austin, Texas State Historical Association, 1983.

Rivera traces the importance and development of community in Mexican-American literature.

———. "Richard Rodriguez' *Hunger of Memory* as Humanistic Antithesis." *MELUS: The Journal of the Society for the Study of the Multi-Ethnic Literature of the United States* 11, no. 4 (Winter 1984):5–13.

A thorough critique of Rodriguez's *Hunger of Memory* as based on narrow presuppositions and cultural dimensions.

Robinson, Cecil. *Mexico and the Hispanic Southwest in American Literature*. Revised from *With the Ears of Strangers* (1963). Tucson: University of Arizona Press, 1977.

A study of the sociohistorical relationship between the Mexican-Hispanic Southwest and Anglo-America as revealed through American literature. The 1977 edition includes a section on Chicano literature.

Rocard, Marcienne. *Les fils du soleil: La minorité mexicaine a través la littérature des Etats-Unis.* Paris: Maisonneuve et Larose, 1980. English translation *Children of the Sun: The Mexican American in the Literature of the United States.* Trans. Edward G. Brown, Jr. Tucson: University of Arizona Press, 1989.

The author presents the changing image of the Chicano in American literature from the "romantic" aristocracy of the hacienda of Mexican California through the contrasting image of the "inferior, immoral, lazy" Mexican to the sympathetic portrayals of migrant workers of Hemingway, Steinbeck, and Saroyan and finally to the contemporary Chicano facing the dilemma of assimilation or ethnic preservation.

———. "La Lutte du Chicano sur le plan de l'écriture: Ou la face littéraire du mouvement chicano." *Les Langues Modernes* 80, no. 3 (1986):45–52.

As essay outlining the difficulties of Chicano literature as the expression of a collective consciousness rather than individual statement.

Romo, Ricardo, and Raymund Paredes, eds. *New Directions in Chicano Scholarship.* La Jolla: Chicano Studies Program, University of California, San Diego, 1978. Chicano Studies Monograph Series.

Essays representing a wide range of Chicano research such as: folklore-ethnography, critical literary theory, linguistics, and sociology.

Rosaldo, Renato. "Politics, Patriarchs and Laughter." *Cultural Critique* 6 (Spring 1987): 65–86.

Through a study of Américo Paredes and Ernesto Galarza, the author takes exception to a concept of minor literature which uses canonical European examples not readily applicable to Chicano letters. He asserts that Chicano narrative uses an understated politics of humor and "the border" as a creative space of resistance.

Saldívar, José David. "The Limits of Cultural Studies." *American Literary History* 2, no. 2 (1990):251–66.

An examination of the limitations of the cultural studies movement in the United States through the work of Michael M. J. Fischer, Rolando Hinojosa, Guillermo Gómez-Peña, Renato Rosaldo, and Gloria Anzaldúa. Saldívar moves beyond the static category of ethnicity as a self-contained and totalizing form to a global and interactive perspective.

———. "The Ideological and the Utopian in Tomás Rivera's . . . *y no se lo tragó la tierra* and Ron Arias' *The Road to Tamazunchale.*" *Missions in Conflict: Essays on U.S.-Mexican Relations and Chicano Culture,* ed. Renate von Bardeleben et al., 203–14. Tübingen: Narr, 1986.

Studies the shared political and aesthetic world views through the unfolding of both fictional plot and history in the mentioned works by Rivera and Arias.

———. "Towards a Chicano Poetics: The Making of the Chicano-Chicana Subject, 1969–1982." *Confluencia: Revista Hispánica de Cultura y Literatura* 1, no. 2 (Spring 1986):10–17.

Saldívar analyzes the development of the Chicano subject through the work of three Chicano contemporary poets: José Montoya, Bernice Zamora, and Alberto Ríos.

Saldívar, José David, ed. *The Rolando Hinojosa Reader: Essays Historical and Critical.* Houston: Arte Público Press, 1985.

A collection of thirteen new critical essays concluding with an interview with Hinojosa. Sections are divided among (1) essays by Hinojosa, (2) essays on his Klail City Death Trip series, and (3) on individual works.

Saldívar, Ramón. *Chicano Narrative: The Dialectics of Difference.* Madison: University of Wisconsin Press, 1990.

A deconstructionist-Marxist study of Chicano narrative from Américo Paredes and José Antonio Villarreal to Cherríe Moraga and Sandra Cisneros.

———. "A Dialectic of Difference: Towards a Theory of the Chicano Novel." *MELUS: The Journal of the Society for the Study of the Multi-Ethnic Literature of the United States* 6, no. 3 (Fall 1979):73–92.

An evaluation and reassessment of Chicano literary theory and criticism through the dialectics of history and "difference."

———. "The Form of Texas-Mexican Fiction." *The Texas Literary Tradition: Fiction, Folklore, History,* ed. Don Graham et al., 139–44. Austin: College of Liberal Arts, University of Texas at Austin, Texas State Historical Association, 1983.

An examination of the similarities and differences between the Texas-Mexican novel and Texas-Anglo novel and their uses of realism, forms, synthesis, etc.

———. "Ideologies of Self: Chicano Autobiography." *Diacritics: A Review of Contemporary Criticism* 15, no. 3 (Fall 1985):25–34.

Saldívar explores the themes of history, time, and space, as well as the issues of self and history, self and place, within the context of the emergence of racial, ethnic, and gender consciousness in the Chicano autobiographies *Hunger of Memory* by Richard Rodriguez and *Barrio Boy* by Ernesto Galarza.

Salinas, Judy. "The Image of Woman in Chicano Literature." *Revista Chicano-Riqueña* 4, no. 4 (Fall 1976):139–48.

Salinas traces the traditional roles and stereotypes of the Chicana in Chicano literature.

Sánchez, Marta Ester. *Contemporary Chicana Poetry: A Critical Approach to an Emerging Literature.* Berkeley: University of California Press, 1985.

A survey of several seminal Chicana poets and the cultural, sexual, political, and critical issues and the appearance of such topics in their poetry.

Sánchez, Rosaura. *Chicano Discourse: Socio-Historic Perspectives.* Rowley, Mass.: Newbury House, 1983.

A semiotic, ideological, social, and historical look at the dynamics of Chicano bilingualism.

———. "La crítica marxista: Propuesta para la crítica literaria chicana." *Revista Chicano-Riqueña* 8, no. 3 (1980):93–96.

An examination of Chicano literature as a product of economic and historical circumstances and conditions.

――――. "Ethnicity, Ideology and Academia." *Americas Review* 15, no. 1 (1987):80–88.

A discussion of the notion of cultural boundaries as related to academia and the status of ethnic studies programs and minority intellectuals.

――――. "Postmodernism and Chicano Literature." *Aztlán* 18, no. 2 (Fall 1987):1–14.

An exploration of postmodernist theory and its possible application to a wide variety of Chicano works. Sánchez concludes that there are no Chicano postmodernist works.

――――. "Voces, códigos y cronotopos en la literatura chicana." *Revista Chicano-Requeña* 13, no. 2 (1985):54–63.

An intertextual analysis of Chicano literature in light of the theories of Mikhail Bakhtin and Edward Said.

Sommers, Joseph. "From the Critical Premise to the Product: Critical Modes and Their Applications to a Chicano Literary Text." *New Directions in Chicano Scholarship*, ed. Ricardo Romo and Raymund Paredes, 51–80. La Jolla: Chicano Studies program, University of California, San Diego, 1978.

A discussion of three modes of literary criticism—traditionalist, culturalist, and historical-dialectical—and their relation to Chicano literature as applied to Tomás Rivera's . . . *Y no se lo tragó la tierra.*

Sommers, Joseph and Tomás Ybarra-Frausto, eds. *Modern Chicano Writers: A Collection of Critical Essays.* Englewood Cliffs, N.J.: Prentice-Hall, 1979. (Twentieth Century Views, A Spectrum Book)

A series of essays concerning the conceptual framework of Chicano literary history and critical approaches, as well as the characteristics of Chicano narrative, poetry, and theater.

Yarbro-Bejarano, Yvonne. "Cherríe Moraga's *Giving Up the Ghost:* The Representation of Female Desire." *Third Woman* 3, no. 1–2 (1986):113–20.

An analysis of sexism, racism, feminism, homophobia, and the complex and the multifaceted structures of oppression created from these issues in relation to the Chicana experience.

Ybarra-Frausto, Tomás. "The Chicano Movement and the Emergence of a Chicano Poetic Consciousness." *New Directions in Chicano Scholarship*, ed. Ricardo Romo and Raymund Paredes, 81–109. La Jolla: Chicano Studies Program, University of California, San Diego, 1978.

Ybarra-Frausto describes the historical emergence of Chicano poetic consciousness as a long process of militance and resistance, from the eighteenth-century concept of revolution borrowed from Mexico to the mobilization of campesinos in California in the 1960s and the emergence of the teatro campesino.

Index

✡

Contributors

Norma Alarcón, Assistant Professor of Chicano Studies at the University of California, Berkeley, teaches courses in Hispanic women writers and feminist theory. She is the founder, publisher, and editor of *Third Woman Journal* and Press. She is the author of *Rosario Castellanos' Feminist Poetics: Against the Sacrificial Contract* (1987) and is presently at work on *Feminism and Nationalism: The Poetics and Politics of Identity.*

Héctor Calderón is Associate Professor of Hispanic Studies and Chicano Studies at Scripps College. He is the author of *Conciencia y lenguaje en el "Quijote" y "El obsceno pájaro de la noche* (1987). He has written numerous articles on Latin American and Chicano literature and is currently completing *Contemporary Chicano Narrative: A Tradition and Its Forms.*

Angie Chabram, Assistant Professor of Chicano literature at the University of California, Davis, teaches courses in Chicano literature and critical theory. She is coeditor of *Chicana/o Cultural Representations: Reframing Critical Discourses,* a special issue of *Cultural Studies* 4–3 (1990) and author of "The Splitting of Chicana/o Subjectivity" in *Chicanas Speak Out* (forthcoming U.C. Press). She is currently completing a volume of interviews with selected Chicano scholars, *Conversations with Chicano Critics: A Portrait of a Counter-Discourse.*

Barbara Harlow, Associate Professor of English and Comparative Literature at the University of Texas, Austin, teaches courses in Third World literature. She is the translator of Jacques Derrida's *Spurs: Nietzsche's Styles/Éperons: Les Styles de Nietzsche* (1978) and the author of *Resistance Literature* (1987) and *Barred: Women, Writing and Political Detention,* to be published by Cornell University Press.

Rolando Hinojosa, an internationally recognized writer, is Ellen Clayton Garwood Professor of English and Creative Writing at the University of Texas, Austin. He is the author of numerous novels in English and Spanish including *Generaciones y semblanzas* (1977), *Mi querido Rafa* (1981), *Rites and Witnesses* (1982), *The Valley* (1983), *Dear Rafe* (1985), and *Claros varones de Belken/Fair Gentlemen of Belken County* (1986). All form part of his series Klail City Death Trip. He received the Quinto Sol Prize for novel for *Estampas del valle y otras obras* (1973) and the Cuban Casa de las Américas International Prize for novel for *Klail City y sus alrededores* (1976). His latest novel is *Becky and Her Friends* (1990).

Luis Leal is a well-known scholar of Mexican and Chicano literature. He is Emeritus Professor of the University of Illinois, Champaign-Urbana, and since 1976 has been Visiting Professor at the University of California, Santa Barbara, where he teaches courses in Mexican and Chicano literature and culture. He has received numerous international awards including Honorary Fellow of the Society of Spanish and Spanish American Studies. He has recently added the following books to his long list of publications: *Juan Rulfo* (1983), *Leyendas mexicanas* (1985), and *Aztlán y México: Perfiles literarios e históricos* (1985).

JOSÉ E. LIMÓN, Associate Professor of English at the University of Texas, Austin, specializes in the folklore of Greater Mexico, American Studies, and the anthropology of symbols. His *Mexican Ballads, Chicano Poems: History and Influence in Mexican-American Social Poetics* will be published by University of California Press. He is also currently completing *Dancing with the Devil: Society, Gender and the Political Unconscious in Mexican-American South Texas.*

TERESA MCKENNA is Associate Professor of English and Chicano Studies at the University of Southern California, where she teaches courses in Chicano and Chicana literature, Third World women in literature, and twentieth-century American literature. She edited *Special Issue on Mexican Folklore and Folk Art in the United States, Aztlán* (1982). She is completing a book manuscript, *Parto de Palabra: Essays on Chicano Literature in Process.*

ELIZABETH J. ORDÓÑEZ, Associate Professor at the University of Texas, Arlington, specializes in nineteenth- and twentieth-century Spanish narrative, Chicana/Chicano literature, and theory and criticism. She compiled "An Annotated Bibliography of Chicana Literature and Related Sources," *Bilingual Review* (1980) and is the author of *Voices of Their Own: Contemporary Spanish Narrative by Women*, to be published by Bucknell University Press. She is currently at work on a companion study of nineteenth-century narrative by Spanish women, *Plots and Counterplots.*

GENARO PADILLA is Assistant Professor of English at the University of California, Berkeley, where he teaches courses in American literature, Chicano literature, and ethnic autobiography. He is the editor of *The Stories of Fray Angélico Chávez* (1987). His research interests include a forthcoming book on Chicano autobiography.

ALVINA E. QUINTANA is Assistant Professor of English and Women's Studies at the University of Delaware. Her interests include cultural theory and feminist criticism. She is the author of "Language, Power and Women," *Critical Perspectives* (1984); "Prisoners of the Word," *Chicana Voices* (1986); "Chicana Literary Motifs: Challenge and Counter-Challenge," *Social and Gender Boundaries in the United States* (1989); "Recoding Women's Space: Narrative Strategies of Denise Chávez in *Novena Narratives* and *The Last of the Menu Girls," Cultural Studies* (1990).

RENATO ROSALDO, Professor of Anthropology at Stanford University, teaches courses in Southeast Asian Studies and Third World culture. He was the recipient of the Harry Benda Prize for Southeast Asian Studies (1983). He is the author of *Ilongot Headhunting, 1883–1974: A Study in Society and History* (1980) and *Culture and Truth: The Remaking of Social Analysis* (1989).

JOSÉ DAVID SALDÍVAR is Associate Professor of Literature and American Studies at the University of California, Santa Cruz, where he specializes in pan-American literatures. He is the author of numerous articles on Chicana/o and Latin American literature, editor of *The Rolando Hinojosa Reader: Essays Historical and Critical* (1985), and author of *The Dialectics of Our America: Genealogy, Cultural Critique, and Literary History.*

RAMÓN SALDÍVAR is Professor of English and Comparative Literature at the University of Texas, Austin, and specializes in nineteenth- and twentieth-century comparative studies, theory of the novel, and Chicano literature. He is the author of *Figural Language in the Novel: The Flowers of Speech from Cervantes to Joyce* (1984) and *Chicano Narrative: The Dialectics of Difference* (1990).

SONIA SALDÍVAR-HULL is Assistant Professor of English at the University of California, Los Angeles. Her research interests include Third World literature and feminist theory. She is the author of "Wrestling Your Ally: Gertrude Stein, Racism and Feminist Critical Practice," *Women's Writing in Exile* (1989) and "Helena María Viramontes," *Dictionary of Literary Biography-Chicano Authors* (forthcoming).

ROSAURA SÁNCHEZ, Associate Professor of Spanish at the University of California, San Diego, teaches courses in Chicano and Latin American literature, literary theory, and linguistics. She is editor of the journal *Crítica* and *Essays on La Mujer* (1977) and author of *Chicano Discourse: Socio-Historic Perspectives* (1983). She is currently at work on a study of nineteenth-century Hispanic writers from California.

ROBERTO TRUJILLO is Curator of Mexican American Collections for Stanford University Libraries and is the editor of *A Decade of Chicano Literature* (1982) and *Literatura Chicana: Creative and Critical Writings Through 1984* (1985).

Library of Congress Cataloging-in-Publication Data
Criticism in the borderlands : studies in Chicano
literature, culture, and ideology / edited by Héctor
Calderón and José David Saldívar ; with a foreword by
Rolando Hinojosa.
(Post-contemporary interventions)
Includes bibliographical references and index.
ISBN 0-8223-1137-2. — ISBN 0-8223-1143-7 (pbk.)
1. American literature—Mexican American authors—
History and criticism.   2. American literature—
Mexican-American Border Region—History and
criticism.   3. Mexican-American Border Region—
Intellectual life.   4. Mexican-American Border Region
in literature.   5. Mexican Americans—Intellectual
life. 6. Mexican Americans in literature.   I. Calderón,
Héctor.   II. Saldívar, José.   III. Series.
PS153.M4C7   1991
810.9'86872—dc20   90-25853 CIP